What We Need

What We Need

EXTRAVAGANCE
AND
SHORTAGES
IN
AMERICA'S
MILITARY

Barrett Tillman

ZENITH PRESS

First published in 2007 by Zenith Press, an imprint of MBI Publishing Company, Galtier Plaza, Suite 200, 380 Jackson Street, St. Paul, MN 55101 USA

Zenith Press titles are also available at discounts in bulk quantity for industrial or sales-promotional use. For details write to Special Sales Manager at MBI Publishing Company, Galtier Plaza, Suite 200, 380 Jackson Street, St. Paul, MN 55101 USA.

To find out more about our books, join us online at www.zenithpress.com.

Designer: Tom Heffron

Library of Congress Cataloging-in-Publication Data

Tillman, Barrett.
  What we need : extravagance and shortages in America's military / by Barrett Tillman.
    p. cm.
  ISBN-13: 978-0-7603-2869-9 (hbk.)
  ISBN-10: 0-7603-2869-2 (hbk.)
  1. United States—Military policy—21st century. 2. United States—Armed Forces—Equipment and supplies. 3. Manpower—United States. 4. United States—Armed Forces—Appropriations and expenditures. I. Title.
UA23.T49 2007
355.8—dc22

                         2007013179

Printed in the United States of America

Contents

To the memory of
Lieutenant Colonel Jeff Cooper, USMCR, 1920–2006.
Warrior, scholar, teacher, mentor, friend.
Training was his calling; competence his standard;
excellence his passion.

Preface

I learn something from every book I write, and researching *What We Need* has been more educational than most. My primary sources are military personnel who have left bootprints in Afghanistan and Iraq since 2001. Because few were willing to be identified—either from modesty, security concerns, or fear of officialdom—I have identified most individuals by pseudonyms or *noms de guerre*. I pledged anonymity to all who requested it, though their locales and times of service are accurate.

A few individuals were known to me before 9/11; many are more recent acquaintances. Some are active duty guard or reserve personnel I've met in the course of conducting training or reporting on such events. In any case, they cover a wide spectrum: "straight-leg" infantry, armored cavalry, airborne; rangers, marines, and SEALs. Snipers and recon dudes, base security guys and gals, mechanics and heavy equipment operators, helicopter pilots and tactical jet crews, airlifters and electronic warfare specialists. Not to mention Department of Defense (DoD) attorneys, civilian trainers, academics, consultants, beltway bandits, and other journalists. The ranks range from E-2 to O-6, with multiple delegates in most grades.

I would never claim that *What We Need* represents a scientific sampling. The methodology includes everything from scribbled notes on a firing line to email correspondence and frequent reference to professional journals. The number of Internet sites consulted runs into dozens.

However, there was enough similarity among the responses to form a reasoned opinion as to what we need. The near unanimity in some areas was astonishing: as of 2006, everybody in combat zones wants more socks, and I mean everybody. Far too many still complain about shortages of personal and vehicular armor. The fact that the United States government does not provide such basic items five years into the Global War on Terror (hereafter the Terror War) represents a freaking outrage.

Write your freaking congressman.

Very few infantrymen—the primary combatants in this conflict—think we need stealth fighters or new ships, and if their views are parochial, they are unarguably pragmatic.

Across the board, I also found wide agreement on the big items: we need more people (those we have are approaching exhaustion), more training (including ranges and ammunition), and more linguists (Arabic and Pashto for starters), plus more information.

What We Need does not pretend to describe everything the U.S. military requires from now into the indefinite future, nor could it. The input received was as varied—and as limited—as its sources, and I found that situations change almost month by month. Consequently, predictions are risky enterprises.

A few topics are too esoteric to be covered here, especially intelligence. "Intel" is of supreme importance in the Terror War, but I admit to no spooks among my friends, colleagues, or acquaintances, so I will refrain from addressing that critical matter (and whatever revelations may appear on that score shall be left to the *New York Times*).

Though the emphasis is primarily upon the Global War on Terror, we should remember the biblical injunction that there will always be wars and rumors of wars. Whether the Terror War is truly a war is yet uncertain: it began as a short conventional war and almost immediately evolved into an Iraqi insurgency with a guerrilla movement in Afghanistan. But that could change with sunrise tomorrow. In any case, the next conventional ("real") war will feature many if not most of the concerns addressed in these pages. Therefore, *What We Need* may be used as a continuing reference—a "reality check" if you will—for the concerns of shooters, logisticians, producers, and planners.

While communicating with a diverse military population has been educational and enjoyable, this project carries an inherent frustration. It was bound to be at least partly outmoded upon publication, for such is the progression of the open-ended fight to which we are committed. Eventually most (not all) problems will be identified and solved but inevitably others arise or, Jason-like, recur. In a huge bureaucracy like the U.S. armed forces, there's just no escaping it. Therefore, we probably should not be surprised if some of the same considerations remain topical when *What We Need* is reprinted in 2026.

Clausewitz 101

This book addresses the Great American Dichotomy: we allocate vast sums for our military, yet inevitably we spend most of that treasure on technical marvels that we do not use. And if we do not use them, we are entitled to ask how much we need them.

To quote Hamlet, "Ay, there's the rub."

Determining what we truly need requires study of one of the things that we humans do best: war.

The military bible is called *On War*. It was written by Karl von Clausewitz about 175 years ago and has been universally read and translated ever since.

Von Clausewitz (1780–1831) was a Prussian general who thought deeply upon his profession. His unfinished treatise has been studied by at least seven generations of military students and theorists, many of whom have committed his nine "rules of war" to memory. I prefer to make acronyms out of long lists, and condensed von Clausewitz to "mouse," i.e., MMMOUSSSE.

Mission, Mass, Maneuver, Objective, Unity (of command), Security, Simplicity, Surprise, and Economy (of force). Some people like to add another S, for Speed.

In Clausewitzian fashion I'll define the Objective, with a capital "O," of *What We Need*. It is twofold:

1. Identify some important military requirements that are not being met and try to bring them overdue scrutiny.

2. Suggest some possible methods of meeting those unfilled needs and offer a sense of priority based upon operational requirements, rather than parochial pork from the sausage makers of the military-industrial-political complex (hereafter MIPC).

Yes, I concede that the likelihood of achieving the last-stated goal is slightly less than banishing hypocrisy from politics, but it's worth a try.

Strap in tight, fasten your oxygen mask, and turn up the gun sight. It's gonna be a dogfight.

* * *

In presuming to address what we need in America's military, the title of this book begs the question: but for what purpose?

The Pentagon's "requirements"—which in truth represent American political-industrial preferences—are based upon two conflicting realities. While the MIPC prefers to purchase high-high-tech equipment for an optimal scenario (all-out conventional war against a major power), it is nonetheless engaged in a continuing insurgency against low-low-tech opponents who do not even represent a specific nation-state.

What to do?

The art in military science is determining the best "high-low mix" and acting accordingly. Yet we continue purchasing platinum-plated platforms such as stealth aircraft and next-generation submarines that have absolutely 0.00 bearing upon the present conflict. And therein lies the dilemma. We know that we will be fighting the Terror War for a very long time—decades if not generations. It will be fought in cities and mountains, at home and abroad, in the news media and cyberspace, and especially in peoples' minds. Many of those people are yet unborn.

On the other hand, it is conceivable that at some point in the next few decades, we may see something resembling the scale of

Korea or Vietnam. We certainly will not see anything remotely resembling World War II: wars have become far too expensive to support the massive force structure and enormous amounts of "stuff" for conflict on that scale. One standard of comparison: in June 1944, the U.S. Army Air Forces lost 1,457 aircraft in combat worldwide, not counting training losses (the *average* monthly combat loss that year was over 1,100). Today we cannot buy enough modern airplanes to absorb one day's attrition at that level. The proportionate loss (forty-eight airplanes plus helicopters) might force us to park most combat aircraft and reassess the situation.

For the foreseeable future, we will be engaged in what retired Lieutenant Colonel Ralph Peters calls "a war of flesh, faith, and cities." Wars in which traditional American strengths (air supremacy, sea control, artillery, and logistics) are largely negated against the willing flesh of jihadists. Increasingly, our technological advantages are being consigned to irrelevance. New submarines, stealth fighters, and futuristic land warfare systems have no war to fight—and have not had much opportunity for decades.

If immediate priorities are our guide, logic would dictate that we adjust our military policy to give priority to the Terror War rather than to an indefinite event sometime downstream. That is not happening. How else to explain units that deploy to Iraq or Afghanistan with insufficient personal and vehicle armor, too little ammunition, and inadequate training?

Yet we need to keep one eye on the horizon, against the day when our national interests may be challenged by a well-funded, well-equipped nation-state or consortium. The favored scenario is China (see Chapter Seven) but logic and history dictate otherwise. More likely a conventional war will come out of "nowhere," low and fast beneath the geopolitical radar. Consider recent history: Who would have predicted that Britain and Argentina would fight in 1982? That America would ever find itself engaged in Afghanistan? Or defeat Iraq in 1991 and feel the need to return in 2003?

Yes, we need to continue building high-tech (if not *high*-high tech) gear to be ready for the improbable scenario that takes us by surprise. We need to maintain our industrial base for aircraft and submarines to provide the materiel for a possible conventional war. But let's be honest: the greater motivation is to keep congressmen and senators in residence in D.C. by providing their constituents with porcine projects. (It's probably no accident that the F-22 Raptor is built by subcontractors in forty-six states and Puerto Rico.)

Broke on $440 Billion

In early 2006 the U.S. Army Chief of Staff noted a seeming anomaly: the previous Christmas, Americans spent more on holiday gifts and decorations than was spent on the military all year long. The purported $438.5 billion amounted to less than 4 percent of the total economy. (Retail analysts noted that the actual figure, some $435 billion, included Thanksgiving turkeys. At this point we shall eschew any comparison with military turkeys that provide less bang for the buck.)

However the military-industrial-political budget is spent, the general's concern highlights an important point, though not the one he had in mind.

Do me a favor.

Take out your wallet and examine a dollar bill. It's a smidgen over six inches long. Now, use your imagination and envision 440 billion greenbacks placed end to end. How far would they go?

Actually, they would extend 220 billion feet, or 41,600,000 miles. That's 1,664 times around Planet Earth at the equator.

If the greenbacks had Andy Jackson's picture instead of George Washington's, that line still would run well over two million miles. That's about four trips to the moon and back.

So, then . . .

On roughly $440 *billion*, how is it possible that DoD lacks adequate funds?

On $440 *billion*, how is it possible that soldiers still lack sufficient body armor, training facilities and ammunition, and high-tech bandages?

On $440 *billion*, how is it possible that there is not enough money for vehicle maintenance and repair?

On $440 *billion*, how is it possible that GIs still write home asking folks to send socks and sheets and batteries?

The answer is painfully simple. There is *lots* of money for DoD. The problem is, the military-industrial-political complex often refuses to spend enough of the existing largess on the low-end, unglamorous, routine items that troops really need, or to ship the needed items to the operating areas.

At an *admitted* $286,000, you could buy one hellacious amount of body armor and bandages for what goes into the canopy of one stealth fighter.

The flip side of the equation has to do with supply and distribution. Actually, the Army has plenty of socks. Sometimes it just does a poor job of getting them where they're most needed. That is not the fault of those who deliver stuff to the operating forces. The logisticians, whether aloft or afloat, do not determine what's loaded onto airplanes and ships for overseas transport. Those guys and gals just roll the containers onto the ship or plane and take it where they're told.

The trouble is found much farther up the food chain, where priorities are established. We shall examine that subject in some detail, overleaf.

Throughout the text are segments titled "Been There, Done That" (BTDT) as a demonstration of previous experience with all manner of topics: conflicts, weapons, equipment, procedures, etc. If by studying the past we can avoid only one unnecessary lesson relearned, the time and effort invested in this book will be well spent.

—Barrett Tillman
November 2006

Chapter One

War? What War?

"Men do not fight because they have arms. They have arms because they deem it necessary to fight. Take away their arms, and they will either fight with their bare fists or get themselves new arms."

—Hans. J. Morgenthau, 1967

During a World War II history symposium in 2005 the question arose: "What's a major war?" The question went unanswered.

Now, understand that we're discussing war as opposed to combat. In a gunfight, it doesn't matter whether you're a soldier firing an M16, a cop confronting gangbangers, or a homeowner repelling an intruder. If there's lead in the air, you're in combat.

But what's a war?

There are different ways to define the term. Wars can be judged by duration: Europe suffered through the Hundred Years War, which lasted 116 years in the fourteenth and fifteenth centuries, and the Thirty Years War of the seventeenth century (the French and English never tired of disputing with one another).

War can be defined by casualties. The United States lost 405,000 men to all causes in World War II; about 36,000 in Korea and 58,000 in Southeast Asia. Certainly those were major wars.

But definitions are subject to change, including standard of scale. The Great War of 1914–1918 was eclipsed by the next global feud, such that we began numbering our world wars. Sequencing even applies to far lesser conflicts, as in "The First Gulf War." Today we don't officially have wars, but merely operations: Desert Storm, Enduring Freedom, Iraqi Freedom, and so on.

There are all kinds of wars: declared and undeclared, legal and illegal, conventional or guerrilla, hot or cold, wars of survival, and wars of liberation—even theoretical nuclear and push-button wars. But whether it's a war, "police action," or "conflict," young people still die.

Taking the "big ones" as a standard, we are now into the longest period in American history without a major war. In January 1973 the United States signed the Paris "peace" accords and abandoned the Republic of Vietnam to its fate. Now, some thirty-four years later, we have gone longer than the intervals between any of our "real" wars: from the Revolution to 1812; 1815 to the Mexican War; 1847 to the War Between the States; 1865 to the Spanish-American War; 1898 to World War I; 1918 to World War II; 1945 to Korea; and 1953 to Vietnam, however that mess is reckoned.

Between some of the "real" wars were prolonged "conflicts" such as the Indian Wars (more or less constant until the 1890s) and the post-Spanish insurrection in the Philippines. The latter may offer the best comparison with the current situation: an undeclared guerrilla war against irregular Filipino and Muslim forces between 1899 and 1913.

On the other hand, as of 2006, American military casualties from all causes since 9/11 far exceeded the fourteen-year Philippine toll. But at present rates, the losses are certainly supportable: about seventy deaths per month in Iraq and Afghanistan combined, though the wounded far outnumber the KIAs. In contrast, America sustained several thousand killed per month in the world wars; one thousand in Korea; and well over five hundred per month for Vietnam. Some people argue that anything much under the latter figure may not represent a major war.

There are, of course, other yardsticks. Recently the Pentagon cut people in favor of stuff, and that fact alone makes it hard to accept that we're engaged in a major war. Additionally, some ask if a war can be "major" without significant combat by the Air Force and Navy.

For the moment, let's take the long view. America fought the Indian wars roughly from 1775 to 1890. That's "only" 115 years, resulting in some four thousand military deaths or about 260 per year. Call it twenty a month.

No—that's not a major war. But it's an awfully long *conflict*—a prolonged insurrection against a guerrilla enemy without uniforms, armies, or even a country. Today we face similar enemies, products of a culture that might be compared to Japan in World War II.

In fact, Imperial Japan may provide the upper level of comparison for civilian involvement in a major war. In 1945, with cities burning nightly and three hundred thousand dead civilians, Tokyo ordered total mobilization: schools were closed and women and children were issued spears to repel the expected American invaders.

In contrast, today well under 1 percent of all Americans belong to the armed forces, and years after 9/11 many citizens' greatest engagement is removing their shoes when boarding an airliner. The economy continues growing, apparently immune to the stresses imposed upon our military personnel.

So, to return to the beginning: does it matter how we define a war?

To the troops at the sharp end, it matters little. But to the nation, and perhaps to Western Civilization, it could matter a great deal. After all, how we define ourselves affects the way we conduct ourselves. So let us not argue whether the war on terror is a major military conflict—clearly it is not. Instead, let us concede that we may "only" be entering the longest multigenerational clash in our history, sustainable as long as we possess enough resolve.

Therefore, let's recognize it for what it is: perpetual insurrection; a rifle fight writ large. In this new era, jets count vastly less than stamina; tanks less than persistence; and artillery less than willpower. Let's acknowledge that we are conducting a low-intensity conflict that we are unlikely to win in our lifetime.

That's a major challenge by any standard.

Meanwhile, the question remains: how do we define the Terror War? Is it a "conflict," an "insurrection," or something else? Whatever description we eventually pin on it, one thing is certain. Its central front occurs in an area we have seen previously—and that does not just mean Operation Desert Storm.

Been There, Done That, Part I

The Short Guide to Iraq is a small military reference that begins, "Herr Hitler knows he's licked if the people united against him stand their ground. So it is pretty obvious what he and his propaganda machine are trying to do. They're trying to spread disunity and discontent among their opponents whenever and wherever they can."

Sound familiar?

That was the perspective circa 1943. Farther along, the guidebook noted that Iraq was a "strategic hot spot," literally and figuratively. "Iraq is thus a strategic part of the great 'land bridge' between Europe and India—the road Hitler HOPES to use to join hands with his back-stabbing allies, the Japs. Also, the Persian Gulf is an important back door for us to get supplies to our Russian allies. And even more, Iraq has great military importance for its oil fields, with their pipelines to the Mediterranean Sea. Yes, Iraq is a hot spot in more ways than one."

The forty-four-page pamphlet warned GIs that their new environment was far different from what they might have expected. The stifling heat and appalling smells would be quite unlike "a lot of things the movies didn't warn you about."

Apart from sections describing manners and customs, religion, Muslim females, and "the evil eye," the guidebook had several déjà vu observations. For instance, it described Iraqis as "first-rate guerrilla fighters." And it concluded, "American success or failure in Iraq may well depend on whether the Iraqis like American soldiers or not."

Here's another example of how little things change over the decades:

"You won't be going to Iraq to change the Iraqis. Quite the opposite. We are fighting this war to preserve the principle of 'live and let live.' "

Can you say, *plus ça change?*

* * *

As the saying goes, that was then and this is now.

Way Back Then, we were engaged in a major war and everybody recognized that fact. In contrast, here's an illuminating look at the present, proof of a disconnect not just between the military and civilians, but within the armed forces themselves:

In 2005 the U.S. Air Force proposed buying a $49 million airshow gadget called Thundervision, a big-screen video and sound system for the Thunderbirds flight demonstration team. However, the concept drew unwanted attention amid charges of cronyism and undue influence among some very senior generals, both active and retired. Finally the FBI was called upon to investigate. But the legal niceties overshadowed the larger issue: why, in the midst of a shooting war, the Air Force wanted to appropriate enough irrelevant PR funds to purchase millions of gallons of jet fuel, nearly 2.5 million rounds of 20mm ammunition, or 580 Sidewinder heat-seeking missiles.

But the problem extends elsewhere.

In 2006 the Navy Office of Information's Visual News Service released *The U.S. Navy in 2005 Year in Review*. It featured about one hundred high-quality images of naval activities. They included Navy personnel playing basketball, playing football ("Beat Army!"), playing music, recruiting new people, training sailors, servicing race cars, sailing ships, flying aircraft, and enjoying liberty. Over one-quarter of the images depicted disaster relief in the Pacific or the U.S. Gulf Coast.

After nearly seven minutes the video ended with the notation, ". . . the war on terror continues."

Think about that.

There was not one image of combat. Not one. The closest the producers came was a photo of a Medal of Honor recipient's funeral . . . and a shot of the Army-Navy game.

The Navy's public information office labored long and hard to produce a portrait of the service's missions four years after 9/11 . . . and failed to demonstrate any activities related to inflicting violence upon the nation's enemies.

Our rating: A+ for quality; F for relevance; and F- for awareness. There was no hint of combat activity: of SEALs' frequent deployments to Afghanistan and Iraq, nor of helicopter squadrons taken off ships to augment army units in the war zones.

As inane as the foregoing production appeared, it demonstrated a deeper concern. As this book is published in 2007, we are six years into the Terror War, an endeavor bound to last many years more—likely well beyond the life span of anyone now breathing. Thousands of Americans and many times that number of friendly and innocent Iraqis and Afghans have perished, not to mention unknown thousands of our enemies.

But is it a war?

Glad you asked:

The Best Kind of War

A dear friend of mine was a committed warrior, now happily ensconced beneath Valhalla's golden dome, sipping a heavenly brew served by busty Valkyries and swapping yarns with colleagues such as Genghis Khan, Horatio Nelson, and Manfred von Richthofen.

My friend—callsign "Pirate"—was a two-war veteran, and he had a favorite toast. He would clink glasses brimming with whatever was going and intone, "Short war." Though an aviator, he thought that the Spanish-American War was about as good as it gets: four months' training, sail off to battle with bands playing valiantly and teary-eyed maidens waving hankies, a brief period of combat, and home. Maybe six months block to block.

The best war with airplanes ("they lend dignity to an otherwise vulgar brawl") was the Falklands-Malvinas feud of 1982. Pirate always insisted that few human problems could not be solved by a well-flown division of A-4 Skyhawks, and the Argies came close to proving his point. There was even a decent amount of air combat, though it was resolved wholly in favor of the Royal Navy. However, the entire campaign only lasted about seven weeks. "That really was too short," Pirate averred. "You want a war to last long enough so you get a good feel for it. It's not much fun if you hammer the other guy too soon."

But as they say, that was then and this is now. The days of short "fun" wars are over.

That's the semantic problem. When does an operation or a campaign evolve into a no-kidding war?

So we are still left with the question: what *is* a war?

Here's the conventional answer, right out of *Webster's*: "(1) a state of usually open and declared armed hostile conflict between states or nations; (2) a period of such armed conflict."

But the Terror War doesn't fit that definition. We are not fighting states or nations, nor even nation-states. We are engaged across a very broad front with generally unorganized forces motivated by religion and politics, drawn from many sources. The enemy has no standing army and does not even issue uniforms.

Fill in the blanks as you wish, but a major war requires certain characteristics, starting with dedication and sacrifice from most or all of the population. The world wars fit that description; to a lesser extent so did Vietnam. The Terror War does not. The economy does not suffer overmuch, nor does the American public feel an inordinate strain. Casualties are limited to a very small portion of the populace.

Our friends, enemies, and neutral geopoliticians all agree on one point: the defining measure of America's participation in a given endeavor is longevity. The conventional wisdom holds that the United States lacks staying power, and there's something to that view. Our three bloodiest conflicts (the War of Northern Aggression and the world wars) all lasted four years or less, as did Korea. Yet the specter of Vietnam (fifty-eight thousand dead in roughly a decade) presumably meant that nineteen KIAs were enough to force us out of Somalia, although whether we had any business there is a separate matter.

Having said that, what would John Q. Public think if America had been engaged in a fourteen-year counterinsurgency that claimed four thousand of our soldiers? That's about as many as died fighting in the eight-year Revolution and almost matches the combined toll of the War of 1812 and the dispute with Spain.

How did *that* happen?

Odd you should ask:

Been There, Done That, Part II

The treaty ending the Spanish-American War of 1898 ceded the Philippines to U.S. control. American forces occupied Manila but the rest of the archipelago remained in the hands of Filipino nationalists.

In February 1899, Emilio Aguinaldo opened hostilities near Manila, and though originally his larger force was defeated, he proved durable and skillful. He was finally captured in 1901 and swore allegiance to the United States.

The high (or low) point of the war occurred on the island of Samar that year. Americans had been massacred by guerrillas, prompting the U.S. commander, General Jacob H. Smith, to retaliate in kind. The ensuing atrocities resulted in widespread horror in America, leading to Smith's court-martial. He was found guilty of "conduct to the prejudice of good order and military discipline" and received a reprimand. The outraged public reaction led to President Theodore Roosevelt retiring Smith.

Meanwhile, serious problems began with the Moro population in the southern islands in 1902. Largely Muslim, they proved themselves sometimes fanatic, always resilient, enemies with an awesome reputation for toughness. Combat continued until 1913.

In the fourteen years between 1899 and 1913, over 125,000 U.S. troops were committed to the Philippines; some 4,200 were killed. Seventy soldiers received Medals of Honor (only one posthumously) and the Army recognized eleven battles and campaigns for regimental honors, but Samar is conspicuously absent.

Fourteen years. At that rate, we can expect to be fighting in Iraq and Afghanistan until at least 2015. But for more perspective, let's look farther back.

Talk about the Long War, consider the Crusades. The clash of East and West; Christians versus Muslims, almost a thousand years ago.

Many people today who are aware of the Crusades at all will tell you there were three. In fact, there were at least seven, though some historians count eight or even nine, and hardly anybody agrees on the specific years other than the start and stop dates. The hell of it is, nothing much changed as a result.

Here's the short version:

In November 1095 Pope Urban II ordered a vast mission to retrieve the Holy Land from the infidels. The following August a pack of Crusaders departed, hacking its way through Eastern Europe and points south.

Thus began the First Crusade, which peaked in July 1099 when the Crusaders took Jerusalem. Things percolated for nigh onto one hundred years.

However the individual crusades are reckoned, the key player was not Richard the Lionheart but a modest forty-one-year-old Iraqi named Saladin. To say that he rode rings around the Crusaders would be an understatement. Apart from a keen military mind and rock-star charisma, he benefited from rare Muslim unity. In an active three months of 1187 he recaptured most of the major cities and all the ports except one, thus isolating Jerusalem. After a bitter siege, he made the Crusaders an offer they could not refuse. Thousands vacated the holy site; the stay-behinds went into slavery.

Around 1190 the Europeans were at it again, seeking to recapture Jerusalem.

After a short intermission (computed as these things go) The Next Crusade kicked off in 1198, highlighted by the sacking of Constantinople in 1204. A subsequent Children's Crusade occurred in 1212, intending to reconquer the Holy Land by love rather than by force. Some thirty thousand kids were sold into slavery by shipping merchants, leading to appalling loss of young life.

That was followed by Another Crusade (1215 or so), the last one initiated from Rome. In turn, next came Yet Another Crusade (1248), followed by One More Crusade (1270), et cetera, et cetera. You get the idea.

Somewhere in there (1244) the remaining Christians were driven from Jerusalem, which was sacked by the Turks (and you've never really been sacked until you've been sacked by Turks).

Following the Mamluk capture of Acre in 1291 (almost exactly one century after Christians grabbed the place), the crusades bled to a halt, nearly two hundred years after the first expedition.

However, things got totally out of hand with non-Christian, non-Muslim pagans injecting themselves into the proceedings. Sweeping out of the east in the thirteenth century, lathering their hardy little ponies to a frazzle (trust me: there were few Mongol horse whisperers), the Asiatic Hordes took advantage of the Palestinian diversion and descended like a biblical plague that may have claimed seven million Europeans.

Oh, did we mention the Moors' occupation of Spain? Sorry. The Muslims, who take the long view of history, controlled part or most of the Iberian Peninsula for nearly eight hundred years, from the eighth to the fifteenth centuries. The *reconquista*; El Cid and all that.

Playing number games, if we total the Crusades and add that figure to the Spanish experience and drop in the piddling Philippine insurrection, we get an average of nearly 330 years.

There might be a lesson for today.

* * *

Here's a more recent perspective: the Cold War lasted almost fifty years but that could prove a cakewalk compared to where we're headed today.

For comparison, we might consider that the Crusades occurred in a period when both Christianity and Islam were growing, gaining new converts. In that instance, perhaps a clash was inevitable, especially since both sides claimed the Holy Land. And in that context, neither side could gain the upper hand. Essentially, the Crusades ended in a centuries-long stalemate.

Today, Islam represents the growth industry. In the West, Christianity and religion generally have given way to secularism, permitting Muslims to close the population gap. At present, Christianity and Judaism account for 33 percent of humanity with Islam claiming 21 percent. The next largest categories are the nonreligious (16 percent) and Hinduism (14 percent).

What do those figures mean for the future—and for conduct of the Terror War?

Let's take a closer look. It's possible that the type of conflict will be as important as the duration because the one affects the other.

Where's the Asymmetric War?

A great deal of ink and electrons have been expended in discussion of "twenty-first century asymmetric warfare." The buzz word actually refers to a lopsided situation in which one combatant heavily outweighs the other in firepower, troops, sophistication, logistics, and just about everything else that matters.

However, comma . . .

A shepherd boy named David faced the giant Goliath in perhaps the earliest recorded example of asymmetric warfare: on one side a really big, professional warrior with armor, shield, and a ferocious reach with his huge spear. On the other side: a much smaller, amateur combatant, minus armor (other than the righteousness of his cause) and a simple shepherd's sling.

The final score: Shepherds one; Giants zero.

However, that example need not dismay us overmuch. After all, in the American Revolution, *we* were the underdogs, usually outnumbered and always ill equipped, facing the world's most formidable nation and its thoroughly professional army.

On the other hand, maybe a tad bit of concern would be healthy.

The point is, at the sharp end there is far more symmetry today than the pundits might allow. Think about it. America's traditional strengths—sea and air power—are largely irrelevant to the war on terror. Stealth bombers and fast attack submarines (let alone boomers carrying Trident missiles) simply do not matter. Talk about all dressed up and no place to go.

Consequently, our troops end up in squad-sized rifle fights with opponents similarly armed and well motivated. In that situation, the war looks pretty darned symmetrical, the key difference being training. (See Chapter Three.)

However, al Qaeda and its acolytes keep finding ways around even that advantage. Talk about asymmetric warfare: our enemies consult their Holy Book while we consult the latest polling data.

Reportedly the jihadist creed says, "I kill, therefore I am. I die, therefore I exult."

Our enemies in the Terror War are not interested in fighting us; they devoutly wish to kill us. Hence the proliferation of suicide tactics and IEDs.

That attitude can offset one hell of a lot of asymmetry.

Wanted: A Real War

A "real" war involves massive commitment by the entire nation, or at least a major portion thereof.

The Terror War fails that test.

It's been said that major segments of the U.S. Army and Marine Corps are fighting the Terror War but America is not. That's a true statement. Soldiers and analysts assert that about 70 percent of the Army is engaged in supporting the other 30 percent that is deployed to Iraq and Afghanistan at any one time. Presumably similar figures apply to the leathernecks.

If we accept the premise that the Terror War is a violent clash between cultures and even civilizations, then logically it requires total commitment. However we define the nebulous nature of "winning" and "losing," as this book goes to press, America and the West face not only radical Islam but an unlikely alliance of that faction with Communist ideologues in North Korea.

How do we deal with that chilling reality?

As noted in the preface, some military leaders insist that we're broke on nearly $450 billon per year (a little under 4 percent of the gross domestic product or GDP). Some perspective might help.

During John F. Kennedy's administration, military spending ran around 9 percent of the GDP. In the two decades following Vietnam (1975–1994) the defense establishment absorbed slightly less than 6 percent of the economy. That covered the final phase of the Cold War, and it was enough to spend the Evil Empire into the dustbin of history.

But the old ways die hard, if at all. One example:

In 2002, a year after 9/11, the Bush administration moved to cancel the Crusader artillery piece, a huge 155mm weapon system. The proposal made sense, as Crusader was intended to fight a conventional war in Europe and had little relevance to events elsewhere. But the Army leadership joined forces with politicians from fourteen states that would build the system, insisting that the $11 billion project continue. The Army declared Crusader to be "very important and very necessary and, as a matter of fact, an important part of transformation." (*Congressional Record*: http://cns.miis.edu/cr/02_06_17.htm)

Eventually Crusader was terminated, with part of the remaining funds being transferred to another project. But the transformation concept remained, frequently stressing equipment over personnel in search of the most bang for the buck.

Today, we do need to spend more on the military, but probably not a great deal more. As will be seen overleaf, by spending smarter (i.e., more relevantly) we could realize a huge improvement in efficiency and thereby improve our security. We can accomplish that goal by concentrating on people, training, logistics, and equipment. The big problem is going to be achieving such change in the bloated, parochial, military-industrial-political complex. Briefly stated, that means rethinking the military transformation process, and acquiring less exotic hardware in favor of more personnel—not less.

Whatever else we may argue about in coming years and decades, one thing seems crystal clear: "Business as usual" represents a losing strategy.

Chapter Two

We Need People

"No nation ever had an army large enough to guarantee it against attack in time of peace or to insure it victory in time of war."

—President Calvin Coolidge, 1925

We need more people in the military, especially more of the experienced, knowledgeable men and women who make things work.

We need to focus on getting more of them and keeping a greater proportion of those who join.

So: why do people enlist in the armed forces?

That's a subject of obvious concern to each branch of service, and there's a quick way to determine what the U.S. Army, Navy, Marines, Air Force, and Coast Guard offer their recruits.

If you go to the U.S. Army web site, www.army.com, you'll notice the major sales points on the tool bar: travel, education, and money.

If you go to the U.S. Navy web site, you'll notice the major sales points are careers, jobs, and benefits.

If you go to the U.S. Air Force web site, you'll notice the major sales points are careers, education, and cool stuff (the latter involves airplanes and weapons).

If you go to the Marine Corps web site, you'll notice the major headings are recruiting, headquarters, units, and careers. That's a mission-oriented menu, even if it doesn't include killing our enemies.

If you go to the U.S. Coast Guard web site, you'll notice the major subjects are news, missions, and careers.

In other words, the branch with the *highest* degree of combat involvement and the *non* combat-involved service are the most mission-oriented in their recruiting emphasis (under "What the Army Does," it takes two paragraphs to get around to warfighting).

By their own admission, the Army, Navy, and Air Force see careers, education, and money as the primary inducements for joining those branches. The Marines seem to attract young people who are not only willing but eager to slay the heathen; at the other end of the spectrum, the "coasties" are equally motivated to save lives and protect our security.

Are those accurate generalizations?

For the Marines and the Coast Guard, apparently yes. For the others, it's obviously unfair to say that all soldiers, sailors, and airmen are motivated by what the service can do for them, but *institutionally* that's how the services perceive most of their recruits.

Just thought I'd mention it.

As of mid 2006, all the armed forces were meeting their monthly recruiting goals with the Marine Corps doing best at 112 percent. Furthermore, all branches expected to achieve their desired retention rates, as did the National Guard and Air Guard.

That's the good news.

However, the "accession" from active to reserves was lagging badly. Including direct recruiting as well as transfer from the regulars, only three of the six components gained enough new reservists, with the Army running at 75 percent for the National Guard and 87 percent for the Reserves. The Marine Corps, Air Force Reserves and Air Guard met their goals.

Based on those figures, the personnel picture looks pretty good.

But look closer.

The recruiting and retention figures are adequate to sustain the current force structure, six years into the Terror War. But despite Pentagon declarations to the contrary, we are no longer able to fight two wars: one big one and one small one, which was doctrine for decades. Our active and reserve forces are being worn to a frazzle, with repeated deployments just for the present conflict.

Soldiers say that in many deploying units, the divorce rate runs around 60 percent. That chilling statistic sends shivers up and down the military food chain, since it affects retention, morale, and efficiency.

What happens if *another* war breaks out?

It doesn't matter where: Korea, the Pacific Rim, South America. Wherever it is, we'll need a lot more personnel, trained, equipped, and ready to go.

In that case, assuming that we decide to fight, we probably need between two and three times the people available now. Split the difference and call it times 2.50.

Where will we get them?

In September 2005—four years after 9/11—a series of briefings was provided by senior Navy and Marine Corps officers. The primary focus was Iraq and Afghanistan, but the broader view concerned the military as a whole.

One briefer said, "Supply people and corpsmen are getting hammered in Iraq, even more than aviation. There are reserve 06s (Navy captains and Marine colonels) on their third involuntary tour."

A naval officer noted that the United States has roughly 4.5 percent of the world population, and about 0.4 percent of Americans are in the armed services. However, he insisted, "We are going to meet our needs without a draft."

Actually, that's not true.

We already have a draft. Ironically (or not) it involves conscripting active duty personnel who are eligible for separation from the service. It's called the "stop-loss program." It permits DoD to retain military personnel beyond their scheduled release date or retirement "for the good of the service." It doesn't matter whether the individuals want to remain or not.

An army captain, a former enlisted man who went to West Point, responded to a Thomas Sowell article about the draft in 2006: "A draftee military is not an ideal, but neither is a volunteer force that is overextended, overworked, underpaid, and used as a punch line on both sides. The current stop-loss policy in effect . . . is for all intents and purposes a draft, albeit an extremely selective one targeting people who have already done their part and . . . wish to leave the service." (Thomas Sowell, "A Military Draft?" *Townhall.com*, August 1, 2006.)

Most of the stop-loss conscripts are retained for their particular knowledge or abilities. But if we have de facto conscription of people already in the military—and we do—then the next obvious step is conscripting civilians.
Or is it?

Been There, Done That, Part III

New York, 1863. The first large draft in American history proved something less than a rousing success. While the War Between the States was pitched (with some success) as a campaign to Preserve the Union, it was demonstrably less salable as a means to Free the Slaves. In the Big Apple that muggy summer, antidraft rioters went on a rampage, burning and looting in protest. Just to add emphasis, a Negro orphanage was torched on Fifth Avenue.

Based on growing requirements, all male citizens in the U.S. between 20 and 35, and unmarried men from 35 to 45, were liable to call-up in the lottery (blacks, not being citizens at the time, were exempt). The unwilling lottery "winners" were allowed to hire a substitute or pay a $300 fee, or $5,500 in current value. Nevertheless, resentment boiled over.

On July 13 (barely a week after the Battle of Gettysburg) there began four days of outraged violence. Protesters savaged government buildings; the police commissioner was caught and beaten unconscious. Eventually the heavily Irish mob was estimated at fifty thousand men, women, and youngsters. Martial law was not declared, but elements of seven state and federal regiments were delegated to reinforce police in subduing the protesters. In dismantling barricades, one soldier was killed and some twenty seriously wounded.

Reportedly at least eleven blacks were lynched and more were otherwise murdered. Total deaths may have exceeded ninety. The $1.5 million in damage would equal nearly $28 million today.

President Lincoln ordered an investigation that led to modification of New York's draft mechanism. The commission found bone-deep corruption under the Democratic Party bosses, some of whom were thought behind instigation of the riots to demonstrate opposition to Lincoln's Republican policies.

Lapse-dissolve, fast-forward, fade in to daytime. In 1940 Congress passed the draft by one vote. It went into effect in October, requiring twelve months of military service. The following fall, the acronym OHIO began appearing in hastily painted scrawls on military bases. It had nothing to do with the seventeenth state. It meant, "Over the Hill In October."

Some dogfaces did desert, but considering what occurred in the Territory of Hawaii two months later, desertions didn't matter. Recruiters were busy from Monday morning, December 8, onward.

Though far smaller, a similar result occurred in the wake of 9/11. Such was the wave of patriotic enthusiasm that Americans who had never considered the military rushed to enlist. The upshot was at least a four-year bump in military personnel, but inevitably the numbers fell off.

Then what?

The D Word

We fought World War II mainly with draftees, and though the end result was deemed wholly satisfactory, there were lingering problems. Obviously, we don't need 16 million uniformed personnel any more, although certainly it would be easier to get them from a population of 300 million than of 130 million, even allowing for different demographics, especially since more jobs are open to women now.

In the wake of the Vietnam debacle, the American people through their elected representatives decided to end conscription in favor of a professional military. The debate waxed hot and cold with advocates on both sides of the political aisle. In 1971, while blood still flowed in Indochina, Democrat Senator Thomas Eagleton of Missouri predicted, "An all-volunteer army will be a poor boys' army . . . Congress has a rather immaculate record of not deeply concerning itself with the pleas of the poor."

But six years later, Eagleton's colleague from Wisconsin, Senator William Proxmire, wrote, "The fundamental argument for the volunteer army is that it's just, it's fair. People are in the Army now because they want to be there. They're not in the Army because they're forced to be there. And in a society which is at peace, that's the way it ought to be."

Now we're caught somewhere between those views, committing a volunteer force to an open-ended conflict increasingly demanding troops on the ground.

(An aside: in 1987, journalist Arthur T. Hadley observed, "To be accurate, we do not have a 'volunteer' armed force . . . We have a 'recruited' armed force, an important distinction.")

The problem with deciding the size of the military is complicated by Iraq. We could use at least another 50,000 troops there (some say 150,000), but will we still need them in two years? If we're going to liberate North Korea, Syria, and Iran, then yes, we need that number and many more. There's enough stretch in the economy, especially among the mouth-breathing slackers who hang out at malls, so that the economic impact need not be great, and could even be positive. Paying an additional fifty thousand kids twenty grand a year comes to only a billion bucks, but of course there are lots of other immediate and downrange costs associated with each soldier (and let's face it: they would mostly be soldiers).

It might be possible to recruit fifty thousand more kids without resorting to a draft, but the costs would be greater. The big question for a draft of that size is how to select such a small number out of some four million eighteen-year-olds.

Presently we have fewer than 1.5 million active personnel, beefed up with the guard and reserves. Even if we want to double the size of the active army, plus adding some swabbies to run more fast transport ships and airpersons to operate more cargo planes, we're looking at most at an additional million personnel. Presumably that would include bringing back some recently retired senior noncoms and officers to impose order upon that mass of conscripted teenagers yearning to breathe free.

At the end of the Cold War, we had around 2.1 million active, although a higher proportion of Navy and Air Force than are needed at present. So, with 2.5 million, we could probably even make a decent stab at sealing our borders, including beefing up the Coast Guard and maybe Navy patrol units.

(A plug for the coasties. No outfit gives the American taxpayer more return on the dollar, bar none. You heard it here first: if there's ever a draft, the Coast Guard will skim the cream off the top of the conscription bottle, and you probably won't be able to get near a USCG recruiting office.)

So even in this maximal (indeed extreme) case, with two-year draft terms, we would need only five hundred thousand a year, or one in eight kids turning eighteen. You quickly narrow the pool to high school grads with clean records, acceptable test scores, adequate physically and psychologically, and you still end up with a highly *selective* Selective Service requirement. Various proposals have been offered as to how to handle the situation, including costly inducements to volunteer.

A question: is two years sufficient to be useful for most military occupational specialties?

One answer: probably not. Among others, it is sufficient for truck drivers, cooks and bakers, and line infantrymen, but not for the more technical positions so critical to supporting a modern military.

Then there's the other end of the equation:

Without seeming antidemocratic (small D), let's be adult enough to admit that there are a few youngsters possessed of abilities too rare and valuable to risk in combat or to waste their time in the Army. If some of them want to enlist, by all means let 'em in, but remember that the thoroughly professional German army took pains to identify staff officers early on, and usually kept them away from the front. The Japanese went the other way—they dragged electronics specialists away from industry and into the army at a time when the Mikado's warships lacked radar.

There should be room for a middle ground.

* * *

The foregoing remains separate from the moral issues. Apart from the pasty-faced bed-wetters opposed to all militaries, there exists far more latitude to debate the morality of enforced servitude in the cause of freedom—however "freedom" may be defined. The United States government drafted millions of unwilling young men to fight and die in both world wars, conflicts widely portrayed as crusades to liberate the oppressed and to protect American freedom (point of fact: America's freedom cannot be threatened from overseas, but that's a separate issue).

Eventually—probably sooner rather than later—the Pentagon will expend its manpower pool, especially in the sustainability of the crucial National Guard and Reserve. The rush to the colors following 9/11 began to fade four years on, when the initial patriotic fervor had subsided, especially absent a recurrence of those attacks.

The dilemma, of course, is represented by the Two-Headed Conscription Beast. One head bellows that a draft is politically impossible; the other that if it were possible, it would not work. There is no third head claiming that even a limited draft would solve more problems than it would create.

If you spend any time on blogs and Internet forums, you quickly discern a pattern. There are scads of chest-thumping posts along the lines of "Any American/Texan/marine/whatever can lick ten/twenty/whatever Arabs/Chinese/whatevers." But if you take the effort to separate the kernels of wheat from the blowhard chaff, you find occasional pearls such as this:

"I don't know anybody who'd want to share a foxhole with somebody who didn't want to be there and didn't believe in what he was doing."

That's a far more important concern than many people are aware. Yes, draftees can get the job done. After all, the "Greatest Generation" fielded an army and navy composed of 61 percent draftees. But despite billions in war bonds and Kate Smith belting out "God Bless America," the fact remains that, in by far the most popular war in our history, the large majority of young Americans waited to be drafted. And not all of them were so young. The average serviceman was twenty-six, and some were thirty-four. In fact, the record may go to a forty-five-year-old private first class who received the Medal of Honor (hey, some of those old guys are dangerous).

In what appears one of history's great ironies, the ratio was reversed during Vietnam, with more volunteers than draftees. However, thousands of draft-eligible males enlisted in the Air Force or Navy to avoid infantry combat, and that fact must skew the statistics. (It didn't always work that way, as today a successful artist laughs at himself: "I joined the Air Force so I wouldn't become a grunt, but they made me an air policeman and sent me to Vietnam, running ambush patrols out of Tan Son Nhut!")

* * *

There's another prospect: a limited draft.

It hasn't been discussed much, and then mainly in favor of sending conscripts to the Guard and Reserve. The theory is that eventually many draftees will extend their service and provide a net growth in available troops. However, that concept is chained to the onerous prospect of being sent to a war zone against one's will.

Another option is drafting only those individuals possessing special skills, such as advanced computer programming or speaking Arabic. The downside is that it unfairly places the burden on a few people who have gone out of their way to acquire specialized knowledge.

Let's consider something else.

In order to make maximum use of the all-volunteer force, drafting soldiers and sailors for noncombat service would release thousands of more willing personnel for overseas deployment. In the Terror War, it is not realistic to think that we can send conscripts to Iraq, Afghanistan, or any combat zone where they will not be exposed to ambushes, rockets, mortars, and IEDs. But by employing draftees for two-year stints in the U.S. (and perhaps Europe), a more efficient use of available manpower might be obtained.

Even a limited draft would not be popular, but it would avoid the worst of the unpleasant consequences of the Civil War and Vietnam.

Meanwhile, anybody can join the regular armed forces; only citizens are eligible for the National Guard.

That's the good news.

The bad news: well, take a number and wait in line. We haven't even begun to talk about "gender." (The government means "sex" but insists on misusing the grammatical term. In this book, we're all big kids and we can talk about the Sexes with a capital S.)

The Female Dilemma

Demographers tell us that about 4,180,000 Americans turn eighteen every year. With the all-volunteer force, that figure is sufficient to maintain 1,422,000 active duty personnel amid a total force structure of 2,360,000. In extreme emergency, there are some 135 million Americans aged seventeen to forty-nine as prospective conscripts.

Of the aforementioned 4,180,000 persons becoming draft-eligible each year, 52 percent are female.

Hmmm . . .

A new draft would require some careful scrutiny, and Job One might be women. Are We the People ready to send eighteen-year-old females into enforced military service? It's not like other wars in which uniformed women largely stayed at home or served behind the lines. There are no lines in the Terror War: it's aptly called the 360-Degree War.

(That raises a question that the Pentagon devoutly wishes to avoid. Women are still legally prohibited from serving in the infantry, armor, and field artillery. But how do we maintain the combat exclusion clause when females already are engaged in gunfights and have been killed and captured by the enemy? Most likely DoD will continue ignoring the situation and pretend that the contradiction does not exist.)

One example: In April 2006 the *Navy Times* published an article about a group of sailors being trained at Fort Bragg to replace an army unit in Afghanistan. Photos showed two females in full battle gear shooting weapons with the men.

Combat exclusion? No such thing.

The sailors—men and women—were assigned to a provisional reconstruction team, a security and civil affairs unit. The commanding officer of the ad hoc organization was a former helicopter squadron commander, training a ground unit to engage in infantry combat. Concluded a Navy Department spokesperson, "This is an appropriate mission for navy personnel."

By year end the Navy expected to have five thousand people in Afghanistan.

So, contrary to the law, women are already serving in ground combat roles, but does that mean that we should draft women?

Female conscription is not unknown. In fact, it is currently practiced in an astonishing variety of nations and cultures. Among the countries already conscripting females to varying degrees are Israel, North Korea, Peru, Eritrea (1994), Taiwan (2004), and even Muslim states such as Libya (1984) and Malaysia (2000). Whether Americans want to join that eclectic group remains to be seen.

It's an extremely touchy subject, but if you buy enough beer for veterans of Iraq and Afghanistan—especially NCOs—you'll start to hear what you won't see in print. The bottom line: a great many men believe that most women in deployed units are simply not worth the effort to keep them. The exceptions occur in units where officers enforce one standard for all.

Here's "Darren," a first sergeant with nearly thirty years' military service, including an Iraq tour in 2004–2005:

"We had twenty women in our company, and you can count the number of good ones on one hand. When you're done you'll have four fingers left over. For the others, most of them were useless. They caused me and the other NCOs unnecessary problems every damned day. The officers wouldn't deal with it—they were terrified of getting cross-threaded with the higher-ups.

"Most of the women didn't want to wear their helmets because that mussed up their hair. They didn't want to lift anything heavy because (A) they couldn't and (B) they might break a nail. They'd flirt with the guys who were dumb enough do their work for them, and spent the rest of the time bitching about the heat, the food, and the accommodations. Don't even ask me about the incoming mortars . . .

"I don't have the official figures, and maybe they don't even exist. But in my time near Baghdad, I talked to a lot of guys from a lot of units. It looked like about 20 percent of the females in-country got themselves knocked up, either through carelessness or a way to go home. So guess what? The rest of us—mostly men—got to pick up the slack."

It's not only the Army. Just when you thought it was safe to go near the Navy again, here's "Tom," executive officer of an Atlantic Fleet warship:

> "The worst part of cruise now is when we pass Gibraltar headed home. That's when all of the cruise romances break up. My 'brick' (radio) goes off. 'XO, we have another altercation on the mess decks.'
>
> " 'Let me guess . . . '
>
> " 'Yessir. It's one of our women trying to claw a guy's eyes out. She's shrieking, 'He never told me he was married!' "

The Navy's "female problems" began in earnest immediately after Desert Storm. Amid the Bush 41 administration's Tailhook witch hunt, the Navy could not promote women fast enough to meet the perceived need to be seen Doing Something. Nobody expected any star wearers to tell Representative Patsy Schroeder to get stuffed, but the fact that almost a full generation of navy admirals and marine generals failed to demand due process for the male troops speaks volumes. The tone was set by the chief of naval operations (CNO), who did what submariners do in time of trouble: he dived deep and ran silent.

In 1992, after CNO delivered a speech at Naval Air Station (NAS) Miramar, a Tomcat pilot remarked, "We sure have a lot of five-knot admirals trying to run a five hundred–knot navy."

Shortly thereafter, in just one selection board, every carrier-qualified pilot and naval flight officer was passed over for commander in favor of female admin officers.

Lapse-dissolve, fade in to day. At Tailhook '94 an officer coming off a tour in Personnel quoted his admiral as saying,

"Retention really sucks. I'm beginning to think we may have a morale problem."

Well, duh!

Things are better now. But the fact remains, during the greatest personnel reduction (aka "rightsizing") in half a century, when *man*power was no longer a problem, the U.S. Navy fell all over itself to appear politically correct, and drove hundreds of combat-experienced aviators out of the service.

So let's cut to the chase.

Can females perform in combat? Definitely. Even allowing for the excesses of Stalinist propaganda, many Russian women proved themselves as snipers, pilots, tankers, and guerrillas in the Great Patriotic War. Nearly ninety were awarded their nation's highest honor, being declared Heroes (Heroines) of the Soviet Union.

American women also have been there and done that:

In March 2005, Sergeant Leigh Ann Hester, a twenty-three-year-old Kentucky National Guard MP, participated with her dismounted squad in a counterambush action southeast of Baghdad. With Staff Sergeant Timothy Nein and Specialist Jason Mike, Hester outflanked the hostiles and assaulted their position with an M203 grenade launcher on her M16. She personally slew at least three insurgents. In all, seven GIs killed twenty-seven of the enemy and captured others. Hester was the first woman awarded the Silver Star in almost sixty years, and few would argue that she did not deserve it.

In the same action, five-foot, two-inch Specialist Ashley Pullen received the Bronze Star for suppressing enemy fire and crossing open ground to treat a wounded noncom.

Contrast that event with the far better known ambush of the 507th Maintenance Company two years earlier. Private First Class Jessica Lynch's unit was unprepared for combat. Weapons maintenance—a known critical factor in the desert—had been neglected. Later she stated that her rifle jammed on the first round and the last thing she remembered was praying on her knees. Eleven soldiers were killed and five others were captured with Lynch, who was later rescued.

How to explain the difference?

In a word: Leadership.

Hester and Pullen's CO said that he never doubted the women's ability to function under fire, because it was what he expected of all his soldiers. Though the two events occurred in different areas under different circumstances, the similarities invite comparison: an insurgent ambush of military convoys, one ending in total defeat, and the other a clear-cut victory.

There's a lesson here.

Women are never going to be as strong as men. Not even the United States government can alter that elemental fact. Nor are most military women nearly as eager for combat as most males (few female naval aviators seem as enthused about bombing and strafing as they are about flying the space shuttle). But in the rare instances when commanders establish a uniform standard of behavior and performance—and stick to it—the results speak for themselves.

The problem occurs when commanding officers—especially the uniformed politicians with stars on their shoulders—invoke a double standard. In just one instance, when women were allowed aboard warships, a rear admiral told his officers, "Gentlemen, if you're smart you will not fraternize with female officers on leave. If she changes her mind 'the morning after' and complains to me, I will be required to believe the lady."

It's better now than during the 1990s, but then it *had* to get better.

Still, there are potential PR problems with women in combat, and none more sensitive than female POWs.

Of the three army women known captured in two Iraq wars, apparently all were raped or sexually assaulted. Those few instances—especially Lynch's—generated much comment, but eventually they faded from public attention. Apparently most Americans have adjusted to the likelihood of female soldiers being raped in captivity, though ironically (or not) there is far more coverage of real and alleged sexual assault on college campuses, from Duke to Annapolis.

The world isn't what it used to be. And neither is America.

* * *

There are some short-term alternatives to drafting people, and one of the options is expanding the potential enlistment pool by raising the age for volunteers.

That's exactly what happened.

After attracting too few recruits in 2005, the Army and the Reserve acknowledged that they could not attract enough young people to meet the required 80,000 enlistments each year. Originally the upper age limit was raised from thirty-five to forty, but that was inadequate. Therefore, in June 2006 the minimum acceptable age was raised to forty-one (one recruit reported to Fort Jackson, South Carolina, at 11 p.m., sixty minutes before his forty-second birthday). The campaign involved higher enlistment bonuses and increasing some pay levels. Greater reenlistment incentives also were offered.

To an extent, it worked. In some instances, parents and sons or daughters completed basic training within weeks of each other. The extra numbers have not been terrific—some 1,100 recruits over thirty-five as of that August—but the program had not been widely promoted by then.

Even with the new age limits, it appeared that the washout rate was reduced. According to Dr. Lawrence Korb, assistant secretary of defense under Reagan, during the first six months of 2006, only 7.6 percent of new recruits failed basic training, compared to 18.1 percent a year before.

The inevitable result of lower standards is fewer fully qualified soldiers. Korb noted that the number of army recruits scoring below average on the standard aptitude test doubled in 2005, a figure matching the number of enlistees without high school diplomas in 2006. Those factors contribute to a descending spiral: placed under greater pressure to enroll more people, recruiters have been found falsifying entrance qualifications by an increased factor of 50 percent. (Lawrence Korb et al., "Tapped Out," *The New Republic* Online, September 13, 2006.)

What does that mean to the Army or the other forces downstream?

Hard to tell, but it certainly means nothing good.

The Transformation Thing

In the Pentagon game, you pays your money and you takes your chances.

Following collapse of the Evil Empire, President Clinton and the Republican Congress eagerly sought the "peace dividend." Ignoring history and human nature, the demise of the Soviet Union was interpreted as "peace in our time," leading to major reductions in the military. But while the Cold War force structure was dismantled, brushfires sprang up around the globe: Bosnia, Kosovo, Haiti, Somalia—and Kuwait. All that was before 9/11. There was an inverse relation between force reductions and deployments: the former down 40 percent; the latter up as much as 400 percent. Something had to give.

It was people: retention suffered.

Consequently, DoD sought to offset the deficit by spending more money on technology with smaller, more flexible combat units. Considering the 1991 world view, that might have made sense. But the world refused to cooperate.

Then came 9/11. The poles had shifted: suddenly we faced a broad-front conflict in two dissimilar arenas: Afghanistan and Iraq. We were going to need more people, not fewer, to wage a long-term campaign against a tough, committed enemy.

Yet after 9/11, DoD continued with plans to turn the Army into a smaller, more flexible force. In the eighteen months between Operation Enduring Freedom in Afghanistan and Operation Iraqi Freedom, it was pretty much business as usual. High-high tech gear continued eating massive portions of the defense budget, to the detriment of the kind of warfighters we needed: ground troops and support personnel.

In 2004, 27 percent of active duty forces were serving in foreign countries, a figure almost identical to the Desert Shield/Storm level. But the deployed units (as opposed to those permanently based overseas) were four to five times greater than the decade after Desert Storm, and the total personnel serving abroad was nearly 50 percent more. (Carl Conetta et al., "Is the Iraq War Sapping America's Military Power?" *PDA: The Project on Defense Alternatives*, October 22, 2004.)

In short, however you slice or dice the numbers, the computer keeps spitting out the same result: we need more people.

Where are they to be found?

Elsewhere, the hardware tail is wagging the personnel dog. In Defense Secretary Rumsfeld's transformation movement, the Air Force decided to reduce its manpower to offset increased cost of the F-22 Raptor and other new, expensive systems. As of 2006, the service's strength of 351,800 people would be reduced by 40,000 personnel, with 16,000 of that reduction by the end of fiscal year (FY) 2007.

It's not just the Air Force, of course. This comes from a former navy electronics warfare officer who made forty trips over the beach in Desert Storm:

> No matter what we say, combat time is not very important to a career in the military. I was at a brief today [2006] where we saw that the EA-6B community was below average this year for promotions to commander and captain. The reason stated was, 'The rules have changed.' Time at sea is not critical, command isn't even what it used to be [they had the highest passover rate in history this year for O-5s with command at sea who failed to make O-6]. Time on joint staffs, schools, and a master's degree are what you need to get promoted. EA-6B types have a bad habit of spending a lot of time in operational functions. For instance, 11 percent

of the EA-6B community officer force is in Iraq right now—on the ground with the Army! Yet this doesn't count for critical 'joint' time because it's at the operational and not staff level. It's starting to kill them.

Had a long talk with a navy 'pers' O-6. He tells me we're eating ourselves from the inside, and that as we continue cutting manpower [which is the most expensive part of the budget], there's little long-term vision for what the impact will be years from now. Pretty depressing, actually.

A look at ship/squadron manning comes from "Ray," a former naval flight officer now in industry:

My most recent trip to D.C. was a real eye-opener, in that I had a chance to talk with a couple of old flying buddies now in OpNav. They're both postcommand captains who are pretty disillusioned and getting out. One's in personnel [N-1] the other in plans [N-5]. I won't go into details, but I consider both to be very good officers who have given everything to the company—and now see things unraveling at the seams. CNO/OpNav is talking about six-year sea tours 'because sailors belong at sea.' No word on what that will do for retention, particularly since we continue the march toward contracting everything possible to reduce costs [which means no shore billets for sailors]. Total personnel cuts are, without doubt, cutting muscle now, and there's more to come. Massive individual augmentee assignments: *every* staff has people yanked to go over to the desert—some serve two six-month tours in an otherwise normal tour, but the gouge is we're still fine for pers.

The fact that USS *George Washington* recently [spring 2006] deployed off Venezuela with a hollow air wing went largely unnoticed—only half of its normal strike fighters, an E-2 outfit and antisubmarine warfare

[ASW] birds, but no VAQ [electronic warfare] onboard. I'm sure somebody would try to tell you that it was 'right sized' or some other such nonsense. The much-bally-hooed 'TacAir Integration Plan' is a shambles. The Navy has sent only two units over to Japan so far in trade for all of the marine units that have gone to carrier air wings, and my jarhead friends tell me that the navy squadrons are not prepared to the level that the Corps trains its squadrons [small arms, self-defense, chemical-biological-nuclear (CBN)), et al]. Yeah, we're doing great out there.

There's something else to consider, and it receives precious little attention. Even assuming that we obtain sufficient numbers of new personnel, then what? That means we need more housing, gear, and training. There are not enough training facilities or firing ranges now (see Chapter Three). We need planning for expansion of barracks, uniforms, food, and equipment, plus weapons and ammunition.

From the perspective of the MIPC, none of the foregoing holds much attraction because it does not equate to big-ticket programs such as sophisticated aircraft, new submarines, or futuristic "combat systems" that produce jobs and votes. The whole idea behind Transformation is to do more with high-high tech stuff in order to get by with fewer people. Yet the Terror War is a people-intensive endeavor, requiring enough of a force to keep sufficient boots filled wherever the sharp end occurs at a given time.

Transformation is based on four concepts: joint operations; greater intelligence gathering and distribution; concept development and experimentation; and developing transformational capabilities (whatever that means).

Among the transformation goals that make sense is an increase in special operations forces. The Terror War offers fertile soil for special operations forces (SpecOps): Green Berets, rangers,

SEALs, and other commandos. They are flexible: trained and equipped for rapid, violent door-kicker missions as well as covert operations to gather intelligence or put a laser designator on an interesting building while a fighter or bomber puts a precision guided munition (PGM) through the second window on the right. The Clausewitzian term is "economy of force," a war college way of expressing more bang for the buck.

But the insurgency we face in Iraq, and potentially almost anywhere else, also requires conventional forces. "Boots on the ground" are essential in securing large areas, patrolling hot spots, and providing "presence." Those crucial goals cannot be achieved by gear, hardware, or stuff. They can only be accomplished by large numbers of well-trained troops thoroughly educated in the local culture, serving enough time in a specific op area to learn the lay of the land: physical, social, and environmental.

Even in the twenty-first century, there's no substitute for a rifleman with a good pair of boots.

We Need Civilians

The Defense Department has seven hundred thousand civilian employees, so why not add some more?

Aside from administrators and clerical workers, DoD has used nonmilitary people for decades. Many of those in the most important positions are former military personnel doing the same kind of work they did in uniform. Contract maintenance is just one example, but it's better than most.

Captain Lonny "Eagle" McClung was a career navy fighter pilot and Topgun skipper. He has personal experience with civilian contractors.

"I became alarmed when we contracted the maintenance for my T-2s and A-4s at NAS Kingsville. They did a good job—most were ex-navy—but the product was no better than what the contracting officer wrote on paper. It took lots of growing pains to get it right. I share the concern about contracting out services. There is no substitute for the skill, initiative, versatility, and work production of the USN bluejacket, but manpower costs are driving the train.

"When we were having trouble getting instructors to the training command, there were discussions about using retired guys like me for pilot training, just like the T-39 guys who trained the naval flight officers (NFOs) on a contract basis. Since our retirement was already paid for, the bean counters figured there was a savings there. Might be worth a relook. I would gladly do that—at least on a part-time basis."

Imagine you're a fresh-caught student pilot drinking beer with your buds that evening.

"How'd your hop go, Studly?"

"Hey dude, I got an up-check. And guess what? My instructor used to be the CO of Topgun!"

We have an enormous pool of knowledgeable, enthusiastic civilians who are eager to contribute to the military, but the pool is largely untapped.

Other civilians are intimately involved in military operations, but strictly in the private sector. The fact is, DoD does not have enough qualified instructors or facilities to meet the needs for combat training, and that subject is addressed in Chapter Three. But for the moment, we could be making far better use of civilians across the board: career retirees, those with prior service, and probably a few million who are just interested in lending a hand. Consider the knowledge and experience among the population surrounding most military and naval facilities: computer programming, clerical and stenographic help, vehicle repair, and marksmanship training to name a few.

They're out there. Let's go get them.

Aside from aviation, the Navy needs people so badly that it has taken to hiring professional mariners to "drive the boats" by conning warships in and out of some ports. The reason: many ship captains are only "sea buoy to sea buoy" operators. The result is increasing reliance on what amounts to nautical valet parking, even in home port. Though more ship handling simulators have been available since the mid 1980s, skippers do not get enough hands-on time to master the intricacies of port entry, departure, and docking. Even the gadgetry appears lacking, however: in 2006 a navy captain described the equipment as "third rate" and unworthy of presumably the world's greatest fleet. (Stuart Landersman, "Where Have All the Shiphandlers Gone?" *U.S. Naval Institute Proceedings*, August 2006.)

Logistic support ships previously operating as commissioned navy vessels now belong to Military Sealift Command, conned by master mariners and usually crewed by civilians.

One officer familiar with the situation is Phil, a navy captain who commanded a supply ship in the Pacific Fleet. "One good example of civilians manning our ships is the flotilla that is anchored in the lagoon at Diego Garcia. It is a number of ships loaded with spare parts, supplies of all kinds, weapons, ammo, etc. They sortie occasionally with civilian masters and the fleet is commanded by a civilian commodore."

Nor are civilian contractors limited to security personnel in Iraq and Afghanistan or to seagoing venues. Increasingly, the military relies on commercial aviation enterprises beyond the Civil Reserve Air Fleet (see Chapter Four, Logistics).

Some firms tread the line between administrative support and combat training. Arguably the best flying job in the world is a civilian aggressor pilot: an experienced tactical aviator who, if he plays his cards right, can yank and bank with F-16s or F/A-18s and sleep in his own bed that night.

Just before Desert Storm in 1991, the Air Force disbanded its aggressor squadrons that provided realistic threat training. The theory went that at the end of the twentieth century, the air-air missile had finally matured, and air combat maneuvering (dogfighting) finally had passed into history.

The aerial results of the Mesopotamian live-fire exercise seemed to vindicate the decision, since F-15s ran up a 34-0 score while navy squadrons went 2-1 (additionally, two A-10 Warthogs and a Tomcat snuffed three helicopters). All the kills against Iraqi fighters were the result of missile shots with very little maneuvering for position, as most of Saddam's pilots were intent on "getting out of Dodge at the speed of heat." Air supremacy was quickly established, and in Round II a dozen years later, the Iraqi air force remained a no-show. In fact, some of its airplanes were buried in the sand.

In 1996 the Navy disestablished its last regular adversary squadron, leaving two reserve units for aerial combat training. Consequently, a few civilian companies stepped in to fill the gap. Firms such as the Arizona-based Advanced Training Systems International provided 1960s-vintage A-4 Skyhawks for dissimilar air combat maneuvering (DACM). Other firms use biz jets to fly cruise missile profiles, usually low and fast. Circa 2002 the CEO of one such organization exclaimed, "Hey, we sank a carrier last week!"

Nor is that all. In 2004 the Royal Air Force, with just two tanker squadrons, decided to transfer in-flight refueling to the private sector. AirTanker, Ltd., won the contract, flying modified Airbus 320 jumbo jets for refueling missions. A long-term agreement was inked, averaging almost $1 billion per year.

In the U.S., Omega Aerial Refueling Services of Alexandria, Virginia, provides two converted 707s that essentially provide KC-135 capabilities. Thus, it appears certain that for the foreseeable future, private enterprise will only grow in importance in supporting the military.

So much for all that 1990s "rightsizing."

The Revolving Door to Combat

There's a challenge inherent to personnel policy, and it's permanent as gravity. Apart from the obvious questions—how many people are enough, and how do we get them?—remains the equally important matter of rotation policy.

During the Vietnam War, the Army and Marines rotated individuals in and out of permanently assigned units "in-country."

Like anything else, the policy had advantages and disadvantages. The advantage was that the unit (squad, platoon, company, etc.) generally retained enough old hands to provide institutional knowledge, so that the same hard lessons did not always have to be relearned. The downside was that, with constant turnover, unit cohesion and therefore morale could suffer.

Today it's different. Generally, units are assigned to a fixed term of service Over There (six months or a year) with the troops permanently assigned. Consequently, once the company, battalion, whatever learns the ropes, it's an all-up round for "the duration." Personnel learn the job, the working environment, and the local tricks of the trade. Additionally, the officers and NCOs learn their subordinates' strengths and weaknesses: who can do what; who can be relied upon and who can't.

The trouble, of course, is that when the next unit rolls in, there's an unavoidable loss of corporate knowledge. Without some old-timers who have BTDT in that job and that locale, the new guys and gals start over. Yes, there are "turnover" and "in-chop" briefings, but even when they're conscientiously applied, troops report that they can be cursory ("Let's get the hell outta here") or rendered marginally useful owing to an evolving atmosphere.

What to do?

The Army has suggested one or two ideas; I'd like to suggest another.

To its credit, in 2005–2006 the Pentagon began considering an "on-off" tour for middle and upper-level officers: battalion grade and higher. The concept would place lieutenant colonels and colonels in semipermanent billets to oversee a continuity of operational doctrine and plain old know-how. One version would put officers in-country for six months "on" and back home for three or four "off" before repeating the cycle. For an incentive, the officers would be eligible to select their next assignment, especially career-enhancing slots such as war college. It's worth a try.

Now let's consider another prospect.

Since we're engaged in an open-ended conflict likely to last decades or more, long-range planning should be possible. Ergo, shorter-term planning should pose no great challenge. Once a unit's place in the deployment schedule is known, send one or two officers and NCOs to the unit currently in-country two or three months early. Integrate those "scouts" into the unit that's nearing completion of its tour so there will be some corporate knowledge on the ground when the newbies roll in.

Yes, it may require longer deployments by the advance "scouts" but maybe not. Possibly rotate them home after six or twelve months and receive the next outfit's scouts.

It's worth a try. And it might save some lives or limbs.

Army Mules and Canoe U.

What about the military academies?

There are two predictable news stories about West Point, Annapolis, and Colorado Springs. Either the Cadets, Middies, or Falcons make the Big Game, or the entire male student body is suspected in the latest date-rape case. It's almost as if military science is an afterthought, though the taxpayers might ponder why those institutions have been sustained since 1802, 1845, and 1955, respectively.

There seems more public concern over evolving (or declining) standards at Annapolis than at West Point or the Air Force Academy. In 2006, citing concern over an increasingly politicized atmosphere of the Naval Academy, a World War II alumnus wrote, "Its only reason for existing has been that it trained fine naval officers; not fine engineers, not fine mathematicians, not fine scientists, but fine naval officers."

The situation had been noted long before. A 1945 graduate was the late Captain Wally Schirra, the only astronaut to fly in America's first three manned space projects. Circa 1980 he was invited to address his alma mater, which by then had admitted women. As a combat fighter pilot, Schirra reckoned his operational service was more pertinent to the audience than his time with NASA. Therefore, he tried to put things in perspective by observing that the midshipmen would graduate as engineers, but their purpose was war. He ended by claiming, none too modestly, "I can say that because in my time I was the finest hired killer in the U.S. Navy."

Years later Schirra notes with a wry grin, "You know, I haven't been invited back!"

All too often, troops (and some officers) see the academies as careerist hatcheries. Says "Ray," commissioned as an ROTC officer, "The primary role now is diversity. We think we can train women for combat because they're 'equal' to men, yet the girls are seen as potential victims who need to be protected from the male students. It's a contradiction that isn't even being discussed. Many of the alums don't seem to care: they're either more worried about the football team going to a bowl game or trying to get their daughters in so they don't have to pay tuition at a 'real' school.

"We have way too much careerism. Real warriors are not welcome any more. All of the services seem to be more concerned with training officers for staff duty than combat because, as I've been told, 'We'll all do about the same in combat. Being there is all you need. What you do there really isn't that important because we can assume that any other officer would've done the same job.'" (This was from a personnel type in 1991.)

The matter of "combat equivalence" is a genuine sore point among mission-oriented personnel.

For generations, combat experience was almost *de rigueur* for promotion to flag rank, but it has become irrelevant in the Navy, long dominated by submarine and surface officers. Of the nine CNOs since Vietnam, only three have been combatants; just one of the last seven. The latter aviator slipped in when Admiral Michael Boorda committed suicide in 1996.

Boorda was a refreshing change in some ways. When appointed, he was the only non-Annapolis CNO since, well, forever. As a "blackshoe" (surface) officer he had sailed off Vietnam and years later received an unauthorized "V for valor" device on his Southeast Asia service ribbon, unaccountably granted by former CNO Elmo Zumwalt. That was controversial enough. But Boorda was widely criticized for failing to support his vice chief against Senate Republicans who withheld the admiral's next assignment owing to sexual politics. Having expended his dwindling capital, the CNO ran out of allies. In perhaps the most telling comment, one uncharitable pilot quipped, "Well, I see that Mikey Boorda finally got shot at." The resentment ran that deep.

In contrast, all nine army chiefs of staff have been to war, as have the ten marine commandants. Eight of ten air force chiefs have flown genuine combat missions.

Apart from a Clintonesque inquiry as to "What is combat?" perhaps a more pertinent question is whether combat experience truly matters in the rarified D.C. atmosphere. Certainly political connections and beltway savvy are more useful among the Potomac helium breathers than demonstrated skill at slaying the nation's enemies, but there should be room for both. After all, in theory the politicians (uniformed and otherwise) exist to support the shooters, but as will be examined downstream, all too often the services fail to put their money where their rhetoric is.

Unfortunately, that rhetoric interferes with the mission. Time and again, contributors to this book cite examples in the United States and Iraq (not so much in Afghanistan) of commanding officers who cannot be bothered with mundane details, such as whether weapons function. A former NCO quoted one brigadier general as saying, "That's far below my level of responsibility."

Consider this:

In the Air Force, if jets don't fly, somebody with birds or stars on his shoulder usually gets hammered.

In the Navy, if ships don't sail, somebody with birds or stars on his shoulder usually gets hammered.

In the Army and Marines, if guns don't fire, frequently nobody gets hammered. We need to make functionality a requirement for promotion, but "the System" successfully resists that impulse, probably because of a deadly binary: indifference and careerism.

The next time you hear an officer say "Our people come first," ask him (or her) whether the troops' rifles are zeroed—and operable.

Who Should Serve?

Many of today's potential military recruits are a contrast to the draftees of the World War II era, when Americans were more accustomed to physical hardship and less inclined to complain. Additionally, in 2005 about 17 percent of applicants for military service were found unfit. Many recruiters note that the biggest reason for refusing potential soldiers is "auditory exclusion." So we'll have to be more selective, but there's a much bigger pond to fish in, so it's pretty much a push.

According to the Selective Service web site, some two thousand local draft boards are staffed with eleven thousand trained members in case conscription is initiated. Regardless of what is considered politically possible, we need to recognize that at some point in the multigenerational Global War on Terror, thousands of young Americans may find themselves reading those eight dreaded words: "Greetings from the President of the United States."

Chapter Three

We Need Training

"A government is the murderer of its citizens which sends them to the field uninformed and untaught, where they are to meet men of the same age and strength, mechanized by education and discipline for battle."
—Major General Henry "Light Horse Harry" Lee, c. 1812

Gentle Reader: In order to remove any doubt, I will step off the page and address you face to face. *Step-step.* None of the following is based on hearsay, Internet blogs, or urban legend. There is no "anecdotal evidence." *All* of it is based upon first-person observation.

I have seen graduates of military sniper schools who do not know how to use a shooting sling; who have never been allowed to do anything but single-load their rifles, owing to range safety concerns.

I have seen a soldier who did not know how to load cartridges into her magazine.

I have seen a five-stripe sergeant load his magazine to capacity—with the bullets pointed to the rear.

I have seen a soldier point a loaded M16 at an instructor—twice.

I have met an automatic weapon instructor who has never fired the gun.

I have met a helicopter pilot bound for Iraq who had not fired a rifle or pistol in two years.

I have met an air force reserve officer bound for Afghanistan who had not fired a weapon in eight years.

I could go on, but there's no need. You get the picture.

In other words, I was freaking *there.*

Back into the page. . . .

Rocks to Rockets

Since the age of rocks, armies have scrimped on training. The reason that history records so few world-dominating armies is that few have devoted as much attention to training as the Romans. Indeed, Caesar's army boasted that its training was bloodless battles and its battles were bloody drills.

Even at the height of World War II, the German army allotted sixteen weeks to basic training. At the same time the Western Allies devoted something less, even with vastly greater resources.

Frequently at or near the bottom of training priorities is marksmanship. In the British army of the 1850s, even the elite Guards regiments allotted each soldier an average of ten rounds per year. Change came grudgingly and glacially: sixty years later His Majesty's soldiers fired 1,100 rounds in a competition, of which five were scored as hits.

It was only slightly better across the pond. During the 1870s, America's Indian-fighting army reportedly included regiments that never conducted weapons training while apparently the most progressive units provided ten rounds per trooper per month. It took until the next decade to begin redressing the situation.

It's not always a lot better. After Desert Storm, which featured very few rifle fights, a former marine sniper officer said, "The Army has reduced marksmanship training, because some people think it tends to personalize killing."

Let's step back for a moment.

While nearly everyone can agree that soldiers should know

how to handle, load, and fire their basic weapons, how often do troops actually use them? Beyond that, how many times do Americans lose rifle fights?

Very, very seldom.

But if *your* parent, child, or friend stands in the line of fire, you probably want that loved one to possess the military's most basic lifesaving skill: hitting the target, quickly. After all, the enemy (currently from a culture with almost no marksmanship tradition) occasionally gets lucky. And considering that we're engaged in a multigenerational conflict, the enemy certainly will improve his weaponcraft.

We need to do the same.

More recently, two certified members of the Gun Culture compared notes in the D.C. area. John George fought the Japanese in World War II and authored a "combat jock" memoir, *Shots Fired in Anger*. His colleague was John Pepper, a Korean War veteran who produced an innovative target system and has conducted realistic rifle training for decades. Pepper relates, "We got to talking about how many infantrymen will look at their sights and control the trigger in combat. Based on what I saw, I'd guess 10 percent. John said, 'No, that's too high. It's more like 6 percent.'"

Actually, they may both be right.

Lieutenant Colonel Dave Grossman's widely read *On Killing* accepts Marshall's figures and tracks the "engagement ratio" from the black powder era through Vietnam. He concludes that improved training techniques and cultural desensitizing have produced steady increases in the firing rate, but that should not mislead us.

Understand that we are not discussing the ratio of *active* shooters, but of *effective* shooters. S. L. A. Marshall's widely quoted figures of 15 to 25 percent active shooters has often been discounted, partly because of his desire to get the Army to issue more automatic weapons. In the 1980s a retired major general said, "You'll never get 100 percent shooters, but if Marshall was right, I would've died in Korea."

In statistical terms—what the Pentagon best understands—
the difference between active shooters and effective shooters is
the distinction between probability theory and marksmanship.
We used to grasp that concept, once upon a time:

Been There, Done That, Part IV
"Rifle practice is a waste of money."
—New York Governor Alonzo B. Cornell, 1880

After the Civil War (aka the War of Northern Aggression) some
former bluecoats realized that the Union was preserved at bayonet point because so few of them could shoot straight. A wartime
survey of one Union corps revealed that one-third of the men
had never fired their weapons. In contrast, the mostly rural
Confederates were far more proficient with firearms.

Seven years after the war, two officers—Lieutenant Colonel
William C. Church and Major General George Wingate—decided that if the Army would not train soldiers to shoot, they would
do so themselves. Church was a journalist (publisher of the
Washington Sun and reporter for the *New York Times*) and later
cofounder of the Metropolitan Museum of Art. Wingate, a prewar lawyer, served in a New York regiment and later supervised
construction of Brooklyn's elevated railway.

In November 1871 the pair established an organization with
the stated goal of "providing firearms training and encouraging
interest in the shooting sports" among the general population.

Thus was born the National Rifle Association. The first president was General Ambrose Burnside, and former U.S. President
Ulysses S. Grant became NRA president in 1883. Wingate's manual for the New York Militia became the basis for the army-wide
document.

Years passed before the NRA reforms took effect.

Records from the Indian-fighting army indicate the same
abysmal pattern: unit after unit, year after year, soldiers were
denied adequate weapon training. By regulation, each soldier

was allotted ten rounds per month (an outrage for such a perishable, lifesaving skill) but even that miserly standard was seldom kept. Evidence from the Seventh Cavalry shows that most troopers had averaged seven rounds in the year before they rode to posthumous glory at Little Big Horn. In some units, years passed without shooting at all. In those days, recruits often received basic training in their units, with disastrous results to uniformity and competence. Something approaching adequate weapon training only began about twenty years after the War of the Rebellion.

* * *

Watch the History Channel or the Military Channel sometime. If you look long enough, you'll see a grainy black-and-white film of army maneuvers circa 1939. Soldiers "training" with wooden machine guns. "Training" with beer cans dropped down imitation mortar tubes (one assumes that the cans were empty, not that it matters). Mechanized units training with antique trucks bearing crudely painted signs proclaiming the vehicles "tanks."

You can see the rookies mouthing the sounds: "Bang-bang." "Rat-a-tat."

Absurd?

Yes.

Scandalous?

You bet.

At least it couldn't happen today.

Could it?

Well . . .

Fort Sill, Oklahoma, 2005. Listen to Warrant Officer Dave Long, a helicopter pilot training before deployment to Afghanistan. "We didn't have enough pistol ammunition, so we ran around with our Berettas, going 'Bang-bang.' Although we're an aviation unit, we had to train for convoy escort, but there was no training ammo for the .50 calibers or Mark 19 grenade launchers. So we did like Sergeant Rock, going 'Budda-budda' and 'ka-boom, ka-boom.' It was laughable and pointless."

That was not an isolated case. At Fort Bliss some National Guardsmen had M16 ammunition but there were too few range facilities. They waited their turn, and by the time they got to the firing line, darkness had fallen. "All we could do was function-test our rifles," said an NCO. "Yup, they all worked, but we had no idea where they shot. But we checked that box and off we went to war."

* * *

Combat troops are not receiving the hands-on weapon training they need. A case in point: in 2004 Staff Sergeant David Bellavia of the "Big Red One" was engaged in close quarters fighting in Fallujah when he confronted several insurgents in a basement. He had a flash-bang grenade, intended to stun and disorient enemies, but he had never used one before. Uncertain whether the violent sound and light would harm himself or his soldiers in that circumstance, he elected not to use it. Instead, he killed the enemy with his rifle and a personal knife.

Sergeant Bellavia has been nominated for the Medal of Honor.

Pop quiz:

What do Alvin York, Samuel Woodfill, Audie Murphy, and Charles P. Murray have in common?

Partial answer: They all received the Medal of Honor.

Full answer: Among millions of others, they also learned to shoot as civilians.

Lesson to be learned: We need more recruits who know how to shoot before they report for basic training. But assuming that marksmanship becomes a national goal (a huge assumption), how could we accomplish it?

The Gun Culture

Most of the progress in firearms and weapons training came from the private sector. Rifles themselves were civilian inventions, as were revolving pistols, metallic cartridges, smokeless powder, and the machine gun. Today's practical pistol doctrine was wholly the result of private endeavor. So we need to understand that, whatever institutional reluctance may exist, the military still can learn a great deal from civilians.

In the Terror War ("the three-block war") everybody needs to be trained to a combat standard because our truck drivers and supply people are almost as likely to be involved in a firefight as our infantrymen. Currently it's not possible to train all personnel to the same level, owing to shortages of ammunition, ranges, instructors, and priorities.

The one item we're not lacking is Official Indifference.

Unfortunately, far too many soldiers receive familiarization or qualification that passes for training. However, there is a difference—a huge one. It's more than the distinction between a qualifying time at the Indy 500 and the ability to race in traffic.

It's the difference between living and dying.

Faced with the impossibility of providing relevant training, the *Rawhide* syndrome kicks in: "Head 'em up, move 'em out." Get the troops through The Course and we've done our job. It's Miller time.

The real tragedy is that many of the troops do not know the difference. Soldiers shoot a qualifying score on the indoor electronic range (similar to an arcade game) and honestly believe that they're ready for combat.

Fortunately, civilians are willing to plug some of the gaps. I have seen active and reserve soldiers and marines attend club events just so they can get some trigger time. Three NRA instructor friends have been approached by troops bound for combat, seeking refresher training on small arms. In each case the instructors not only provided the guns and ammo, but declined compensation.

One of the shooters was a junior noncom named Mike. When I met him in late 2004 he had returned from Kosovo, where he was declared a sniper on the basis of his qualification scores. "They gave me a rifle, a can of ammo, and a manual and told me I was ready to go. That's when I decided I needed some real instruction."

Many months later I got an email from Mike in Iraq. He said, "After the things I've seen here, I just want to go home and live a better life."

"Kent" was a fresh-caught marine helicopter pilot whose squadron was leaving for Iraq in 2005. Because his unit would be flying from advanced operating bases, he wanted to get up to speed on M16 rifles and M9 pistols. Some family friends pointed him toward an instructor who obtained the guns and gear and provided three days training during Kent's two-week home leave. Kent said, "I really appreciate what Rick's doing. We're supposed to qualify annually but I haven't shot a rifle or pistol in the two years since Basic School. I'm not sure that anybody in our squadron has, either."

The following comes from Seth Nadel, a retired federal law officer and national-class pistol shooter:

> In the late eighties I worked with a reserve special forces major. They had not qualified in two years! The range of skills in my office, which, for law enforcement, was 'gun oriented', went from guys like me, to guys who had to shoot two or three times to qualify. And we shot four times a year, not once a year like the Army.
>
> At one of our club's machine gun events in 2005, two army guys showed up to shoot a privately owned M60. Seems they could not get enough time to shoot on duty (they did bring some ammo). They got more trigger time in that one day, than they had in the last few years! I hope the Marines are living up to their 'every man a rifleman' creed, so they can bail out the Army.
>
> Lots of GIs do not get enough ammo or trigger time (or useful trigger time) on their guns. What is useful trigger time?
>
> John Farnum has been doing pistol courses for the USMC. They carry loaded guns on the range, and draw from their holsters. Virtually every marine (up to and including the rank of colonel) says that is the kind of

training they need. Not the sterile 'Fire five rounds slow fire, and unload' they are getting on the ranges. Realistic targets at realistic distances, starting with loaded guns. We expect them to carry loaded guns on duty, but never let them train with loaded guns!

Reportedly our air force pilots and aircrew are not even allowed to load magazines! The range staff has to do it for them, allegedly because they 'might take ammo'! Where is the realism in that?

The NRA was founded to enhance marksmanship. We did a lot of training in the world wars. We are back at it. And with more interest in full auto marksmanship, the shooting community is stepping up to help our troops survive the GWOT.

I've lost track of the numbers of NRA shooters helping to train troops about to deploy, but it goes way back. Don't overlook the letter of thanks from Harry Truman and George Marshall after World War II for the help the NRA provided training shooters. There was also such a letter from Pershing after World War I.

Writing in late 1945, President Truman said, "The tradition of a citizen soldiery is firmly, and properly, imbedded in our national ideals. Initiative, discipline, and skill in the use of small arms are essentials for the development of the finished citizen soldier."

General Marshall, army chief of staff, wrote, "The nation is fortunate in having such an organization upon which it can rely for the continued development of proficiency in the use of small arms by the citizens of this country."

Admiral Ernest J. King, chief of naval operations: "The National Rifle Association of America came to our assistance with facilities and expert instruction which proved invaluable to our small arms program. Such assistance rendered willingly and unstintingly in the interests of our country is deserving of highest praise—and is sincerely appreciated."

Not surprisingly, criticism of DoD training priorities is resented by many military instructors (and students, for that matter). But ask yourself: if the armed forces are adequately funding weapons training, why is there a backlog of military units and individuals at so many civilian shooting schools?

I'll let one civilian instructor speak for many.

Among the most active civilian trainers is William Graves, who manages the McMillan Rifles sniper school in Arizona. His classes have been full for the past several years.

"The military sniper schools can fail 40 to 60 percent of their students. They see that as keeping up the quality of their programs, but they're always short of the numbers they need. That's why we have a full schedule: our classes are 100 percent shooting. There's no time for physical training, no politically correct programs, and not much admin down time. Trigger time is what counts."

We should not think that the military fails to provide basic firearms instruction to its personnel. Every recruit receives some degree of familiarization and initial qualification.

However, in far too many cases the soldier/airman/whatever is not allowed to perform basic tasks: loading cartridges in magazines (they're issued preloaded for accounting purposes); clearing malfunctions (that's what instructors are for), or even zeroing the weapon properly (it's done on twenty-five-meter laser ranges). Troops shoot an acceptable score on indoor ranges and walk away thinking they're ready for a rifle fight.

Says "Darren," the National Guard instructor, "We're *still* sending people to war who don't know how to defend themselves. It was bad enough with Jessica Lynch's unit in 2003. In 2006 it's a (bleeping) outrage."

The next problem, time after time after time, is lack of follow-up. If a unit has not conducted annual (let alone biannual) qualification with rifle or pistol, the individuals will soon lose whatever ability and knowledge they ever had. Shooting is a highly perishable skill—especially pistol shooting. Therefore, it needs to be reinforced at regular intervals and, equally importantly, reinforced *properly*. (Remember your high school coach? "Perfect practice makes perfect performance.")

Question: if a service member serves under an uninterested commander, what can the subordinate do?

Answer: he or she can go to a civilian school or facility. After all, institutional indifference does not absolve soldiers of the right or the responsibility of taking care of themselves. If a service member wants to shoot, there are civilians more than willing to provide the opportunity.

Meanwhile, the best solution is to learn weapons skills before enlisting.

Red Mike's Letter

He was a stocky, icy, red-headed marine who knew everything worth knowing about rifle shooting. He trained his Raiders to shoot fast and straight, and one September night in 1942 they held the vital ridge in tropic darkness against Japanese human-wave assaults. Had the enemy broken through, Henderson Field could have been lost, and with it the Guadalcanal campaign.

Merritt Edson received the Medal of Honor to wear with his Distinguished Rifleman badge and two Navy Crosses. A decade later, a retired major general and executive director of the NRA, he wrote a letter to the mothers of America.

Unfortunately, the letter no longer exists but I saw a copy in the 1980s. Basically, Red Mike said, "Mother, in wartime the military might not teach your son to shoot well enough to save his life. The best thing you can do for him is to ensure that he learns to shoot a rifle as a boy."

Contrary to conventional wisdom, in World War II, Colonel Edson issued automatic weapons to some of his best shooters. He insisted, "Firepower is important, but it is effective only insofar as it is accurate; the more accurate it is, the less firepower is needed. Teach basic marksmanship first. Given that, a man can devote his whole mind to the meeting of combat conditions without being in doubt of his ability to kill his enemy, once that enemy is met."

Today the value of premilitary marksmanship training still supports Edson's letter. In 2006 a Vietnam veteran forcefully stated the position on a web site as his son deployed to Iraq:

"The shooting, gun handling and firearms maintenance skills he learned *before* entering the military will compensate for the inadequacies of military training and procedures. What he brought to the military will greatly improve his survivability—and that of his buddies. Every person who calls for a ban on military style guns is a direct threat to the safety of our children who serve in the military and is unfit to hold public office."

Edson's comments were echoed five decades later by weapon evaluators who were also dedicated shooters (two roles that are not necessarily compatible, however logical the connection may be). A retired colonel recalls, "I was part of the army study group before I moved to my present position. From the outset, Dr. Martin Fackler, I and others provided critical points of information, such as 'incapacitation' (undefined) depends on shot placement; 'bigger' (whether in caliber or projectile weight) is better; more hits are better than a single hit; probability of hits is in direct proportion to the shooter's training/ability; and enhanced sighting devices (e.g., ACOG, EOTech, etc.) are of no value *if the soldier has not been properly trained in basic marksmanship* and how to use it."

In other words, gadgets will not compensate for lack of skill. It's a lesson that we Americans continually have to relearn. Yet the same officer reflects, "The Army spent three years and over $3 million to come up with little more than these conclusions. But it does not want to change to a different bullet or caliber because of costs, and because the ammunition manufacturing industry today is running at max speed just to keep the Army in bullets as it is."

Gun Games

The best training pits soldiers armed with loaded weapons against other soldiers in fluid, unpredictable scenarios. The guns are real: the ammunition is light beams.

Dating from the early 1980s, the multiple integrated laser engagement system (MILES) permitted realistic "force on force" training. Basically, MILES is laser tag with transmitters on weapons ranging from rifles to tanks. Receivers register hits on a vehicle or a soldier's harness, removing the "You're dead—No I'm not" aspects of the game. Additionally, weapons are coded to prevent a rifle from "destroying" an armored vehicle. More recently, MILES has been upgraded to prevent a "dead" soldier from continuing to play, and later models, upon taking a hit, disabled the victim's weapon until reset by an umpire.

Increasingly, we can expect to see more urban operations, what the British call FISH (fighting in someone's house). Most soldiers, the saying goes, are FISH out of water, poorly trained for that specialized type of combat. But fortunately, the Army and Marines have taken corrective measures.

Among the military's most useful training facilities are sample Afghan or Iraqi villages, complete with Arabic or Pashto speakers carefully coached in role playing and varied scenarios. Since troops are going to walk and talk a great deal more than they're going to shoot, such emphasis makes a great deal of sense.

The shortcomings of innovations such as MILES and representative environments are twofold. First, they do not replace live-fire training in which troops learn to use their weapons or reinforce the fundamentals. Secondly, no matter how sophisticated or how well designed and administered, there simply are not enough opportunities to put everybody through the advanced training. Priorities necessarily go to the combat arms—mainly infantry and special forces—while the larger numbers of support personnel often are left wanting. The situation is compounded in that one or two sessions with MILES or a couple of scenarios in "the village" are not enough. Repetition is the heart of learning, in the combat arts as in all things.

In short we need more ranges, more facilities, and more instructors for the kinds of training that the military does best.

Then we need to fix the lapses in the training that the military does poorly.

Simulators and Stuff

Our training deficit exists in areas besides infantry weapons. Tactical aircrews flew fewer hours in 2006 than in recent years: sometimes by considerable margins. A senior navy pilot called "Chuck" is typical: "A few years ago I was getting from 250 to 300 hours, which was great. This year I'll be under 200, and some guys in my squadron might be lucky to get much over 150. That's simply not enough to remain combat-ready, considering the multitasking we do. The jet (the F/A-18 Hornet) is a multimission airplane, and with our limited operating allowance, we just can't stay fully proficient in all areas."

One way of trying to offset the deficit in flight hours is more simulator time, and with computer and software advances, that's a factor. But it only goes so far. Simulators are definitely useful for procedures and switchology, and in fact they make economic sense in that regard. It's not necessary to have altitude beneath you and runway behind you in order to ingrain the subtle hand and finger movements that keep an airplane operating most efficiently.

However, the psychological component inherent to flying is totally lacking in simulators. A former naval flight officer working with a major manufacturer explains, "The Navy is starting to rely on sims more now. I believe they're called 'M-coded' which means that for some events a sim can replace an actual flight for training purposes. I have mixed opinions. Nobody ever died in a sim, which means the fear factor shouldn't be there, although I've known people with 'sim fever' who had trouble functioning in trainers—it's all psychological.

"There's just some stuff you can't duplicate in the sim, but I'm not sure we've figured out where that is yet. Then there's the problem that many people don't take sims seriously—we tried in the '80s to get squadrons to do back-seat work in the sim, yet time after time it turned into a less than successful evolution.

When the crew wore khakis, they canceled at the last minute ('Too much paperwork'—almost always senior NFOs in this case) or expected the junior aircrew to do all of the flight and mission planning for them, which is 50 percent of the learning experience. One of my COs used to insist that an LT do all of the mission planning and have a kneeboard card ready for him with all of 'the gouge' on it so all he had to do was show up and push buttons. Not much training there."

The situation has been known for many years. In 1999 an F-22 test pilot said, "We are more fiscally constrained, which forces us to work smarter and more efficiently. Boeing has a flying test bed with a full avionics suite to help us. Lockheed Martin is building an air combat simulator to expose pilots to a wartime environment without having to fly the airplane. We have fewer flying hours and fewer planes at an equivalent point in the development cycle, but we are further [sic] along because we have more experience and better tools."

But even the most advanced simulators still lack the feel of the real thing. "Every pilot knows that the simulator always flies a little differently than the airplane. The sensors usually work better in the sim. Ideally, we would demonstrate the effectiveness of the F-22 in the air. We would have one hundred targets show up, all the threats light up, and the electronic environment of a war. Even if we could do all this on the range, we would still have to simulate missile shots. At some point, then, we have to back off from reality. In the Air Combat Simulator, we will use computers to simulate denser threat environments with more surface-to-air missiles, more aerial threats, and more complex electronic environments. We can also simulate the data link and all the avionics on the ground. We would rather do it all in the air because it would be more realistic. But we can't; it would be too expensive." (Lieut. Col. David Nelson, interview by Eric Hehs in *CodeOne* magazine, January 1999.)

The goal in simulators is called "high fidelity"—a high degree of realism not only in visual displays, but in "feel," the feedback a pilot receives through his controls. Says "Andy," an experienced weapons and tactics instructor, "One person's interpretation is not the same as another's. Sims are great for teaching and training some skills, but not all. The issue is fidelity again. There are a lot of 'models' to predict how the real world will react to different economic stimuli. But like a model airplane, any model is not and cannot have 100 percent fidelity to real life. So, compromises are made to fidelity in various areas, and as such, no sim is ever a full substitute for real ops.

"As a fighter instructor, I found that in order to challenge experienced aircrews I had to crank up the speeds and closure rates in intercept training to well above real-world speeds because the sims were too easy. Why? Lack of fidelity. The real world has infinite variables constantly in play. But in a sim, the only variables are the ones modeled so the rest are held as constants due to fidelity constraints. That's why you can't have the majority of your tactical training in sims.

"The short course: Sims are invaluable for procedures and part-task training and mission rehearsal, but in the near term it is probably penny-wise and pound-foolish to assume you can replace any significant portion of tactical flight training with them."

What to do?

Buy airplanes that are affordable enough to fly frequently, and make up the deficit with technology.

It's so simple a solution that it has absolutely no chance of being adopted.

Chapter Four

We Need Logistics

"I don't know what the hell this 'logistics' is that General Marshall is always talking about, but I want some of it."
—Admiral Ernest J. King, c. 1944

Logistics have been called "the sinews of war," and nobody does logistics better than the United States military. Nobody. As one example, recall that Lieutenant General William G. Pagonis, who ran logistics for Desert Shield/Storm, retired to run Sears' supply chain and RailAmerica.

However, American admiration for logistics can go the other way, as well. During the Korean War, U.S. airmen said the one person they most wanted to meet was the commander of Communist supply and logistics. General Pen Te-huai oversaw the combined Chinese-North Korean army, and for three years his G4 officer did a magnificent job in the face of Allied air supremacy.

A definition is in order. Logistics is the process of moving large quantities of materiel (the proverbial "stuff") from where it's made or stored to where it's used. It's separate from the acquisition and production process, both of which tend to resemble the old-old adage about sausage and politics: Nobody should have to watch either being manufactured.

There are three ways of providing logistics: By land, sea, and air. America is a creature of the sea and the air more than the land, but we have considerable reason to brag there, too. Recall that the War of Northern Aggression was the first in which large troop movements were made by rail, and the semifamous "Redball Express" supplied beans and bullets to GIs in the European Theater of World War II.

The trouble with logistics is not nearly so much the process of transporting fuel, food, ammo, and stuff across long distances. The difficulty more often is coordinating the needs of the end users (the troops) with what is actually shipped. One example will suffice.

Been There, Done That, Part V

West Germany, 1962. A U.S. Army officer fresh off the Berkeley ROTC campus (you know that was long-long ago) was thoroughly enjoying his government-paid tour of Europe. Having been around Germany and Oklahoma twice, he thought he knew the lay of the land. He had a blonde Teutonic girlfriend who turned out to be a KGB agent (her fondness for vodka and recordings of the Red Army Chorus provided what Military Intelligence is pleased to describe as "a clue"), and when he was informed, the Sooner gasped in shock. "Omigod! I'll dump her right away!" he promised the counterintelligence types.

"No, no," the spooks replied. "We want you to keep her happy. As long as she's with you, she can't get information from somebody who knows something like a major or a colonel."

The second lieutenant chewed on that sentiment and had to concede the argument. After all, how much did Moscow really want to know about a deuce-and-a-half truck?

As officer in charge of his battalion's motor pool, the Oklahoman had little to do because he had a damn good first sergeant. (That left ample time to comply with the onerous orders from MI to keep the blonde KGB agent diverted. True, it was a rough job but Patriotism and Duty called, and besides, *somebody* had to do it.)

Among the vehicles that came and went from the motor pool was a mobile crane. A large, heavy mobile crane, big enough to hoist a truck. For one reason or another, the engine had lost its dipstick, and a replacement was duly requisitioned. Time passed. Still no dipstick. More requisitions followed, each more urgent than before.

Finally, one morning the NCO stuck his head in the office where the Oklahoman was reading a well-thumbed issue of *Road and Track*. "Lieutenant, your crane is here."

"My crane? What're you talking about, First Sergeant? We haven't ordered a crane."

The noncom stepped back and swept his hand outward, palm up, in a *Ta-da!* gesture.

Sure as God put oil in Garfield County, there was one-each, crane, mobile, priority delivery from ConUs. By air.

It even had a dipstick.

We Need Organization

The pattern is reliable as sunrise. We go to war. We're short of everything in-theater. Troops improvise, as they always have. They get in trouble for circumventing the system. Eventually the supply pipeline catches up and troops are inundated with stuff: double and triple what they need or what they ordered. Corrections are made. More shortages arise. Push-pull; shove and tug. Soldiers, sailors, and airmen learn to play the logistics accordion.

There must be a better way. But in 230 years we have not found a way to change the situation. At least not for the better.

Doesn't mean we should quit trying, though.

* * *

There's perhaps more reason for optimism in logistics than other areas. America has at least one hundred major sealift ships, most of which can be activated in two weeks or less. They include eight fast SL-7s (more than thirty knots) that SecDef John Lehman purchased in the 1980s.

Additionally, civilian-registered ships can be chartered from the commercial market. The cost to "park" each fast sealift ship (FSS) is pretty cheap by Pentagon standards: about $4 million a year. That's practically a bargain to maintain an asset that can carry tanks and stuff from the East Coast to Europe in six days; to the Persian Gulf in less than three weeks. With their roll-on, roll-off containers, the FSS "boats" can load and unload rapidly, as proven consistently during Desert Shield in 1990-1991. One of them broke down due to deferred maintenance, but the ship still delivered much of the 24th Mechanized Division's gear in ample time.

Considering how hard-pressed we might find ourselves for a massive airlift, it makes sense to tweak the logistics "train" with even faster, larger ships. The quest now is a program of very fast cargo vessels that can cruise all day at upward of fifty knots. That's hauling the mail, boys and girls: it's faster than most destroyers. The primary question is: can we afford them?

The second question is: in the Terror War, do we need large quantities of heavy stuff delivered rapidly? Probably not.

However, it's advisable to maintain fast sealift against the unexpected requirement of getting an armored brigade or even a division to a new hot spot "soonest." Therefore, maintaining the optimum force level remains—as always—a tricky business.

Meanwhile, maritime prepositioning ships are another bonus. It just makes enormous sense to place ships loaded with assorted Stuff within easy reach of potential trouble spots. When days count in the Next War, it's comforting to know that vehicles, ammo, and MREs are afloat in places like Diego Garcia.

We Need Airlift

Officially they're "airlifters." But pilots who fly pointy-nosed airplanes beginning with F sneer at them as "trash haulers."

Airlift has always been the poor cousin if not the bastard child of Uncle Sam's Air Force. (Never mind that the airborne invasion of Europe would have been impossible without C-47s, nor the China-Burma-India theater kept in the war without cargo flights over the Hump. Nor the only decisive Cold War victory achieved solely by airpower: the Berlin Airlift.)

Let's face it: transports are not sexy. I mean, in the way that school buses are not sexy. Park a big yellow bus next to a sculpted red Ferrari, and which one draws the crowd? Did you ever see anybody walk around a bus three times?

Neither have I.

But so what?

Plain fact is, unpointy airplanes like transports are used 24-7. All day, every day. They'll still be flying when the last manned fighter is replaced by a robotic that pulls forty Gs, and the trash haulers will make denigrating comments about fighter pilots and "artificial intelligence."

Meanwhile, fighters are seldom called upon anymore, and they're almost *never* needed to destroy other airplanes, which is what fighters are built to do. What we call fighter pilots these days actually are attack pilots—a profession at least as old and as honorable as the F guys.

Just for the record, here's the U.S. Air Force Medal of Honor count, all the way back to 1918:

Bomber crew: 31
Fighter pilots: 12
Attack pilots: 3
Observation crew: 2
Helicopter pilots: 2
FACs: 2
Trash haulers: 1

Don't let the numbers fool you. Of the dozen fighter pilots, only seven were decorated solely for gunning hostile airframes. The others did some righteous air-to-mud work.

Trash haulers have it pretty darned easy most of the time. They enjoy a big, roomy flight deck in a big, roomy airplane. They don't have to bother with oxygen masks, helmets, or G-suits. They can get up and move around, go to the lavatory, and have a lie-down in a bunk. Really nice on a TransLant or TransPac. And they can usually get something to eat or drink. Some display a plastic spoon with perverse pride, carrying it in a flight-suit pocket on the left sleeve.

Fighter pilots don't do that. Nor would they want to.

But that's beside the point.

What matters is, while we're eye-deep in F machines, we're running out of C machines—and we use cargo haulers every hour of every day.

For a possible glimpse of the future, cast your eyes backward just fifteen years. During Operation Desert Shield—the buildup to Desert Storm—the Air Force literally flew the wings off its cargo planes. At that time the C-141 Starlifter made up the greatest portion of our military airlift capability. But the unexpected demand for long-range supply flights from the continental United States to the Middle East placed enormous strain on the airlift community. The Civil Reserve Air Fleet was activated but the 141s continued hauling most of the load.

Here's a retrospective from "Hal," an air force employee who saw the results firsthand:

"We literally flew 'em to death. I remember about 1993–1994 when I was at Scott AFB (Illinois) and we got a briefing on their wing problems . . . *really* serious. We actually had a wing fail on one while it was on the ground. Some airplanes after that were coded by weight, as to how much they could haul, and many were essentially DOA . . . We shoulda had more."

Been There, Done That, Part VI

Stalingrad, January 1942.

Hermann Goering had made a promise to Adolf Hitler. The *Luftwaffe*, scourge of the Eurasian landmass, could supply General von Paulus' encircled Sixth Army by air for as long as necessary. It was the only way to prevent nearly a million Axis soldiers from surrendering and being prodded at bayonet point into the black hole of Stalin's gulag.

Goering lied.

Like most air commanders, the Fat One had grown up flying speedy, fun machines. After all, he had been a fighter ace in the Great War and had built his Air Force into a highly effective tactical instrument: just the thing to bludgeon a path for Guderian's panzers in the new form of warfare called *Blitzkrieg*.

The lack of a strategic air arm had become evident in the Kentish summer of 1940 when Goering's twin-engine Dornier, Heinkel, and Junkers bombers were unable to knock out British industry. But the next year his trimotor Junkers 52 transports had delivered a knockout blow to the vital Mediterranean island of Crete in one of the significant airborne operations in history.

That was the good news.

The bad news: Germany lost about 220 Ju-52s to the British and New Zealand defenders—losses that were not made good in time. After Crete, the *Reichsluftministerium* allowed an increase in transport production, but only from 503 in 1941 to 570 in 1942. It wasn't nearly enough.

By then, there was more need for fighters, and the transport units were left under strength. When they were called upon to deliver at least three hundred tons of supplies into the Stalingrad pocket every day—in some of the worst weather of the century— they simply could not meet the demand, averaging only one hundred tons. The Germans had about 150 available transports when 800 were needed, owing to maintenance, attrition, distances flown, and offloading at the seven fields inside the pocket. In barely two months the Luftwaffe lost nearly 500 transport and modified bomber aircraft.

Consequently, some 400,000 Germans and 450,000 Italians, Hungarians, and Romanians were killed, captured, or wounded.

Throughout World War II, Germany built barely three thousand dedicated transport aircraft. The U.S. built over ten thousand C-47s alone.

Buddha and Fred

Really big jet transports ("jumbos" in the commercial world) are mighty fine things. They get large amounts of people and gear where they're needed in a hurry, and because they fly rain or shine, they're often taken for granted. The U.S. armed forces have been flying jet transports for nearly fifty years, and today's crop of airlifters claim a proud heritage harking back to World War II if not before. They're an important part of the logistics story.

With retirement of the last C-141 Starlifter in 2006, U.S. Air Mobility Command (AMC) was left with two jet transports: the Lockheed C-5 Galaxy and the newer McDonnell Douglas/Boeing C-17 Globemaster III.

Depending on the load, both aircraft can fly about 2,500 nautical miles unrefueled. However, the Galaxy is rated at 270,000 pounds of cargo versus 171,000 for the Globemaster.

Both have their admirers and detractors.

The C-5 was a troubled project from the start. First flown in 1968, it was plagued with technical problems and went well over budget, requiring the government to bail out Lockheed in the process. (In the 1970s the unit cost topped $40 million, a Double Whopper of a price tag for one airplane. The follow-on B model went much higher.)

Eventually the Galaxy proved its worth. Speaking of the huge (223-foot wingspan) C-5A, aviation historian Robert F. Dorr said, "After being one of the worst-run programs, ever, in its early years, it has evolved very slowly and with great difficulty into a nearly adequate strategic airlifter that unfortunately needs in-flight refueling or a ground stop for even the most routine long-distance flights. We spent a lot of money to make it capable of operating from unfinished airstrips near the front lines, when we never needed that capability or had any intention to use it."

With an ugly profile that only a mother or an engineer could love, the Galaxy acquired the acronym FRED, for "Freaking" Ridiculous Economic/Environmental Disaster owing to the high number of maintenance manhours for each flight hour. The total "buy" was limited to some 130 airplanes, with fewer than that in service at a given time. In comparison, the Air Force bought 285 C-141s in the 1960s.

Meanwhile, during the Cold War (it was in all the papers) the Air Force ordered 222 Globemaster IIIs, but amid all the "rightsizing" by Bill Clinton and his GOP congressional colleagues, the buy was reduced to 180. That at a time when the C-141 was nearing the end of its service life.

When the C-17 entered squadron service in 1995, great things were expected of it. However, it was soon dubbed "Buddha" on the basis that it's very fat, it sits still, it refuses to move, and everybody worships it.

As always, there was good news and bad news.

The good news: The "Globe Three" was new construction and presumably would be around for many years to come.

The bad news: Demand was such that it was quickly run into the ground. Its relatively short range became a drain on tankers, and there were not enough of them as it was. As one observer noted, "The C-17 can travel long distances and carry a lot of stuff, but it cannot do both."

Some of the airlift slack may be taken up by the KC-10 tanker, which is reputedly going to double as a transport, but too few can be purchased to make much of a dent in the airlift backlog.

In summer 2006, Boeing announced plans to begin closing its Long Beach facility producing the C-17. The Air Force front office had decided that there was a greater need for F airplanes than C airplanes, never mind that F airplanes hadn't done any "F-ing" in seven effing years, and precious little at that.

The response was noteworthy not for what was said, but not said.

Predictably, the pols huffed and puffed. Governor Schwarzenegger was vehement that Kal-y-fornia's economy depended on military contracts, and closing the C-17 hatchery would put 5,500 people (read: voters) out of work.

Nobody protested that we're short of airlift and getting shorter.

With other local, state, and federal officials, the Governator stressed that the C-17 program "has a multibillion-dollar impact on the local economy," then as an afterthought conceded that it serves a useful military purpose.

In other words, never mind the Mission: "It's the Economy, Stupid."

Actually, with Globemasters still on order, Boeing could keep the factory open until 2009, but the situation boded ill for the military-industrial-political complex nonetheless. Southern California, once the hub of the aerospace trade, has fallen upon perilous times with fewer and fewer manufacturers.

In any case, an AMC analyst who wants to keep his job says, "We need both the C-17 and the C-5. The latter still has horrendous reliability issues and an appalling mission-capable rate but it is a true strategic airlifter. There has been no serious discussion of taking C-17 production beyond 180 that did not also include retiring C-5s. But 'Fred' is far more capable than 'Buddha' and always will be."

Generally the airlift community shares an attitude like the circus: everybody rushes to lend a hand when anyone hollers "Hey Rube!" But there are partisans in the transport business, and that concerns "Bob," a former air force officer working inside the Beltway:

"In an ideal world, where the government collects enough taxes to pay for what it needs rather than borrowing $400 billion per year, both would be affordable. But in the C-5 Galaxy community, many worry that C-17 proponents will try to get what they want by nudging some or all of the C-5 fleet to pasture.

"If that happens, it won't be the first time the Air Force retired an old plane that works perfectly well but has no support in Congress in favor of a newer aircraft with proponents on Capitol Hill.

"There is serious discussion today about retiring some of the Galaxy fleet, possibly the sixty-two planes that were built as C-5A models almost two decades before the forty-nine C-5Bs. The Air Force is already in the position of burning the furniture to save the house—retiring some 1,124 aircraft over the next few years in order to buy new ones. It must be tempting to retire the C-5As, which have reliability problems and few friends in Congress."

As is often the case, the crunch comes down to leaders willing to make decisions. Bob concludes, "I wish we could afford to purchase more than 180 C-17s without retiring a single C-5. We cannot. Things might be different if we had real leadership, if some leader of either political party would stand up in the spotlight, acknowledge that our nation is drowning in debt—our government, our corporations, our people—and push for drastic tax increases to meet the minimum needs of national security. There is no example in history of a nation surviving with the level of debt the United States has now accumulated. But the debt is a fact of life and that means hard choices. One painful choice we must make is to halt C-17 production.

"We cannot, and should not, retire a single C-5."

Q: How can we take up the slack?

A: Call the civilians—again.

As of 2006, Air Mobility Command had about 145 C-17s and 110 older C-5 Galaxies. Airlifters say that's an okay level but leaves almost no velvet, even with twenty-five more "Globes." If we have another major surge effort such as Desert Shield (which gobbled up huge amounts of the C-141's remaining fatigue life), we're in trouble. Plan B involves the little-known commercial air fleet option, placing civilian airliners and freighters under military control for a specific purpose.

The Civil Reserve Air Fleet (CRAF) receives almost no press but provides a much-needed backup to Air Mobility Command. The CRAF involves some forty airlines that have committed more than 1,100 transport aircraft to emergency use nationally, internationally, and for medical evacuation. In order to promote participation in the CRAF program, airlines are offered a percentage of government contracts during peacetime or nonemergency periods. In return, each company pledges to make 15 to 30 percent of its eligible aircraft available for call-up, with qualified flight crews.

An air force insider with personal knowledge of the CRAF compares 1990 with 2006:

"We did seventeen million ton-miles per day in Desert Storm using Stage Two of the Civil Reserve Air Fleet plus every airlifter we had. I doubt we could do that today. I think we're now moving about fifty-five thousand tons a day . . . but we are *seriously* stressed on the large capacity (not necessarily load, but size) side . . . which is a powerful argument for more C-17s."

There's a people side to the airlift equation, and the people drive the program, literally and figuratively.

Because transports are flown all day, every day, it's easy to assume that the "C birds" will always appear on the ramp, awaiting the next load. But apart from maintenance down time, there's the critical matter of "crew time"—the number of flight hours allotted to pilots and loadmasters in a given period. Shuffling airmen with sufficient unused flight time to where the next crew-expired airplane is parked calls for planning and coordination that would tax the world's best commercial airline. And that does not even address the equally critical matter of available tankers to get the next C-5 or C-17 across the Atlantic, let alone Pacific.

What to do?

During Desert Shield/Storm, air force reserve units were called to active duty because "crew time" was an operative factor. The USAF Associate Wing program is a terrific concept: it puts reserve crews flying airplanes belonging to the "host" active duty wing. That system worked in 1990–1991 because there was a finite "ramp-down" schedule that released reservists to their civilian jobs. But as one AMC analyst says, "If we ever tax airlift resources for an indefinite time, that mechanism could become a serious personnel problem."

We need more transport airplanes and more people to fly and maintain them. That's the obvious solution, but it's so simple a concept that it eludes easy remedy. The Air Force is not terribly enthused about "C" types, much preferring "F" types. In turn, the situation requires Congress to provide adult supervision lest the blue-suit kids continue playing with their supersonic toys. Some budget reallocation is badly needed—and unlikely to occur anytime soon.

We Need Tankers

Ken Tomb, a retired air force master sergeant says, "There's no stairway to the stars in airlift or refueling." That goes a long way toward explaining why the blue suits continue purchasing high-high-tech fighters and bombers: there's no cargo or tanker "mafia" à la the late John Boyd.

Today we have about 550 KC-135s (median age forty-five years and counting) and a shade under sixty KC-10s. Now, 610 tankers sounds like a lot but it's really not, especially when you consider the average number of planes down for routine maintenance, let alone depot-level repairs and whatever "special tasking" is imposed from on high. If only 20 percent of tankers are typically unavailable for whatever reason, that means about 480 to meet not only the needs of the U.S. Air Force but the Navy and many allies as well.

Say what?

It's true. During the Bush 41 administration, excessively high hopes were pinned on the A-12 Avenger II, a futuristic design intended to replace the tried and true Grumman A-6 Intruder, which doubled as a carrier-based tanker. DoD and the politicians were so certain that the Avenger II was going to fly (so to speak) that they hastened to retire the Intruder.

Bad idea. Really-really bad idea.

While perfectly good A-6s were being turned into fish habitat, the A-12 crashed and burned, figuratively if not literally. That left the Navy without a "bomb truck," without a deep-strike capability, and without indigenous tanking. For the first time since the 1920s, naval aviation found itself without any dedicated attack aircraft.

In that absurd situation, the dark blue guys dialed 911-USAF and began cadging gas from the light blue guys. Meanwhile, the F-14 Tomcat was turned into the "Bombcat," capable of flying long distances with useful ordnance loadouts into places such as deepest-darkest Afghanistan. But in 1992, then-SecDef Cheney, evidently in a snit toward the New York congressional delegation, had ordered the F-14 production jigs destroyed, thus preventing reopening the Tomcat assembly line.

(There was an intriguing story circulating in 2006 when the Tomcat was approaching retirement. Reportedly a middle level manager in the Pentagon's labyrinth of cubbyholes had exercised some Individual Initiative and had the jigs trucked to a government warehouse in the Midwest, thus retaining the option of building more F-14s. One likes to believe the tale, if for no other reason than the assurance that somebody out there thinks with his brain rather than his glands.)

Whatever improvements accrue to the F/A-18 Super Hornet and/or the vastly expensive F-35 Lightning II, we're still going to need more tankers.

We Need Heavy Lift—Fast

America has the ability to deliver a lot of stuff almost anywhere on earth, relatively fast. The question is: can we deliver *enough* stuff *fast* enough?

Maritime prepositioning ships are an excellent idea, especially when the "afloat reserve" contains enough big items such as trucks, tanks, and fuel to support an initial landing or invasion. But strategists inevitably fall back to the concept of "sustainability," the muscle to keep a powerful blow driving forward. It's exactly the sort of situation that Germany lacked in 1914 against France and in 1941 against Russia.

America recognized the need to establish sustainability before the first Iraq war. Desert Shield was nothing if not logistics—stashing enough people and gear to maintain a relentless campaign to drive the Iraqis out of Kuwait. And it worked: the six-month buildup to Desert Storm proved a luxurious opportunity to set the stage before the curtain was raised.

But what if we need a huge amount of people and equipment delivered somewhere in a matter of days, not months? What if we need lesser amounts delivered to two places simultaneously? Say, Iran and Korea. Or Israel and Indonesia. Or Bosnia and the Philippines. Close your eyes and poke your finger at any two places on a world map. One combo is as likely as another.

We can't do it. In the first place, we do not have huge amounts of people, and if we did, there's not enough stuff to support them. Food, housing, training, transport, weapons, ammo, radios, socks, whatever. We'll undoubtedly have enough of some stuff but certainly not adequate amounts of everything. That's not possible, since we don't have everything we need right now.

Consequently, we should be reinforcing our logistical base: producing stuff and the means to move lots of it over long distances, rapidly. That means more airlift, maintaining or increasing fast sealift, and perhaps more prepositioning assets.

Chapter Five

We Need Guns and Gear

"Man became man, in part, because he held a weapon in his hand."

—Robert L. O'Connell, 1989

For a variety of reasons, including NATO politics, the United States armed forces have shunned most home-grown firearms for decades. At this writing, both of our infantry machine guns as well as the standard sidearm are of European origin: Belgium and Italy, respectively. In some instances our service rifle has been made in Belgium and much of our ammunition is produced abroad because the military-industrial-political establishment would rather buy high-high-tech stuff than low-end gear such as small arms.

It's enough to rile the shade of John M. Browning, of honored memory. And if you don't know who he was, you're probably reading the wrong book.

Meanwhile, here's a pop quiz.

Quick: You have one minute to arm yourself for an unavoidable gunfight.

Do you choose the current small-caliber, high-capacity assault rifle that often fails to knock down a determined assailant, or an older, heavier weapon of less capacity that can kill an elk with one round?

I own both types but the older, heavier one rests at the front of my gun safe, with two loaded magazines nearby.

It's been said that the infantryman's primary weapon now is the radio, which may be connected to an artillery battery, a helicopter gunship, or an F-16 at the other end. However, as Clausewitz noted a couple of centuries ago, combat still remains the small change of warfare, and when it's time to "drop a dime" on a hostile, the soldier wants to launch a bullet that arrives with authority.

Bottom line: It's more about ammunition than guns. But because infantrymen literally live or die with their weapons, it's instructive to hear their opinions.

In late 2005 a widely circulated email provided a grunt's evaluation of guns and gear in Iraq. The author was a first-tour marine, the son of a retired staff sergeant who copied the world via a cutout source to preserve his boy's anonymity.

The youngster's assessment of standard infantry weapons is not universally held, but it's representative of the majority opinion among dozens of contributors to this work. Therefore, some of his comments are included as typical of the opinions of front-line shooters:

"The M16 rifle—thumbs down. Chronic jamming problems with the talcum powder-like sand. It's everywhere. They all hate the 5.56mm round: poor penetration on the cinderblock structures common over there, and even torso hits can't be reliably counted on to put the enemy down." He added that random autopsies of enemy KIAs showed "a high level of opiate use." (Déjà vu again: much like the Philippine Moros of a century before.)

"The M9 pistol is a mixed bag: good gun, performs well in desert environment but they all hate the 9mm cartridge. Use of handguns for self-defense is actually fairly common. Same old story on the 9: bad guys hit multiple times are still in the fight."

Conversely, the 7.62mm M14 rifle and the .45 Colt pistol received enthusiastic thumbs up.

The M240 machine gun rated well: "accurate and reliable, and 7.62 puts 'em down."

The young marine concluded, "Most of the good fighting weapons and ordnance are over fifty years old." That is certainly true of the beloved M2 .50 caliber Browning heavy machine gun, called "the ultimate fight stopper." The original design dates from 1918, and the current iteration dates from before World War II. There's nothing comparable, and it'll still be front-line equipment when it hits the century mark in a couple of decades.

In fairness to "the black rifle" it should be noted that the M16 functions reasonably well when properly maintained. Probably the most notorious example occurred when the 507th Maintenance Company was ambushed early in 2003, and everything from rifles to machine guns to grenade launchers malfunctioned. Because the unit had been on the move for two days or more, there had been little attention to weapons, with drastic consequences.

But institutionally, the Army still had much to learn about the '16. Nearly two years later, a senior noncom in central Iraq found that despite all the Bright Star exercises with Egypt, let alone the desert warfare training center in California, soldiers still were lubricating their rifles. "We knew before going over that Iraq has extremely fine sand like talcum powder," the sergeant said. "But the Army was still telling us to lube the guns, and any kind of oil will attract dirt and grit that'll jam the weapon after a while. Finally we took all the guns, broke 'em down and dunked them in solvent. Then we wiped 'em off, air dried them in a safe area, and ran 'em with dry lube. After that we had few problems."

We'll never know how many Americans died with inoperable weapons in their hands—probably few. But one is too many.

"Use Enough Gun"

In 1966, author and big game hunter Robert Ruark published a popular book titled *Use Enough Gun*. What he meant was, in pursuit of dangerous game, carry a rifle that shoots a bullet large enough to kill whatever you're after.

Certainly that wisdom applies to the hunting of man.

The standard rifle ammunition in the U.S. military is the 5.56mm cartridge, M855. It's a .223 caliber bullet weighing 62 grains, compared to the 115 grains of a 9mm military pistol round and typically 150 grains in 7.62 NATO rifles. The 5.56's greater velocity (some three thousand feet per second) is reputedly the reason for its superiority over other calibers, while more ammunition can be carried by individual soldiers. The rule of thumb is one-third more 5.56 ammo than 7.62mm.

However, there are problems.

The M855 bullet contains a hardened steel penetrator in the point of the green-tipped projectile. The bullet is calculated to penetrate a 3/8-inch steel plate at one hundred meters, and a GI helmet at six hundred. You can start a decent fist fight in a military club either by praising or damning the 5.56 cartridge: it has vocal supporters and visceral detractors, probably with a majority among the latter.

Both sides claim an enormous amount of evidence to support their views. Over the past forty years or more, the 5.56 family of cartridges (they're by no means all alike) have been praised for their lethality and damned for lack of same. There are war stories of one-shot kills at five hundred meters and horror stories of six or seven nonlethal hits at muzzle contact. Whom to believe?

The answer: everybody.

Plain fact is, 5.56 is a marginal mankiller, dating from the M193 cartridge of the Vietnam War. But its adherents are mostly elite forces or some variety of doorkickers who train hard and often, unlike the huge majority of people who wear uniforms to work. Frequently, those who can shoot well are satisfied with M855, though many would prefer other types of 5.56. Those who criticize it most rigorously often belong to the transitional generation of riflemen who grew up shooting humans with .30 calibers and saw the often indifferent results of 5.56s. In the words of military and police trainer Bill Jeans, a marine of 1966 vintage, "I never shot anybody with my M14, or saw anybody shot with one, who did anything but lie right down and assume ambient temperature."

Another leatherneck rifleman is Jim Coxen, an Eastern Oregon squirrel shooter who used rifles, pistols, and shotguns to kill VC and NVA. Like so many Vietnam veterans, he remains skeptical of the 5.56mm cartridge. "No matter what they do to make that poodle a pit bull, it will still be a mutt. I have not liked it since 1967, when I had to trade in my beloved M14 for an M16. The .223 is fun to play with and the rifle's light to carry, but the best use I've found for .223 is my favorite 'red digger' round.

"As a marine who has shot several people with each, 5.56 and the 7.62 NATO, I can say without any reservations that if I had a choice, it would be 7.62 every time. I have shot literally hundreds of man-sized and larger game animals and would not ever consider any round with a smaller diameter than .280. If I am limited to full metal jacket (FMJ) ammo, then I would never go smaller than .308. In fact, I'd feel a lot better taking a .308 bolt-action scout rifle to war than any of the new stuff—as long as I could pack my ivory-gripped M1911 at the same time."

In 2005 a National Guardsman reported from Afghanistan: "The 5.56 might be OK if every fire team had at least one 7.62mm weapon, but it's just not suited to combat. It's great for shooting squirrels but wasn't even designed as a military cartridge. It lacks penetration and killing power. I don't know how many BGs (bad guys) I saw shot multiple times without killing or even incapacitating them. And for enemy behind protection, it's useless until they stick their heads up. A marksman able to make snap headshots can use it, but for everyone else, it sucks. Both grunts and SF guys complain about all 5.56 weapons, although the M4 carbine with M203 is the least hated."

There's also a physiological component. Says "Red," a long-service army NCO and firearms instructor, "The current M855 doesn't work real well on skinny people. We saw that in Mogadishu where emaciated Somalis took repeated hits and kept on shooting. The 5.56 just seems to zip through torsos without much muscle to cause the round to deflect and do more tissue damage."

From a military perspective, it matters little whether an opponent is killed or merely wounded, as long as he stops shooting at us. The operative word is *Stop.*

Stopping power is like real estate: location, location, location. That means bullet placement, which means marksmanship. That is not (repeat not) to say that a peripheral hit with a 7.62 will end the fight, but it's just about certain that a peripheral hit with a 5.56 will not.

In short, the best way to stop a gunfight with 5.56 is to score a central nervous system hit: brain or spine. But that's usually a tall order, considering that most people devoutly wish not to be shot at all.

About the time of 9/11 a new military cartridge was requested by special operations troops. It was the 6.8mm, a .27 caliber round with more range and energy than the 5.56 (.223), and equally serviceable in rifles and light machine guns. Its primary advocates were found in the Fifth Special Forces Group, Green Berets who had used the M16 and M4 carbine in battle and found them wanting.

After a period of development, Remington produced the new cartridge in 2004 and it was tested in M14s, but more importantly in M16s with new barrels, upper receivers, and magazines. The "proof of concept" was successful: it was found reliable, powerful, and accurate. In fact, it delivers about 50 percent more energy than the 5.56 at ranges from the muzzle to five hundred meters. A few 6.8mm rifles were combat-tested in Afghanistan in 2005 and reportedly performed very well indeed.

Meanwhile, other cartridges in the .27 caliber range were being tested. Andrew C. Tillman was a small arms evaluator for *Jane's International Defense Review* for nearly twenty years. He recalls, "In 1980–1982, when I began testing for IDR, I shot every military caliber possible into common building materials. I found that 7.62 x 39 [the AK-47 round] was minimum bullet weight that would perforate a cinder block. Even tungsten-core Hertenberg 5.56 or mild steel core 5.54 x 39 [AK-74] would not.

"Based on that experience, I decided a 6.5mm of 125-grain weight with mild steel core [B-50 Rockwell is the hardest steel you can impact extrude], in a cartridge case like .257 Roberts would be ideal military automatic rifle [AR] and light machine gun [LMG] cartridge.

"That means we need an entirely new rifle that can handle recoil of a 6.5 at 2,650 to 2,700 fps. The AR15/M16 family will not do it."

Despite the foregoing, the plain fact is, we are not going to inject a new caliber into the military supply system, though the corporate knowledge exists for future reference. The downside is seen as greater pressure on production and supply, which are already stressed. Therefore, we're going to continue with 5.56 or—best case—we'll accept 7.62 as an adjunct rather than a replacement.

The D.C. view is provided by a retired colonel and former scout-sniper platoon leader who says, "I am a diehard 7.62x51mm guy, both as to lethality and long-range accuracy. But feminization of the Army and the fallacious argument that soldiers cannot be taught aimed fire in all likelihood will keep us with 5.56mm.

"Understand, too, that many of our military gunfighters do not wish to change from the 5.56 M4—they are deadly with it at all ranges, and they are reluctant to depart from its excellent ergonomics. For a 7.62 rifle, I believe the Heckler & Koch 417 is far superior to the SR-25 that's been in service for several years.

"Bottom line: the Army has stuck with M855 for a variety of reasons, mainly acquisition and logistics. 'Big Army' has never asked for anything else."

Ultimately, it comes down to politics, bureaucracy, and logistics. A great many female soldiers already have problems managing the M4 carbine, let alone the full-size M16, and would not welcome a heavier weapon. In addition to institutional resistance to change, the Army believes it would be too expensive to replace the M16 family, and has enough problems maintaining enough M855 ammunition.

W. Hays Parks, a DoD attorney who studies law of war and writes rules of engagement, notes that contentions of 5.56mm inadequacy often depend on the experience and competence of the soldier. "I should point out the 'lack of lethality' argument has not been offered by the 'high-speed, low drag' unit members with whom I work, because they know how to shoot. They have had no failure to incapacitate with the M855 (when they've used it) or the 75-grain Match King and 77-grain Hornady Match that was approved for them.

"By the way—reportedly more effective bullets have been prohibited because of alleged political/legal constraints, but it simply isn't so. Special forces operators have received everything they want. However, they don't want hollow point or soft-nosed projectiles because they do not provide adequate penetration (twelve to eighteen inches), particularly when fired out of the M4."

Our Rifle

Americans seldom lose rifle fights. It happens so seldom as to be considered remarkable.

That's the good news.

The bad news: some shooters think we've been lucky.

In any case, we are engaged in a global rifle fight that will certainly outlast the current generation. Therefore, rifles and riflery matter as never before.

Through various iterations, the M16 has been with us since 1965; over forty years. That's a record for American military rifles: just consider the arms of the past century or so.

"All of those weapons fired .30 caliber cartridges of various sizes—an unbroken record of seventy-eight years. Therefore, depending upon one's perspective, the M16's 5.56mm cartridge represented either Progress or Heresy, with boots coming down on both sides of the line.

Even if we accept that we need bigger bullets than we're now shooting, we should recognize that the System feels about Change exactly as J. Edgar Hoover felt about Crime. But once you get past that hurdle, you start looking at a bigger, better bullet launcher: another rifle.

Consequently, many SpecOps shooters have received M14s taken from deep storage. Having seen problems with M16s and M4 carbines, the trigger pullers are willing to lug a bigger, heavier rifle with fewer rounds in favor of landing a more decisive blow.

It would be easy—and tempting—to conclude that all we need to do is resume production of M14s (the Springfield M1A with 18-inch barrel would be just dandy) and get on with the war. But Derrick Martin, a world-class rifleman and gunsmith, summarizes the downside: "The problem is, with no parts in the inventory, and very few armorers who have ever worked on a '14, it's hard to maintain. If you take one to a war zone, you'd better have a pocket full of spare parts and know how to install them."

There are other problems relating to the Rifleman's Rifle. The armed forces now have large numbers of what the Army is pleased to call "small stature soldiers." Male chauvinists call them "soldierettes." The fact is, few women can comfortably carry an eight-pound civilian AR-15 for an hour, let alone a nine- or ten-pound hunk of iron like an M1A. Additionally, the ergonomics of the M16 family are superior to the M14, and the .30 caliber recoil is unpleasant to most females and some males.

So: What We Need is to allow selected units to carry M14s or other 7.62s with adequate supply and support. Meanwhile, a more lethal 5.56 round should be procured—with hundreds of tons of ammunition. And a lot more ranges and training time should be devoted to basic rifle marksmanship.

I'll say that again: we need *a lot* more ranges and training time devoted to basic rifle marksmanship. When you watch seven of ten soldiers consistently miss life-sized silhouettes at one hundred meters, from a steady rest with no time pressure, you realize that The System has failed the troops. Badly.

Since the armed forces—especially the Army and Air Force—frequently do an inadequate job of teaching people to fight with rifles, the civilian sector becomes more important. Elite forces such as airborne, rangers, SEALs, and marine recon make good use of civilian training schools and instructors, and we need to recall that most advancements in firearms training (and often design) come from nongovernmental sources. A short list includes the rifle itself; metallic cartridges; smokeless powder; repeating arms; and the machine gun (the radio and airplane are beyond the scope of this discussion).

Meanwhile, the problems accumulate.

Even assuming that some units are allowed to carry .30 caliber weapons, the troops need to train with those guns. That's not so easy. Today there are fewer military ranges certified for .30 calibers because the primary weapons are .223s, rifles, and squad automatic weapons (SAWs). Because the heavier bullets penetrate more than the lighter ones, the berms and stop plates on military ranges need beefing up to retain .30 caliber strays. That in turn requires Effort, Money, and worst of all, a Change of Priorities.

While the special forces' 6.8mm project dead-ended, other programs are proceeding. A 7.62mm variant of the M249 SAW called the Mk 48 has already been issued to rangers and special operations troopers. Among "trigger pullers" there is still sentiment to develop a 7.62mm service rifle, but that poses obvious weight issues in the design process.

In 2004 the Army selected another foreign-designed product, the SCAR from Belgium's Fabrique Nationale—the same outfit that designed the M240 medium machine gun.

SCAR stands for Special (Forces) combat assault rifle (as opposed to a *peaceful* assault rifle). In any case, it's an innovative concept: a multicaliber weapon adaptable to the U.S. standard 5.56mm cartridge of the M16 family as well as the 7.62x51 NATO (.308) and the Russian 7.62x39mm round. The SCAR is lighter than the M16A2 (7.7 pounds to 8.3) though about 2 pounds heavier than the M4 carbine, based on the M16. In the .30 caliber models the SCAR runs around 8.7 pounds.

Cyclic rate is pegged at 800 rounds per minute, which might be on the high side of controllability for many troops, but in truth full auto is seldom needed outside of room clearing operations: often little more distance than muzzle contact. The M16 family can run as high as 950, which almost always equates to "misses per minute."

Currently it's uncertain how widely the SCAR will be distributed. If in fact it remains a dedicated SpecOps weapon, no doubt it will be well received by the end users.

Meanwhile, we have already addressed the shortage of snipers (Chapter Three) but that also applies to sniper rifles. One example: At Camp Cooke northwest of Baghdad in 2005, a unit on perimeter defense needed some precision rifles to engage hostiles beyond the nominal three hundred–meter range of the M16. When no scoped .30 caliber rifles could be obtained, some soldiers went scrounging. They turned up a few Model 1898 Mausers, chambered for the original German 8mm cartridge, and delivered them to a maintenance company. One of the senior noncoms was a custom gunsmith in civilian life. ("Iraq was no different from Arizona: I lived in the desert and worked on guns seven days a week, except I seldom get mortared in Arizona.") He adapted a 7.62mm machine gun barrel to the Mauser action and stock, mounted one of his personal scopes, and sent the package off to the wire. Said the sergeant, "It wasn't pretty, but it worked."

The United States armed forces should not have to rely on makeshift weapons, nor upon civilians to send plans for rifle and pistol suppressors to the Army in a combat zone. But such things happen, and will continue to occur until the DoD front office gets its priorities straight. For the current war, and well into the future, those priorities should place infantry weapons and ammunition ahead of jets and submarines.

Keeping the Guns Working

Far too many people assume that weapons always work—including people who rely upon them.

But think about it. If you went to work every day knowing that your life depended on one item, wouldn't you become extremely attentive of that gadget?

Many people with a dress code do not. They assume that The System will look out for them. Promises that troops will receive some critical gear in-country almost never come true. Here's a true-life example from Camp Cooke, Iraq, early 2006.

"First Sergeant, do you have dry lube?"

"Yes, of course I have dry lube."

"Well, can I get some?"

"Specialist, I have *my* dry lube. I got *my* dry lube before we left Fort Bliss. I do not have enough for you or anybody else who didn't pay attention."

"Well, where can I get some?"

"I suggest that you write home. Have your folks send some. And ask for batteries while you're at it."

"But that'll take weeks!"

"Undoubtedly."

That conversation—and variations upon the same theme—were shared repeatedly by personnel who have deployed to Afghanistan and Iraq. While it would be excessive to claim that shortages are endemic, it is accurate to say that they are common. One soldier reported that when his unit was extended in Iraq, the troops received no cleaning solvent or patches for eleven months. They obtained the items by "care package."

In far too many instances, the unit level armorer system is broken. Soldiers report that scheduled service is duly reported on cards, but not performed because of too few parts and a lack of interest. Increasingly, soldiers are forced to rely upon their own resources—when such resources exist.

Here's an email from a Vietnam veteran to his son in 2005. "Do not rely on your armorer. Good armorers are a delight, but most armorers are not gun guys. They are the supply guys with bad knees and a key to the door.

"There is a major disconnect between unit level and depot level weapons maintenance. Gauging and parts changes are not performed adequately. Depot level guys only do depot level maintenance, and do not do what should have been done by users and those lower than him.

"Unit level firearms technicians typically have little knowledge, no parts, and no incentive to do the job properly (there's little or no penalty). Armorers who do care tend to be wounded infantry soldiers; they appreciate how important this is, but are thwarted by lack of parts and knowledge."

It's hard to believe, but fundamental parts are not always available to the troops. A persistent problem in the Army concerns springs for the M16 rifle and M4 carbine, and one weapons authority who has dealt with the guns for thirty years emphasizes the degree of technical knowledge often lacking in military units. "Ejection is more of a problem with the M4 because it runs at higher port pressure and the bolt opens and cycles faster than the M16. Sometimes '16s develop ejection problems and can benefit from gold springs or O-rings.

"The M4/M4A1 extractor spring is a case in point. The obsolete extractor springs are dark or silver with a blue or black rubber insert. These obsolete springs lack adequate extractor tension for the M4/M4A1. The use of these obsolete springs causes extraction failures where the fired cartridge case prematurely releases off the bolt face prior to ejection. The fired case rides on top of the live round that is trying to get into the chamber, causing a serious malfunction. The immediate action drill is to lock the bolt back, remove the magazine, clear the feedway, remove the fired case (which may have become wedged into the gas tube in the top of the receiver) and then reload, preferably with a new magazine.

"This failure to eject is erroneously called a 'double feed' by those who don't understand that a 'double feed' involves two live rounds and is usually caused by a defective magazine. The springs with the blue rubber insert are the weakest and produce the most failures to eject."

Officially, all M4/M4A1s were to have the new extractor spring assemblies installed by June 2005, but in some cases the change had not occurred more than a year later.

Once it became obvious that The System was not going to correct the situation in every unit, friends and families found other means. Probably the most innovative remedy was a CD containing numerous technical manuals for individual soldiers to consult. Since computers are common among military personnel, an enormous amount of information could be accessed even when the unit lacked the publications. (In one instance, an armorer in Iraq was asked to produce some silencers and suppressors, but the Army had no manuals on the subject. The soldier emailed a civilian shooter, asking for any information ASAP. In days, the taxpayer purchased two books and mailed them to the armorer, who put the material to good use.)

There's a saying among action shooting enthusiasts, "When the last battery dies, iron sights will rule the world." But increasingly, deployed units put optical sights on their rifles because "red dots" are fast and accurate, especially at urban combat distances: frequently under fifty meters.

However, The System has not established an enviable record in supplying batteries. Soldiers who qualify and train with Aimpoint sights often arrive in-country with the same batteries used stateside.

Those batteries could expire at any moment.

Consequently, troops need fresh and spare lithium batteries. (As a point of information for soldiers, the common Airmpoint varieties include Duracell DL1/3N, Energizer 2L76, Sanyo CR1/3N [Radio Shack 23265], or two silver oxide 357 batteries. Wal-Mart only stocks the 357.)

"Shadetree gunsmiths" in combat zones report that other mundane items are often unavailable. Essential are the GI chamber brush and brass rod to make it work, and a GI toothbrush.

"Nice to have" are a shaving brush or one-inch paintbrush, and canned air to blow out inaccessible dirt and grit.

Since the U.S. government does a marginal job of providing such basic gear, the troops should be able to obtain the items without penalty. I recommend that soldiers (including the Army National Guard and Reserve and the Coast Guard) who buy equipment to use on duty, and are deployed or subject to deployment, should be able to deduct cost of equipment from their income tax.

When a million dollars is paper-clip money, Uncle Sam will never know the difference.

Distilled Essence

The machine gun has been called "distilled essence of infantry," and foot soldiers want a machine gun's firepower with a rifle's portability, leading to the light machine gun (LMG) concept. Today's squad automatic weapon (SAW) dates from World War I: the American-designed Lewis Gun, the egregious French Chauchaut, and the heavy yet effective Maxim 08/15.

In World War II the infantry squad's main firepower was typified by the Browning Automatic Rifle, Britain's Czech-designed Bren Gun, and Germany's superb MG-34 and 42 LMGs. Though there's a difference between automatic rifles such as the BAR and true LMGs like the MG-42, the tactical roles are nearly identical: providing suppressive fire while riflemen maneuver against an enemy force or defended position. The main distinction between automatic rifle and LMG is sustained fire, an obvious advantage with belt-fed guns versus magazine weapons.

For well over thirty years the standard American LMG was the M60, heavily influenced by German design features. Adopted in 1957, "the hog" was a mainstay of Vietnam War infantry units, though it was widely adapted to helicopter use as well. It was a belt-fed 7.62mm weapon weighing some twenty-three pounds empty, and according to the source, it was a tolerable companion or a sulking bitch. At any rate, it was retired by the Army after

Desert Storm but was retained a while longer by the Navy and the Marines, who are accustomed to making do with castoff gear.

More or less taking up the slack left by the hog's departure was a Belgian design, the 7.62mm MAG of 1958. It was among the more significant post–World War II weapons, being widely used in foreign service until adopted by the U.S. Army as a tank weapon in 1977. It's an excellent design: reliable and accurate. But it's heavy, weighing something over twenty-six pounds, and somewhat unwieldy, better suited to tripod or vehicle mounts than to carrying by "Mark 1 Mod 0" grunts.

The M240 has a high cyclic rate, which makes it good for helicopter door and ramp use, though the window in the CH-47 Chinook's left door is too small. An M60 would be better there for easier traverse.

There is also another product of Belgium's Fabrique Nationale, the M249, a lighter, more portable gun firing the 5.56mm cartridge of the M16 family. Whereas the M60 was capable of accurate fire beyond five hundred meters, the "Minimi" is doctrinally limited to three hundred. With light recoil, it's fairly easy to control but lacks anything like the penetration of barricade material common to the .30 caliber weapons.

Naturally, you'll get contradictory opinions if you ask more than two soldiers about their weapons and equipment. But based on years of firing-line surveys, the 240 and 249 both lack a depth of enthusiasm among the troops. Some of the most knowledgeable shooters actually prefer enemy equipment.

Perhaps the most produced post-1945 LMG is the Soviet (er, Russian) PKM (*Pulemyot Kalashnikova Modernizirovanniy*) firing a 7.62x54 round, more powerful than the AK-47's. But like much Russian gear, it's rugged and reliable. It's also highly portable and easily maintained. The PKM is lighter than the M240 and has a quick-change barrel—an excellent feature for sustained fire. Most bipoded models run seventeen pounds empty.

The PKM dates from 1969, based on the AK-47 action, which explains its famed reliability. In recent years, some former

ComBloc nations have produced export versions of Soviet weapons. One of the more intriguing is a 7.62 NATO (.308) version of the PKM.

If the .308 PKM is as reliable as it was with the original rimmed cartridge, then we might consider adopting it on a limited basis. For sustained fire, as in a defensive position, it could use a heavier barrel, but in the light MG role, its lower cyclic rate isn't a bad thing.

Another option in former Soviet client states is the older Degtyarov RPD (*Ruchnoy Pulemet Degtyarova*), an extremely successful LMG firing the AK-47 round. At 650 rounds per minute, it's accurate and controllable, tipping the scales at barely nineteen pounds loaded.

The main problem, again, is bureaucratic. The PKM and RPD suffer from the NIH Syndrome, and since they were Not Invented Here, they are certain to encounter resistance from the ordnance establishment.

Meanwhile, the Mark 48 is being produced as a 7.62 NATO gun, with some M240 parts commonality at a lighter weight. Yet another LMG in development is the JSSAP/PMSW from the Joint Services Small Arms Program. Considering that no American-designed machine gun has been accepted since the M60, it's high time. But let us not be overly parochial: if another superior foreign product turns up, we shouldn't be too proud to use it.

We Need Miniguns

Miniguns are wonderful. They provide a heavy dose of reliable, accurate firepower at a reasonable price. The only problem with them is that we cannot buy them fast enough.

The M134 (GAU-2 in the Air Force) is a six-barrel 7.62mm machine gun that can be set to fire either 2,000 and 4,000 rounds per minute. It's relatively light (thirty-five pounds empty), easily mounted on vehicles and aircraft, and extremely reliable. Counterintuitively, despite its awesome cyclic rate, it's also far longer lived than conventional single-barrel machine guns.

The minigun was designed in the early 1960s when General Electric engineers began playing with "mini" versions of the company's 20mm aircraft weapon. Both the Army and Air Force expressed interest, though GE management insisted upon a more complex design in order to make duplication difficult for competitors. Consequently, maintenance and reliability suffered. Miniguns were terrific when they worked, but they required a lot of knowledgeable TLC.

The public came to know miniguns during the Vietnam "conflict" as the weapon of choice on attack helicopters and fixed-wing gunships such as the AC-47 "Spooky." However, after the Southeast Asia campaign, miniguns largely fell into disuse. Not until the Terror War erupted did the armed forces realize that the .30 caliber Gatling was exactly what was needed in many situations, including urban combat and maritime operations.

Miniguns were rediscovered by the military largely through the efforts of one company: Dillon Aero of Scottsdale, Arizona. Describing himself as "an ex crop duster," Mike Dillon enjoyed playing with automatic weapons. After his aviation career he was wildly successful building reloading machines for competition shooters who required large amounts of pistol, rifle, and shotgun ammunition. Along the way Dillon became one of a handful of civilian owners of licensed miniguns. He began tinkering.

Lapse-dissolve, fast forward, fade in to day. Dillon Aero rebuilt the M134 from the inside out, making its mechanism far stronger than before and much more accessible for corrective action in the field. Operators liked what they saw. A lot.

With much improved reliability and ease of maintenance, Dillon Aero's miniguns found an immediate market. Joint Task Force 160 purchased M134Ds for its helicopters, and was so pleased that it gave Dillon Aero a commendation for its improvements to the Gatling. Considering JTF-160's prestige in the counterterror business, other organizations began ordering miniguns. So did overseas allies, including at least six nations in Europe, the Middle East, South America, and Asia.

The advantages of miniguns over single-barrel machine guns are many and varied. Aside from the obvious superiority in firepower (a factor of 3 to 7.5 in cyclic rate), miniguns are more efficient and cost-effective. They produce more hits per rounds fired, and they last longer. Recent reports from users indicate that the 7.62mm M240 carried by infantry squads and vehicles falls short of its goal of 100,000 rounds service life. Soldiers say that many 240s top out at 70,000 rounds, owing to their riveted receivers. On the other hand, Dillonites point to individual miniguns approaching one million rounds and still going strong.

The minigun's only drawback is that it cannot be used by dismounted infantrymen. Contrary to Jesse Ventura's appearance in *Predator*, no individual can carry the gun, battery pack, and enough ammunition to make use of a 3,000-round-per-minute cyclic rate.

However, when mounted on tripods, vehicles, aircraft, or ships, miniguns more than pay their way. They're surprisingly accurate, providing an extremely high volume of rounds with a narrow cone of fire that permits engagement of targets even in crowded urban areas. Where shoulder-mounted rockets (let alone artillery) can cause collateral damage, miniguns can still be employed.

Naval use of miniguns also is on the rise. In-port security is enhanced when rules of engagement permit firing upon potentially hostile small craft. In such instances as the USS *Cole*, the limited time available to sight, track, and engage suicide speedboats is highly limited. Consequently, an accurate, high-volume weapon such as the M134 offers considerable advantages over single-barrel "gas guns."

Empirical tests provide the proof. At the minimum rate of 3,000 rounds per minute, a minigun fires about three times the ammunition of an M240 or M60 but puts nine times more holes in the targets. The reason is that focused cone of fire noted above: even at about five hundred yards the M134 leaves precious little room for bad guys to "run between the raindrops."

Consequently, a counterintuitive reality emerges: despite their buzz-saw cyclic rate, miniguns can use less ammo than single-barrel guns, not more, while obtaining far more hits.

One veteran of Iraqi Freedom speaks for thousands when he says, "The only problem with miniguns is that we don't have enough of them."

Pistol Packing

Battles are not won with side arms, and certainly not wars. But gunfights are determined by the triumvirate of accuracy, speed, and *power*. And since the pistol is almost always a reactive (i.e., defensive) weapon, it needs to launch a powerful projectile that can save the shooter's life.

Pistols probably matter more today than ever before. Because most of the shooting in Iraq is done in cities—often within rooms and basements—the pistol's agility lends itself to interior tactics. Even carbines such as the M4 can prove a disadvantage when searching confined spaces, and sometimes it's impossible to avoid leading with the muzzle—exposing the long gun's barrel before a soldier turns a corner. Therefore, we need pistols, bigger ones than we now issue.

When the Army decided to retire the best combat handgun in human history, it replaced the Colt M1911 with the Beretta Model 92, designated M9 in the military. Now, don't get me wrong: Beretta has a distinguished record in the firearms field dating back to Bartolomo himself, early in the sixteenth century. But the firm is best known for sporting arms, not combat weapons.

Thus, the M9 is an Italian-designed, American-made side arm that works splendidly in one capacity: as a badge of office. As a fighting tool, it leaves much to be desired.

Some wiggy stories circulated when the M9 was adopted. One of the better tales involved Italian special forces' successful retrieval of U.S. Army Brigadier General James L. Dozier, who had been kidnapped by leftist radicals in 1981. Reportedly, in exchange for fetching back the errant general, Italy's NATO delegates opined that Uncle Sugar owed them one: in this case, the new U.S. side arm.

True or not, replacing the Colt with the Beretta proved just as bad an idea as the big-bore partisans predicted. The M1911 fires a 230-grain .45 caliber slug that arrives with considerable authority. The M9, on the other hand, does not. In GI ball, its 115-grain 9mm (.36 caliber) bullet, though faster than the .45, strikes with less energy. That's nothing new: the 9mm parabellum has been recognized as a marginal fight stopper since it appeared in 1908. While modern bullet design has improved the cartridge's terminal ballistics, the military still issues the full-metal jacket round. Therefore, we need a bigger, better pistol.

We've had this discussion before.

Been There, Done That, Part VII

During the fourteen-year Philippine insurgency (1899–1913) the U.S. Army found itself behind the power curve with "modern," go-faster handgun ammunition. The old, reliable warhorse .45 (Long) Colt, based on the famous frontier six-shooter, had been replaced with a smaller, lighter revolver featuring a swing-out cylinder. It was at least twice as fast to reload as the single-action "thumb buster," and could be fired double-action merely by pulling the trigger rather than manually cocking the hammer. Therefore, Army Ordnance declared it superior to the Colt's revolving pistol of 1873.

Ahem.

As they said in *Tombstone*, the duty load in the .45 Colt was a daisy: a 250-grain lead man-killer propelled by 35 grains of black powder. In fact, at some 550 foot-pounds of energy it remained the most powerful handgun cartridge until the .44 magnum in 1955—a reign of eighty-two years.

Adopted in 1892, the anemic .38 Long Colt (195 foot-pounds) was followed by the long-lived .38 special (200-plus pounds) ten years later. Neither was a reliable fight stopper, though Teddy Roosevelt reportedly dispatched an unfortunate *soldato* with his '92 during the dispute over possession of San Juan Heights one Friday morning.

Because Moros often used drugs or tied off pressure points, the Army discovered a deficiency in its side arms. The then-new .38 caliber double-action revolver was a poor man-stopper, even at point-blank range. Reports from the war zone made for chilling reading: time and again Moro zealots absorbed a cylinder full of .38s, only to remove a Yankee's head with one swipe of a razor-edged *bolo* before succumbing. Or not.

A cinematic depiction of the problem was filmed in the 1939 epic, *The Real Glory*. Army doctor Gary Cooper fills a berserker full of "enough lead to sink a battleship" yet the Muslim warrior cleaves the commanding officer before collapsing with five .38 slugs on board.

The Moro insurrection is oft cited by adherents of the .45 automatic, but seldom with clinical evidence. However, contemporary accounts include the following:

In 1905 a prisoner in Army custody attempted to escape and was shot at arm's length four times with a .38 revolver. Three rounds penetrated a lung and the last went through a hand. The miscreant was finally subdued by the simple expedient of vigorously laying the gun barrel across his head.

In armed combat, perhaps a world record was recorded by a jihadist warrior who absorbed *thirty-two* Krag rifle bullets and, Timexlike, kept on ticking. He was sent to paradise by a .45 that perforated both ears.

Those unsatisfactory results prompted partial reissue of .45 Colt single-actions, leading to the mighty Colt M1911 autopistol.

* * *

Now, nobody familiar with terminal ballistics will claim that the incidents recorded above were typical. But they do make a valid point: if you need a pistol, you need a big one—preferably something beginning with "four."

For a while it seemed that a .45 gat was on the way, a design that is fired like a double-action revolver, with the same trigger pull every time, in contrast to the M9. However, in late 2006 the experimental Joint Combat Pistol was put on indefinite hold, pending yet another review of the 9mm's shortcomings.

Still, the Beretta has its adherents. According to Global Security.org, the M9 is "more lethal, lighter, and safer than its predecessors."

Okay, when loaded the Beretta is almost half a pound lighter. One out of three ain't bad for government work.

But more lethal?

You can start a dandy argument on that point, especially when ballistic numbers are flung. The 9mm round, in the GI ball, is a fully jacketed 115-grain bullet at 1,200 feet per second. Conversely, the old Colt warhorse launches a big 230-grainer at 830 foot-seconds.

The numbers are so nuanced that both bullets are shown superior on various ballistic tables, though the .45 generally rates about 10 percent higher in foot-pounds of energy. But the Colt round is twice as heavy with one-quarter more sectional density and over 40 percent greater momentum. That equates to stopping power.

In fact, the M1911 has a tremendous reputation as a fight-stopping pistol. It's what Alvin York used to destroy a German rifle squad in 1918; it's what fifty-plus other Medal of Honor recipients used from the Great War to Somalia. The 9mm military cartridge simply doesn't have the combat record.

Safer?

Balderdash. The 1911 is so safe that if it were any safer it would be almost useless as a weapon. Good Lord, it has not one; not two; but three safeties: thumb safety, grip safety, and half-cock notch. The trouble is, the armed forces suddenly decided that after seventy-five years the old warrior wasn't safe enough for the Army of One. Because John Moses Browning (may he sit at the Right Hand of God) designed it to be carried "cocked and locked"—round chambered, thumb safety engaged, the hammer fully cocked. Never mind that military pistols are carried in military holsters with flaps that cover the weapon. The very concept of professional soldiers carrying a cocked pistol sent shivers up and down the narrow spines of administrators and managers. Consequently, the M9 was adopted because it has a "decocker" that doubles as safety. With an internal hammer block, the pistol can be carried "hammer down" on a live round. The Soldier with a capital S can produce his or her pistol and press, mash, or otherwise depress the trigger through the heavy double-action pull of the first round, which self-cocks the hammer.

After the first round, the rest in the magazine are fired single-action, which requires less pressure.

That's right: two different trigger pulls. One really heavy pull (the critical first one) followed by fourteen others somewhat lighter but still heavier than the single-action Colt's.

When finished shooting, the Soldier flips the decocker, causing the hammer to fall forward and stop short of igniting another round.

It's a pretty reliable system; it works most of the time.

The point is, however, that in the time required to draw a 1911, the shooter can disengage the thumb safety on the upswing and be on target, ready to press off a single-action round. Fact: most people can shoot a 1911 faster and straighter than an M9. That includes Soldiers.

Let me repeat: there's nothing wrong with Beretta workmanship. The guns are quality items that perform as advertised. But the M9 remains a splendid example of a well-made product of overly complex design that shoots an inadequate cartridge.

Not all 9mm ammo is made equal, of course: some very effective "nines" are available and widely used in police circles. The 124-grain hollow point has earned a good reputation for ending close-range interpersonal confrontations. That's the good news.

The bad news: that ammo is not obtained for military use. Because the U.S. subscribes to international conventions dictating the construction of military ammunition, the legal 9mm fodder is the old full-metal jacket variety. FMJs work fine with big, heavy .45s. They don't work so fine with smaller rounds.

Being objective, the 9mm has one advantage over the .45: penetration. That's been known for decades, and few big-bore advocates would deny it. However, it's seldom much of a concern. What does matter is that handguns have been life-saving tools for hundreds of years, and they remain so today.

Regardless of the pistol, the essential problem, as is so often the case, is training. Or lack thereof.

While three generations of American troops carried 1911s, the Army decided that post-Vietnam Soldiers weren't trusted enough, smart enough, or just plain good enough to carry Browning's timeless masterpiece. Consequently, the seemingly dumbed-down Army of One (composed wholly of volunteers—professional soldiers—go figure) needed a Safer Pistol.

An inadequate, "safer" pistol at that.

Think so?

Let's look at who uses 1911s.

Delta Force, the counterterror specialists.

Marine Corps Special Operations Command.

FBI Hostage Rescue Team.

Numerous metropolitan police departments.

Most of the world's action-shooting pistol champions.

While 1911s are frequently preferred, it's a rare troop who does not want a pistol—any pistol—and especially a big one.

Been There, Done That, Part VIII

In 1953, late in the Korean War, Private John Pepper—already an accomplished shooter and certified member of the Gun Culture—reported to the U.S. Army replacement depot in Japan. He had been advised by a senior noncom to buy a private pistol, though the sentence for owning firearms (let alone selling them to *Gaijin*) was "death or worse."

Pepper chose a .380 pocket model because it fit in almost any garment. Though he never had to use it, he was extremely glad he had it when he got to the front lines. His battalion was short of almost everything except food, clothing, and Chinamen. That first night Pepper was given an M1 carbine with a dozen loose rounds, which meant he possessed a small-caliber, breech-loading single-shot until such a time as he was issued a magazine. He reckoned that the antique .45-70 Springfield Trapdoor in his closet at home would have been far more useful, since it packed a powerful wallop.

Later, when he joined his platoon in the line, Pepper's marksmanship scores earned him a Browning automatic rifle. That was the good news. The bad news: too few magazines. Against his better judgment, Private Pepper inquired why there were insufficient twenty-round magazines to fill his twelve-magazine belt, which by the way had a stubborn rust-colored stain. The platoon sergeant allowed as how the extra mags had been lost when the previous gunner was KIA. Welcome to the war, son. Now get out there and give 'em hell.

Reinventing the Rifle Squad

We need a more balanced infantry squad. But first we need to sort out our ammunition priorities.

Optimally we should standardize on two infantry calibers: 7.62 for rifles and medium MGs; .45 for pistols and personal-defense weapons. (The latter would be shorty carbines for vehicle crews and the aforementioned "small stature soldiers.")

That leaves .50 caliber for the heavy machine guns.

The logistics and supply folks should be pleased. Today we have 5.56mm, 7.62, 9mm, .45, and .50 calibers, without enough of any of them.

Contrarily, if we have to issue M4s and M16s to small stature soldiers and others, so be it. Hell's bells: a hit with a .22 beats a miss with a .30 every dang time.

Yes, I know: the above-noted suggestion is not going to happen—certainly not under present conditions and priorities. But whether or not the Pentagon ever gets with the program and concedes that ammunition should be a higher priority than

Celebrating Diversity and maternity fatigues, a reallocation of funds needs serious consideration. Either we have a professional military or we don't: either we produce warfighters and leaders or careerists and managers.

Either way, We the People are entitled to know.

Meanwhile, we should consider restructuring our infantry units for the long-term GWOT. At the sharp end, the Terror War is a rifle fight writ large, and we need the flexibility to adapt to shifting, unconventional situations.

Every infantry squad should have two .30 caliber machine guns, one per fire team. (You need two belt-fed weapons so one can cover movement of the other. Besides, a crossfire is the best way to prevent trespassing.) We can ditch the .223 caliber squad automatics in favor of the heavier, more authoritative medium machine guns.

If antitank guided missiles are not needed, use two four-man fire teams instead of three-man teams. That squad would carry less ammo than now because of the heavier (and more effective) rounds, but it's still quite a lot of ballistic persuasion. Additionally, it provides the ability to shoot through the kinds of structures often found in Afghanistan and Iraq, and to kill or cripple people at longer ranges.

For an eleven-man light infantry squad, let's consider two four-man fire teams (each composed of a 7.62mm machine gunner, M16/M203 grenadier, M16 automatic rifleman with M136 rocket launcher, and a 7.62 marksman with scope and night vision sighted rifle); a two-man Javelin antitank guided missile (ATGM) team; and squad leader with M16 (for four 7.62mm and seven 5.56mm weapons). Besides three squads, the platoon would include its leader, platoon sergeant, radioman, and medic, for a total of thirty-seven men.

For a nine-man mechanized squad, figure on two 7.62mm machine gunners, two M16/M203s, the Javelin team, fighting vehicle driver, gunner, and squad leader. The platoon leader's vehicle would carry three marksmen, the platoon leader, sergeant, radioman, medic, and vehicle crew, for a total of thirty-six.

Meanwhile, the twenty-first century light infantry squad should look a lot like this: squad leader with 5.56mm or 7.62mm assault rifle; radioman with 5.56 rifle; designated marksman with scoped 7.62 semiauto rifle; two grenadiers with M203s or something similar; two medium machine gunners with 7.62 belt-feds; two riflemen with 5.56 or 7.62 assault weapons and light antitank weapons; two-man antitank team with ATGMs and 5.56 rifles; and medic with 5.56 rifle.

The antitank weapons are not going to be used against enemy armored vehicles very often—if at all. But they can be of tremendous utility in urban areas where vehicle-mounted ATGMs are unavailable.

Legalists may balk at arming medics. Well, get a clue. We're already arming medics, and it's a very good idea. (In Vietnam, at least one army medic carried an M16 in violation of regulations, saying, "I believe in preventive medicine." It's hard to argue with that logic.) Today, in a war where the enemy cuts the heads off living prisoners, there's no excuse for exposing any troops to capture when they can defend themselves.

A final word about supplying extra guns and ammo:

Most certainly complaints will arise from supply officers who cordially detest the idea of providing different kinds of small arms ammunition. Many of them already refuse to stock shotgun ammo because there's little call for it, despite its effectiveness as a breaching or entry method. Well, here's a flash from an infantry perspective: the war doesn't exist for anybody's convenience. If ordnance or supply personnel have to work harder to provide the optimum infantry squad with what it needs, so be it.

Actually, depending on specific squads, the extra burden of supplying 7.62 would not be excessive. It's possible, and in fact likely, that only the two machine gunners and the designated marksman would need 7.62 ammo. Everybody else, including the grenadiers, could use 5.56s as issued today. As postulated above, no more than six of the twelve soldiers would be eligible for the heavier weapons.

In Favor of Bigger Guns

Tanks have little role to play in urban warfare these days, not because they're ineffective but generally because they're far *too* effective. As in, "collateral damage."

As in Fallujah.

While some of the urban combat in Iraq resembles a Stalingrad on the Tigris—a cellar-to-cellar "war of the rats"—most of it is not. Consequently, in some areas, heavy-caliber direct fire offers a viable solution to a knotty tactical problem: ferreting out hidden shooters (not necessarily genuine snipers) in risky room-clearing exercises. The situation can become even more lethal when the enemy decides, "This is a good day to die."

Consequently, despite the concern for excessive damage in residential areas, there's something to be said for the M1 Abrams battle tank. If you look at shell weights, the Abrams' projectiles are a lot less than a 500-pound bomb, and the 120mm rounds are extremely accurate. With a standoff range of a couple kilometers, they can be fired outside enemy observation range, or so far away that they did not appear to be a threat.

The problem arises with the type of available ammunition. Generally, tanks are designed and armed to kill their own kind, much like fighter aircraft. But at least into the early phase of the Iraqi insurgency, the high-explosive antitank (HEAT) round was most often used for buildings and enemy personnel in the open. A 120mm high-explosive round with delay fuse would certainly be more useful, and cause less damage to surrounding structures. Additionally, a laser proximity fuse on conventional HE shells might be preferable since our dual-purpose HEAT shell is not much good as a pure high-explosive round.

Experience in Iraq led to the M908 obstacle-defeating round, based on the M830 multipurpose antitank round. The 830's two-position fuse (proximity and contact) was replaced with a hardened steel cap designed to penetrate concrete buildings as well as rubble common in urban combat zones.

For main-gun employment against hostile people, the XM-1028 canister round has much to commend it. Crammed with 1,100 tungsten balls, essentially it's a huge shotgun, the lineal descendant of original canister and grapeshot from the black powder era of muzzle-loading cannon. Empirical research demonstrated that 9mm tungsten steel ball bearings were the minimum caliber that would disable a Russian heavy transport truck. However, the Marine Corps favors a 10mm ball. Being marines, the Corps likely considers that the .40 caliber diameter has more salutary effects on people.

According to army sources, the canister round was requested by tankers in South Korea who wanted a quick kill against Communist antitank teams, presumably armed with RPGs and ATGMs. In conventional warfare, the tactical doctrine for use of canister would have to be worked out, since infantry ordinarily accompanies armor to deal with enemy AT weapons, and most tanks would be loaded with tank-killing rounds.

What remains to be determined is whether the high price of a 120mm round is cost-effective. The "brochure" says that a 1028 can kill or cripple at least five of ten men with one round and half of a thirty-man platoon with two rounds (the critical matters of distance and enemy dispersion are absent, but coverage is specified between two hundred and seven hundred meters). Presumably blowing $3,000 out the muzzle of an Abrams can achieve a fast, dramatic conclusion to a tactical situation, but in many (perhaps most) cases a far smaller projectile can solve the problem. Man-portable rockets such as the 83mm Shoulder Mounted Assault Weapon (SMAW) have been available since the mid-1980s, and they're popular with the users: depending on the specific ammo, most SMAWs only weigh thirty pounds loaded. Additionally, vehicle mounted antitank guided missiles can provide more than ample blast and penetration of most buildings, leaving the Abrams in reserve to crack the genuinely tough tactical nuts.

The foregoing does not account for the far lower cost of

25mm chain guns on Bradley Fighting Vehicles, let alone what a couple hundred dollars of .50 caliber can achieve with far less "urban renewal" effect. Furthermore, 7.62mm armor piercing (AP) works on light armored vehicles and similar barriers, so the trick is to match the weapon to the situation.

Body Armor and Bandages

In 2004 the Army reported shortages of spare parts for vehicles and helicopters as well as antimortar radars that track the origin of enemy projectiles. Some units were caught without critical spares for five weeks because they had to be delivered from the United States.

The most sensitive topic was body armor, with troops requiring thirty-six thousand sets of ceramic inserts to optimize protection from gunfire and explosives. The topic quickly went political, especially after coverage in the *Washington Post*, while some Administration defenders noted that many soldiers choose not to wear full-coverage vests owing to weight and heat. But the fact remained, that after the insurgents began relying more heavily on IEDs in the summer of 2003, many units and individuals were caught short. Some families began buying body armor off Internet sites and shipping the plates or full vests to loved ones in-country.

In researching this book in 2006, I learned of marines buying their own body armor to obtain side-plate protection often lacking in military issue vests. Asked why such changes had not been made in the previous five years, a leatherneck shrugged eloquently. "Nobody ever asks us what we think, sir. They just tell us where to go and who to shoot."

Body armor is mainly intended to protect against explosive fragments and bullets, and generally it does the job. There's a dramatic video on the Internet showing a GI struck in the chest by an AK-47 round. He's knocked down but immediately rises to his feet, moves to cover, and returns fire. All the while, off camera voices chant "*Allahu akbar!*"

Still, there's room for other perspectives. A reporter embedded with Army units in Afghanistan in 2005 noted, "Sometimes body armor is being carried too far. Grunts I talked to didn't even like having to wear front and back plates because of weight. But it depends on the tactical situation. If you're humping gear through the Hindu Kush, you might not even want the minimum, but if you're riding in a Humvee through the Sunni Triangle, why not side plates, deltoid plates, the whole nine yards?"

Despite much of the media *Sturm und Drang* about shortages of body armor, servicemen who have been overseas note that in many cases, personal armor will not save lives against improvised explosive devices. After the first several months of Operation Iraqi Freedom (OIF), when active resistance abated, IEDs became an increasingly greater threat. Before long they were no longer improvised, but professionally calculated to inflict the greatest possible damage. Roadside bombs with shaped charges were directed toward the level of passenger seats, in which case the vehicles themselves needed upgrading more than individual armored vests.

A problem with body armor that is seldom addressed is difficulty in mating it to weapons. Standard body armor is incompatible with the M16 stock, preventing a decent "cheek weld" for consistency of sighting and firing. However, it works better with the telescoping stock available on some M4 carbines. There are contradictory reports as to whether weapon-compatible armor is being developed, but in any case it appears a low priority.

Anyway, here's the bottom line, as expressed in a veteran's letter to a newspaper in 2006: "Body armor, helmets, boots, language and culture training, improved individual weapons . . . and personal care items are not popular or highly profitable items in the defense industry. There is little sex appeal in a new pair of ballistic eyeglasses or a more functional uniform—at least compared with a 'stealth helicopter.' But it is precisely those individual items that improve the effectiveness of our ground troops and ultimately allow us to take and hold ground.

In a letter to the editor of *USA Today* dated January 19, 2006, Todd Fredericks wrote, "The nation ought to demand that the individual soldier is the highest priority in training, equipment, and weapons procurement. You can buy a lot of body armor for one billion dollars."

Another not so minor scandal in 2005–2006 concerned a shortage of advanced-design bandages. The high-pressure dressings, mainly intended to control heavy internal bleeding, were reported in short supply in Iraq, and administration critics were quick to jump on the perceived inefficiency of the Bush-Rumsfeld regime. The shortage was alleviated when adverse publicity took hold, as even some diehard Republicans had to concede, that poor management of lifesaving gear could not be excused.

As Bad As It Gets

For all the attention focused on inadequate body armor, another problem has received surprisingly little attention. In 2006 the "Soldiers for the Truth" web site carried a continuing story revealing a policy that prohibited medical evacuation helicopters from landing in a "hot" zone. The implication was that star wearers wanted to avoid another "Black Hawk Down" situation like Mogadishu in 1993. Consequently, "dustoff" crews were not authorized to transport critically wounded soldiers from areas where opposition had been encountered. The casualties had to be moved by vehicle—and occasionally by foot—to sites considered safe. As a result, precious time was lost, and with it, some lives.

Among many firsthand accounts was this from a National Guardsman who signed himself, "Grunt with a ranger tab":

"Please be advised that an entire platoon witnessed firsthand when four marines were killed less than three klicks from Abu Ghraib prison gate. We sat by and listened as they called for help. We were ready to go and assist, but the active component refused to send us. As it was told to me by their first sergeant, one marine was not killed instantly and stood a chance, if MedEvac'd in a timely fashion. Instead the marines had to walk back under fire. It took two-plus hours to limp back with their dead and wounded. I will forever remember that night, it was truly shameful."

When a chopper pilot of Vietnam vintage learned of the situation, he declared, "I *never* would've followed an order like that." He knows his subject: Chief Warrant Officer Fred Ferguson survived a harrowing "dustoff" from Hue in 1968 to receive the Medal of Honor. He adds, "If you will remember the DustOff motto, 'Not Without Your Wounded,' we never would leave a wounded Soldier behind. You must at the very least *try*."

As of late 2006, it was not possible to learn the current policy regarding evacuation flights from potentially "hot" areas.

For all the problems, there's near unanimity among returning veterans who rate military trauma treatment as excellent. Front-line medics have never been so well trained, and the combat lifesaving course receives two thumbs up. Similarly, immediate care provided by doctors and nurses in-country leaves little to be desired, though there are reports of disinfectant shortages requiring purchase of commercial bleaches at the local bazaar. Some units also report insufficient laundry facilities to keep pace with requirements.

However, more common problems persist in stateside medical centers, where injured soldiers often endure weeks and months of bureaucratic delays. The 2007 scandal at Walter Reed Army Medical Center in Washington, D.C., was so egregious that a two-star general actually got fired, but regular visitors to the facility report that while facilities had been grossly neglected, treatment was generally good. We will return to that subject in Chapter Eight.

Other Gear

Soldiers are prohibited personal weapons for a variety of legal, logistic, and practical concerns, though nearly everyone consulted for this book would take a privately owned .45 caliber pistol if allowed.

Similarly, one of the weapon-related items that's drawn some criticism is the fifteen-round magazine for the M9 pistol. Early in Operation Enduring Freedom (OEF), reports were heard from Afghanistan that the issue magazines were unreliable. Therefore, some soldiers acquired after-market civilian products, even though many were ten-round models produced before the "assault weapon" ban expired. Evidently the problem was solved, or it was of limited concern, as nothing more was heard, but some troops were understandably upset that the Army had provided poor quality mags.

Meanwhile, specialized ammunition also is difficult to obtain despite demonstrated benefits. Perhaps the most sought after is shotgun slugs, extremely useful for taking doors off hinges in a hurry. Says a DoD official, "Breaching rounds are exactly what's needed in Iraq, and if the soldiers can't get them, it's the fault of the ammo/logistics types. We have approved quite a few types of breaching rounds for special-mission units but again, it appears that 'Big Army' is too slow in responding to requirements."

But the same official cautions, "Be careful what you ask for. Soldiers and marines bend over backward begging for the latest of everything, but often not because they need it but because of the CDI (Chicks Dig It) factor. At the end of the day, they're carrying an additional twenty or more pounds of gear they might need once, if at all. Read S. L. A. Marshall's famous *The Soldier's Load and the Mobility of the Nation*."

Ironically, that remains a valid point in the twenty-first century. Despite the variety of military vehicles, "load tailoring" is almost as important for today's rifleman as it was for the Roman legionnaire. In any combat theater the grunt work is accomplished by dismounted troops, the eternal *mulus marianus*, an overladen foot soldier functioning as martial beast of burden.

This message came from "GI Joe," based in northern Iraq. As one of his company's noncoms he had to deal with a variety of requirements:

"As far as our gear is concerned, we have pretty much everything we need, which I have been pleasantly surprised. The only SNAFU is that our radios and night vision is the same gear that has been here since the beginning, so it is getting beat up.

"I have been asked as to what I need here. Just send food and socks. Some of the marines don't know what a good pair of socks are. For socks, send either Bridgedale or Smartwool in medium or large. Light hiker socks and light colors because of the heat."

Sometimes the tiniest items draw disproportionate attention. In late 2005 a marine NCO was preparing for his fourth combat tour; third in Iraq. Gunnery Sergeant "Marcus" flipped his load-bearing equipment and said, "I finally had to get some civilian web gear. The military stuff that's stitched with cotton thread is no good. It rots in some climates, especially where it's wet a lot of the time." He shrugged philosophically. "You'd think that by now they'd know stuff like that but nobody ever asks us." He noted with more than a hint of irony that if the Boy Scouts can go camping with nylon or synthetic-stitched packs, so should "Uncle Sam's Misguided Children."

Food and "Foot Medicine"

Napoleon's most famous maxim holds that an army travels on its stomach. By that measure, Americans in Iraq are traveling in style. Here's "Stephen," emailing from Mosul:

"Our living conditions here in camp are great. We have a great chow hall with some of the best army food I have ever eaten. There is an Iraqi mess hall, but the doc won't let us eat in it. There is lots of candy and snack food from care packages, which I avoid cause I'm trying to loose (sic) the 20 lbs I put on the way here. As far as food goes, send anything that doesn't melt. We use vehicles mostly so I would greatly appreciate food so I don't have to eat MREs."

Another NCO, a sergeant first class based near Baghdad, has a similar attitude. "Our food was terrific. I had absolutely no complaints but you always have some whiners. A few of our people thought there should've been other kinds of lettuce at the salad bar or more spices for the stir fry but those pukes will gripe about anything."

Even with helos and hummers, food is never far from a soldier's mind. So consider this: a change of tactics in some operating areas mandates more vehicular than foot patrols. Most units prefer to patrol on foot because it permits interaction with the locals and can build good or better relations. But where threat levels remain high, patrolling in hummers and light armored vehicles has obvious advantages. But because the oppressive climate induces dehydration and fatigue, vehicle patrols are command. Therefore, some soldiers report that they actually gain weight in Iraq!

In a combat zone.

Undoubtedly the most peculiar food-related topic arose from Camp Victory at the infamous Abu Ghraib facility near Baghdad Airport in 2006. Internet bloggers released an edited copy of the base's staff meeting, addressing concerns with the chow hall. Among other things, patrons requested Belgian waffles, waffle cones, and additional ice cream flavors. Additionally, onions and pineapples were sought for the stir-fry bar, and there was consensus that dinnertime music was too loud, so might be dispensed with.

It gets better . . .

Or worse, depending upon your attitude.

Some soldiers complained that the lobster tails were too large, suggesting that the portions should be cut in half.

In a combat zone.

The facility manager explained that the tails could not be halved "due to the lack of proper equipment."

A few individuals expressed no concern with the implications of waffle cones and lobster tails in a war zone, assuming that it merely indicates that our soldiers are well fed. But most recognize the widening rift between combat troops and the larger numbers of rear-echelon support personnel, the "REMFs" so despised by Vietnam grunts who humped a ruck and a '16 in the bush. (Article by "Bohica" on *Daily Kos*, "The Lobsters Tails at Camp Victory are Too Big," posted on July 10, 2006, www.dailykos.com/story/2006/7/10/102727/931 [most recently accessed April 17, 2007].)

Besides good food, soldiers always welcome something to drink, and thousands of families routinely send both necessary and comfort items to loved ones deployed overseas. Two years into OIF, some army families in a Western state hit upon a means of providing their soldiers with an especially desirable contraband item: liquor.

The wife of a five-stripe sergeant noted that rubbing alcohol is visually identical to vodka. Therefore, she and her coconspirators purchased quantities of a medicinal substance, opened the bottles and exchanged one clear liquid for another. They devised a way to reseal the cap and sent the precious cargo to Mesopotamia, well insulated amid paperback books, underwear, and other cushiony packaging.

Declaring the contents of the box, the shippers noted that their footsore GIs required socks and "foot medicine." Never mind that the troops were support personnel, not infantry.

Eventually came a cryptic email: "Package received. Send more foot medicine."

As with all good soldiers, where there's a thirst, there's a way.

We Need Maintenance

The U.S. armed forces possess tens of thousands of vehicles, but billions of dollars are needed to put a large share of them back on the road. Deferred maintenance has parked enormous numbers of trucks, hummers, and even tanks, mainly because the Pentagon prefers to buy new stuff rather than support and maintain what it already owns.

The Army has something over 110,000 wheeled vehicles, relatively few of which are intended for combat but are essential for basic transport and supply, including ambulances, fuel and water tankers, tow trucks, and transporters. Yet where support forces are permitted to deteriorate, eventually the shortage appears at the sharp end. The harsh Mesopotamian environment conspired with vastly increased operating tempos to wear out vehicles from four to nine times the peacetime rate.

By one estimate, the Army (including reserves) needed $50 *billion* to make good the equipment shortages. Consequently, in 2005 analysts noted a crisis building, based on robbing the stateside Peter to pay the Iraqi Paul. The only option for providing deployed units even a minimal capability was to ship vehicles from the United States, mainly from National Guard and reserve outfits. Concluded one report, "One of the hidden effects of the Iraq war is that even the troops not currently committed to Iraq are weakened because of it."

The problem is not limited to rear-echelon units. Though they seldom engage in combat, Abrams tanks are often called upon to provide security and "presence" in potentially hostile areas in addition to convoy escort. The peacetime norm allows eight hundred miles per annum, but in recent years the M1s are driving three thousand to four thousand miles and thus using up four to five times their allotment.

It's no better with the Marines. For fiscal 2007, the Corps needed $11 billion to repair worn-out vehicles, let alone replace any of them.

Here's what the numbers mean to those in the field. We've already heard from "Stephen" in this chapter. He's speaking in early 2006:

"The vehicle is a huge disappointment. The humvee I am gunner in (no one else can hit shit with a .50-cal machine gun except one old guy who is half blind) has makeshift armor, no A/C, a lousy turret with thin steel welded by one of the guys on the last team. It's green, not painted tan, and it actually has Korean writing on it. It's one of the ones used in the invasion three years ago and shipped over from Korea. It's a good thing I rarely leave the base. We don't do raids. We only roll out on short missions into Mosul for stuff we can't get sent here—funnily enough, lately it's parts for the trucks."

None of the foregoing is to say that we are not buying new gadgets. The two most important combat vehicles are the well-proven Bradley and the new Stryker, neither of which is very familiar to the taxpayers who purchase them.

After a long, painful development, the Bradley fighting vehicle entered service in 1981, well over budget. It has a three-man crew and carries seven troops over a nominal distance of three hundred miles, capable of as much as forty miles per hour. It's nine feet tall—high profiles are a problem in combat—but after improvements it was rated proof against many mines, RPGs, and IEDs. The Bradley has had many upgrades, but continues doing its main job, transporting soldiers into combat and providing fire support with its 25mm gun and an assortment of other options.

The Stryker is America's first wheeled combat vehicle since World War II, produced in two basic models: a troop carrier and a weapon platform. With a driver and commander it accommodates nine troops and, like the Bradley, it's rated at three hundred miles range. It's quieter than other fighting vehicles and personnel carriers, but can make sixty miles per hour on level ground. Deployed in 2003, more than two thousand have been ordered to date.

Though the Army stresses the concept of Stryker brigades, they're actually mechanized infantry. In fact, Stryker bears a strong resemblance to Canada's Bison, delivered in 1990, possessing very similar layout and capabilities.

There's an irony at work with the fighting vehicles. The Bradley and Stryker were conceived for conventional combat, delivering infantry and providing fire support against enemies similarly armed and equipped. But with the continuing difficulty of upgrading humvees against the growing IED threat, genuine armored vehicles are increasingly valued for convoy escort and patrolling. Thus, both designs exemplify the topsy-turvy nature of asymmetric warfare. Intended for one purpose, they are most useful in another.

We can count on a lot more asymmetry as the Terror War continues.

Chapter Six

We Need Objectivity

"What is the first business of one who studies philosophy?
To part with self conceit. For it is impossible for anyone to begin
to learn what he thinks that he already knows."
—Epictetus, c. 100 AD

We need objectivity. That's another way of saying that we need—we really-really need—intellectual honesty. That's extremely hard to come by in government and most bureaucracies, let alone in a government bureaucracy. But if we're going to start getting a handle on the situation, first we have to admit that the system is broken. It's exactly the same process as starting an alcoholic or drug addict on the road to rehabilitation.

The System is Terminal

If the military-industrial-political acquisition process were a race horse, we would have shot it decades ago. The pony's leg is far too broken to mend.

No one seems to be discussing the real issue: the old-fashioned corporate corruption of our political system. Here's how it works:

1. The U.S. government buys a new weapon system (this scheme works best for aircraft but applies to almost everything else).

2. The defense contractor makes a hefty campaign contribution.

3. The contractor cries to DoD and his recently purchased legislator, saying the firm needs to make more money.

4. Congress allows the contractor to sell the weapon system abroad.

5. DoD complains to Congress that since other countries have the same technology, the United States needs a new weapon system to maintain superiority.

6. The contractor gets more of your tax dollars to develop another weapon system.

7. The cycle repeats. The defense contractor makes buckets of money, and your great-grandchildren get to pay off our national debt.

Everybody is happy with The System: The contractor makes money; the military always has new toys; and the legislator keeps getting elected. Well, everybody is happy but the American people, who fall deeper in debt for no better security.

Meanwhile, our military acquisition system is warped. We spend about $450 billion a year on defense and still can't get everything we "need." An aerospace consultant familiar with classified projects says, "There are *a lot* of good programs being left on the table in the acquisition world. There are way too many 'black' programs that suck money and have no accountability (and I'm not even sure of that, since no one person really knows). I had a friend who was involved in Operation Allied Force tell me that when they got the 'go' word that the skies opened up and a whole host of black and special programs descended on them for use. He said that his boss on the staff there told them to get bent—he'd never trained with them, had no idea what they'd do, and didn't want to conduct some sort of field test to justify their huge budget. That sort of thing happens more than most people would believe."

At rock bottom, the acquisition process is heavily influenced by the American reliance upon technology, not only because that's where the big bucks hang out, but because our institutions now are hard-wired that way. It boils down to the old quality versus quantity issue. It was not always thus:

In World War II, we had enormous quantities of Stuff that was often not great but good enough: witness the M4 Sherman tank. Technologically, it finished well behind the German Panther, let alone the Tiger, and was no better than the standard Panzer Mark IV. But we built *40,000* Shermans; versus fewer than 15,000 *Wehrmacht* main battle tanks built by the Germans, of which merely 1,300 were Tigers. Allied tankers (the British and Russians also used M4s) found they could overwhelm the superior enemy vehicles, and if they lost three or four Shermans per Tiger, that was the cost of doing business. Our losses were replaceable—theirs were not.

Germany also fielded the world's most advanced aircraft, the Me-262 jet fighter. It was one hundred miles per hour faster than anything with a propeller and could pick off Allied bombers almost at will. But only 1,200 were built, with never more than about fifty operational at one time. The swarms of "obsolete" U.S. and RAF fighters that owned Reich airspace hunted the "turbos" to destruction, in the air and on the ground.

Now we have partly adopted the German philosophy, buying very small numbers of extremely expensive, often high-risk technologies, that take years to develop. But the way our military is shrinking in terms of people, we'd be hard pressed to fill those cockpits or ships or divisions even if we did have money for them.

The same consultant said in 2005, "The Raptor will be touted as 'transformational' of course—supercruise, newer, brighter, whiter and all that. Nonetheless, at an event I attended, an air force four-star scolded industry *for selling things that cost too much*. This echoed what the chief of staff was saying: he can't afford all of the $180 million fighters he needs. In other words, it was industry's fault for selling what the services request and Congress approves!"

The parochial cycle repeats like a continuous loop video: the military drafts a requirement for the latest gadget; the gadget maker happily complies; politicians follow their particular constituencies (and their own self-interest) in procuring the gadget.

Or: the maker invents a new gadget; the military wants it; politicians follow their particular constituencies (and their own self-interest) in procuring the gadget.

In either case, since everybody is guilty, nobody is accountable.

What's It Cost?

If you ask how much a piece of military gear costs, you will get at least two answers: program unit cost and unit "drive away" cost. That's if you're lucky.

Program unit cost is the total *acknowledged* cost of a weapon system divided by the number of items delivered. Total acknowledged cost includes research and development, engineering time and effort, startup costs (buying or producing the manufacturing equipment), factory buildings, etc. It does not usually include advertising, greasing palms in foreign (and sometimes domestic) venues, or three-martini lunches.

(A quick aside: in the 1980s a retired rear admiral told me, "In the Korean War, as a lieutenant commander, I could accomplish more during a three-martini lunch than whole boards of admirals do today. The process was much simpler, and usually meant that the customer—the U.S. Navy—actually got what it wanted. But that was when designers like Ed Heinemann knew what we needed before we did!")

Drive-away or fly-away cost is what the manufacturer receives for each new airplane, tank, ship, rifle, or canteen that We the People purchase. One current example: the program unit cost for the F-22 stealth fighter runs around $345 million per copy. But once the R&D, startup costs, etc., have been paid, the fly-away cost is pegged at a little under $190 million.

Inevitably, new and sophisticated machinery costs more than expected, leading to fewer acquisitions. The controversial V-22 Osprey aircraft is a case in point. In 1986 the planned purchase of 923 "tiltrotors" averaged $24 million apiece. But by 2002 the buy had been halved to 458, yielding more than a threefold unit cost of some $80 million each. (Stephen H. Baker et al., "U.S. Military Transformation: Not Just More Spending, but Better Spending," CDI.org, *Military Reform Project*, January 31, 2002.)

If a bean counter really wants to confuse things, he can plug in "real dollars" or "constant dollars" or any inflationary legerdemain he cares to insert.

Fact is, frequently nobody knows exactly what anything costs. That's not surprising in a bureaucracy that occasionally loses track of incidental or "paper-clip money" amounting to hundreds of millions.

From time to time there are news reports about Pentagon ineptitude on an eye-watering scale. Just one example: on January 29, 2002, CBS News correspondent Vince Gonzales reported that the DoD was unable to account for some $300 million. A spokesman conceded, "We know it's gone but we don't know what they spent it on."

It wasn't the first time it occurred, but that didn't matter. Bottom line: nothing happened. It was a one-day story, immediately displaced by something of greater importance: a celebrity's eighth DUI arrest or U2's latest single.

Meanwhile, some military bureaucrats have mastered the dark art of hiding costs in plain sight. Recalls a graduate of a naval aviation safety school, "They used to teach a class on how to pencil-whip mishap costs to lower their reported dollar amount. The case study used was a helicopter that lost power and went into about five feet of salt water. They recovered it after about a week and decided that, even if the airframe, engines, et al, would never fly again, they could, on paper, 'salvage' parts and drive the total cost down below $1M and, voilà, it was no longer a Class A mishap, making everyone happier."

Such intellectual vandalism is not limited to any one service. At least two F-86 aces have stated that during the Korean War, the Air Force typically wrote off aircraft that crashed offshore as "operational" losses because there were no corpus delicti to examine. In Vietnam, it wasn't unusual to see F-100s taking off from Tan Son Nhut with a 250-pound bomb beneath each wing, sending multiple aircraft to deliver the ordnance load of one jet in the continuing "sortie war" against the Main Enemy: the U.S. Navy.

During post-Desert Storm hearings, the Army was caught fibbing about the Patriot missile's performance against Saddam Hussein's Scuds. The Big Green spokesmen asserted that Patriots recorded a 100 percent interception rate—then admitted under knowledgeable questioning that "interception" was defined as passing within a given distance of the incoming Scud, whether the target was destroyed or not. Since proximity fusing could detonate a Patriot up to six times beyond the theoretical kill radius, and some targets were assessed as debris of Iraqi missiles breaking up in flight, the actual success rate may have been under 50 percent, according to GlobalSecurity.org. (In fairness, killing half of the incoming missiles was a noteworthy achievement; the problem is with officers willing to misrepresent the facts.)

In fairness to those who labor within The System, it's so complex that it almost defies comprehension. One aerospace manager reflects, "I will say that how to account for massive contracts over many years actually does take some accounting gymnastics. The contracts people in any company like ours must hate life because their job is never easy. You have to use 'then year' dollars at some point to compare costs over many fiscal years, and program costs aren't a good indicator of what a big device like an aircraft or ship costs, because it includes simulators, training, manuals, etc. The legendary $400 hammers and $600 toilet seats come out of goofy math like this.

"It's things like these that explain why the military is going to 'Enterprise' structures like big business, and why every officer almost needs an MBA now. Despite appearances, it's not really 'cooking the books' (although that does go on). More often it's decent people trying to get the damn system to work."

More Reality, Less Rhetoric

After 9/11 President Bush and just about everyone else within reach of a microphone presumed to explain why Islamic fundamentalists act as they do. "They hate us for our freedom," went the inevitable chant. Al Qaeda, the Taliban, and disaffected Muslims of every stripe seemingly were willing to immolate themselves en route to Paradise because of America's traditional liberties.

Horsefeathers.

Place yourself in a jihadist's sandals. For just a moment, think as he does. *Why* does he hate Americans so thoroughly, so viscerally? Because we have the right to speak our minds; to peaceably assemble; to bear arms; to receive equal justice under the law?

The question answers itself: a resounding *Of course not!*

Islamicists loathe the thought of America not because of its laws, but because of its actions offshore. Our enemies wish us ill because of what we do: because we stand on holy ground in Arabia; because we support Israel; because we invaded an Islamic nation that did not attack us. Many hate us for our culture: the insidious virus that America exports globally: everything from rap "music" to Levi's to McDonald's to women's rights. The list is long but you get the idea.

And another thing. While we're discussing rhetoric, we really-really need to get over the absurd notion of "cowardly suicide bombers." There is, by definition, no such thing. (Having interviewed at least a couple hundred Allied veterans of the Pacific War, I have yet to meet one who mentions "cowardly kamikaze pilots.") If any of the politicians who have denigrated Islamic suicide terrorists are willing to sacrifice themselves for whatever *they* claim to believe in, it's a very well-kept secret, stashed somewhere in that huge warehouse with the Ark of the Covenant.

We need to acknowledge that our enemies in the Terror War are highly motivated, demonstrably courageous, and often smart (they pulled off 9/11 with 75 percent success, didn't they?). To continue belittling them as back-stabbing cowards is merely to deceive ourselves. This is a long-long war—certainly it will last beyond the current generation—and the sooner we recognize that we face serious enemies, the better off we'll be.

As far as rhetoric is concerned, there's one other item on my "rant" list. Pols and commentators occasionally pay tribute to the "fighting men and women" (what's wrong with "the troops"?) guarding America's freedom in the Terror War.

Horsefeathers again.

American freedom is in no way at stake in Iraq, let alone Afghanistan for Pete's sake. Our freedom was never threatened in either world war, in Korea, or Vietnam. Our freedom was never threatened in the half-century Cold War. Our existence, maybe yes; our freedom, never.

The reason should be obvious: since the Revolution, no foreign power has *ever* possessed the ability to invade us and deprive the United States of its freedom. Only Americans can do that, and they've been accomplishing it with increasing regularity over the years. The proliferation of various "Patriot" Acts and the doomed-to-failure rush for greater security at the expense of traditional liberties has been done by Americans, "for" Americans, to Americans.

Just thought I'd mention it.

We Need Equal Justice

We have met "Ray" before. He's a retired naval flight officer and now his son is an enlisted marine. Talk about objectivity—give a listen from 2006.

"Among the talks I had last week was the current rash of charges against junior enlisteds for 'murder'. I was talking to two aviator O-6s and they agreed that we are holding our ground troops to a level of responsibility that we *never* hold aviators to. When a college-educated officer drops a Mk.82 on a house full of civilians, we don't normally make an issue out of it.

"Sorry. Poor targeting or bad luck. Yet when high school graduates are involved in a combat incident, we charge them with war crimes. Look at the difference in personal danger and involvement: we aircrews don't have to worry about IEDs or the guy around the corner with an RPG. The grunts do, and have to make snap decisions, frequently adrenalin-driven with minimal real info on what's going on. Yet they are the ones we're trying. "It's a damn disgrace."

At the other end of the spectrum is astonishing leniency toward Americans convicted of killing or abusing prisoners. A 2006 study cited case after case of blatant instances of murder in which no one was punished to the extent of the law.

During 2002, Army MPs beat to death two Afghans chained to the ceiling of their cell. The commanding officer was charged with dereliction of duty and lying to investigators but only received a letter of reprimand and was released from active duty. Of the actual assailants, two were acquitted and two more were convicted of assault.

Two years later another Afghan detainee was murdered by seven marines, only one of whom stood trial. Because medical evidence was lost or destroyed, he was convicted of assault and reduced to private with no time in jail. Conversely, the facility's commanding officer accepted responsibility, pled guilty to dereliction of duty, and was discharged.

In Iraq during 2003 an army warrant officer forced an Iraqi general with broken ribs into a sleeping bag, then smothered him to death. Though convicted of "negligent homicide," the WO was merely fined and received a letter of reprimand.

The investigation of a 2004 dual homicide resulted in a lieutenant receiving immunity and subsequently being awarded the Bronze Star.

Through 2006 various government and press investigations found that at least eighteen and perhaps thirty-four prisoners in Afghanistan and Iraq had been killed by their jailers. That does not include battlefield incidents such as the alleged murders of civilians in Haditha, Iraq.

The foregoing examples, plus others, contrast vividly with the pattern in Vietnam. There, nearly 100 soldiers and twenty-seven marines were convicted of murdering noncombatants, with Marine Corps sentences ranging from ten years to life. (Gary Solis, "Military Justice?" *U.S. Naval Institute Proceedings*, October 2006.)

Judges and lawyers know that a verdict can reflect far more than what it appears—and far less. There are many variables: how well evidence was collected, how the prosecution was handled, how much "command guidance" came down, and what plea bargains were granted, to name a few. But outside the court, those niceties tend to get lost; what we retain is the image of fairness, or not (after all, OJ is still walking around free).

We need to recognize the enormous harm attending the apparent pattern of leniency accorded American soldiers who murder prisoners, if for no other reason than public and international perception. But the leniency shown previous murderers could rebound if the military ever tries to make punishment proportional to the crime. Defense attorneys may be able to cite unequal treatment if harsher sentences are imposed for identical or similar offenses.

Ironically, nonlethal abuses such as the thuggery at Abu Ghraib Prison may have worse implications. The abuses inflicted upon detainees there—Iraqis forced into pornographic poses, nudity, and other humiliations—may be seen as worse than "simple" killings because they fuel further outrage, enable enemy propagandists to recruit more jihadists, and erode our image among nonaligned Muslims.

Closely related to the foregoing are continuing problems with providing combat troops clear, concise rules of engagement (ROE). While there are general guidelines from DoD's Judge Advocate General, consistent with international law, theater commanders provide more specific rules for their operating areas. That's sensible from a tactical perspective but it can run afoul of legality.

We continue to face a mess of our own making.

We Need Truth In Advertising

Allegedly a Chinese saying holds that the beginning of wisdom is calling things by their correct names. If so, there's precious little wisdom in DoD.

How else to explain the continuing string of irrational, illogical, and downright deceitful prefixes hung on military hardware? Attack airplanes masquerading as "fighters"; nonexistent mission capabilities; unexplained chasms in numerical sequences, and wholesale abuse of what used to be a well-ordered system.

On the plus side there's the A-10 Warthog (aka Thunderbolt II), now alone in the "A for Attack" category. At least it continued the series beginning with Douglas' storied A-1 Skyraider, A-3 Skywarrior, and A-4 Skyhawk series. Attackers through the AV-8 made sense (though the Harrier was a "V" type assigned an "A" number), while Northrop's A-9 was never produced.

As far as air force attack aircraft, the service never liked them—which is why the F-111 (a 100 percent strike bird) was so designated. It began life as Robert Strange McNamara's conceptual TFX (tactical fighter experimental), and retained a 20mm gun as if to prove the point. Intended as a TacAir one-stop-shopping center, the 111 was to become all things to all services (except the Army, of course, which has been prohibited fixed-wing attack aeroplanes since 1947). The prototype Navy version was the F-111B, but an uncommonly ethical vice admiral named Tom Connolly put paid to the beast in 1967 when he told Congress, "There is not enough thrust in Christendom to make that airplane into a navy fighter." RSM got his revenge—as expected—by denying Connolly a fourth star, but the Navy remembered and five years later christened the F-14 the *Tom*cat.

But I digress.

Bombers? Well, we went from the Huff-Daland B-1 (1923) to Convair B-58 (1955) in almost unbroken sequence over a thirty-year period. The Hustler beat out the Boeing XB-59, and then we had the early cruise missiles such as the "B"-62 Snark. Excepting the Douglas B-66, the USAF bomber series leapt to XB-70 about the same time the Lockheed SR-71 materialized. What's *that* about? Insiders intimate that there was a "separate but equal" list of secret project numbers.

However, by rights the S in SR-71 would represent the anti-submarine variant of a recon machine! Somebody (maybe Curt LeMay Himself) determined that in the Blackbird's case, SR represented Strategic Reconnaissance, never mind that no such moniker ever existed.

Then, for absolutely no reason at all, we retreated to the 1920s with the B-1 and B-2 again. What was *that* about?

Then there's the U-2. Now, by rights a "U" designates a utility airplane. Nobody would doubt the utility of the U-2, but how does it fit into the reconnaissance scheme of things? DeHavilland made the U-1 and Cessna the U-3, etc. Reportedly the Uncle prefix was chosen as "disinformation" to spoof the Soviets.

Meanwhile, the "T for trainer" series was doing just fine, thank you: in the high 40s when, for reasons never explained, the USAF decided to call a new multiengined trainer, the T-1. The blue suits also named it the Jayhawk, somehow ignoring that the name already was hung on the Coast Guard HH-60J. According to an insider, the Air Force then tried to name its next trainer the T-2, only to learn that the Navy had been flying Buckeyes since 19-ought-63. Thus we ended up with the low-budget T-3 Firefly but the Navy rebounded with the T-48 for the new NFO trainer. From there we jumped to the T-6 so we could have a nostalgic "Texan II" in honor of the romantic days of World War Deuce.

If you're dizzy from following the bouncing numbers, welcome aboard.

Fighters started all right but became a mess. F-14, -15, and -16. Great. Makes perfect sense, continuing the sequence from 1963 when the Air Force and Navy adopted one standard. The F-17 was Northrop's lightweight fighter that evolved into the F/A-18, which is fine. But: if you check the DoD aircraft designation manual, there's no provision for a slash. None. How did *that* happen?

Then there's the vast leap from the F-20 series of genuine fighters into Puzzle Palace hyperspace with the "F"-117, which isn't even a fighter. What's *that* about?

A thought for the day: the federal government requires truth in advertising. According to FTC rules:

Ads must be truthful and nondeceptive.

Ads must contain evidence to support their claims.

Ads cannot be unfair.

Undoubtedly there's plenty of people willing to hassle in Clintonian terms over the definition of "unfair." So let's just consider the first two requirements.

"Truthful and nondeceptive."

The F-117 is in no way, shape, or form a fighter. It carries no air-to-air weapons and cannot defend itself against interceptors. The Nighthawk, therefore, fails the "truthful and nondeceptive" requirement. It could not legally be advertised alongside automobiles or beer on the NFL Game of the Week.

Compare that to the Grumman A-6 of honored memory. The Intruder never masqueraded as a fighter. Know why? Well, it was a "Type A" personality (as in Attack) and, like the F-117, it was a subsonic strike aircraft with no air-to-air mission, though it could carry Sidewinders for self-defense—something the "Stinkbug" cannot do.

Then there's the vital component of tactical aviation in the Missile Age: electronic warfare. The EA-6B is such a great subject. By rights we should be up to the E or F . . . but are not. In 2005 there was a discussion on that subject in St. Louis. Two of the guys most responsible for the myriad changes in the Prowler are self-confessed sneaky bastards, perfectly happy to do what they can to get new gadgets under the budgetary radar of those who might otherwise Just Say No. (The HARM radar killer alone is a great one—there were lots of Attack types who were really upset about Prowlers getting a missile.)

Moving right along . . . I'm really cranky about gross overuse of the "M for Multimission" tag. By nature, almost all aircraft are multimission, yet the Navy is slapping it on all rotary wing platforms, MH-60 Sea Hawk, MV-22 Osprey, etc.

Oh, by the way, the M means "antimine" when attached to an H-53 . . . "multipurpose" in front of an H-60 and "Special Ops" when placed with a C-130. Please don't ask why; I don't know. Probably nobody does.

* * *

In 2004 the air force chief of staff waved the waiver and declared the F-22 Raptor a multimission bird by dint of the "F/A" designation. Never mind that at the time the Raptor had not even entered service, nor that the original models would have no ordnance capability. Once again, if the FTC licensed combat aircraft, Lockheed and the Air Force would be liable to prosecution.

However, there is some sign of adult supervision in DoD. In late 2005 the new air force chief of staff announced that the F/A-22A Raptor was going to be redesignated—ta-daa!—the F-22A! He correctly stated that the OSD document covering the system clearly states that "F" types can also cover dual-role strike aircraft.

Unfortunately, he then stated that the Raptor can also perform the mission of the RC-135 Rivet Joint and EC-130 Compass Call. Therefore, we should be thankful that he didn't wind up calling it the F/AREC-22.

Come to think of it, that designation would comprise the word "Farce."

Might be a message there.

We just wish someone had thought to invite an FTC representative to enforce truth in advertising.

The Numbers Game

How hard is it to put a sequential number on an airplane?

Apparently it's almost impossible.

The Pentagon, October 26, 2001.

DoD announced selection of Lockheed-Martin's X-35 as the stealthy joint strike fighter, a $200 billion–plus program. (Note:

in 2001 dollars the combined total of World War II's costliest programs—the B-29 and the Manhattan Project—was only $48 billion.)

Since the undersecretary of defense did not offer the information, a reporter asked what the JSF was going to be designated. The undersecretary did not have that information for the biggest military contract in history, and turned to the program manager, a Marine Corps two-star. Here's that portion of the transcript:

Reporter: "What's going to be the nomenclature for these airplanes? What's the designation?"

The undersecretary: "Very good question. It's going to be called—the Lockheed version was the X-35 ... "

Moderator: "Mike knows. Mike knows the answer. Mike, the answer is?"

The major general: "F-35."

Reporter: "How did you decide on that? Where does that come from, F-35?"

The major general: "It's a list of different variants, different companies, different..."

The undersecretary: "The Boeing version was the X-32."

Reporter: "Thank you."

(DoD briefing on the Joint Strike Fighter contract announcement, October 26, 2001.)

Knowledgeable observers were either bemused or awestruck. A Boeing representative in the room said, "The suit had no earthly idea. I'm not sure they had even thought that far ahead."

When the F-35 made its way to the office that assigns aircraft designations, the error was noted and a valiant but losing effort was made to apply the correct (sequential) F-24 designation. To this day, the Pentagon is so sensitive to the hiccup that the first item on the official web site's FAQs declares, "The program manager stated that the aircraft family would be known as the F-35. This was not a mistake."

Balderdash. Otherwise how to explain the leap from the Northrop/McDonnell Douglas YF-23 prototype? A leap of twelve numbers, for no obvious or stated reason, was "not a mistake."

There's more. The breadth of ignorance about the system is shown by recent designations, such as Boeing KC-767 and Airbus KC-330, which became the officially recognized names for two proposed tankers. "These are civil designs and therefore should not have traditional military designations," one Pentagon source said.

Oh, really?

By rights the KC-767 should be the KC-42. But if civilian designs don't need military designations, whatever are we to do about the greatest transport aircraft of the twentieth century? I speak of the C-47 (DC-3), not to mention other stalwarts: the L-series spotter planes (Stinson Reliants and Piper Cubs); and the aforementioned E-3, E-6, E-8, C-18, and C-137 (all Boeing 707s). Not to mention Air Force One, the VC-25 (Boeing 747). The DoD dweeb who issued that asinine statement should be made to write one hundred times on the blackboard: "I will not open my mouth unless somebody tells me I know what I'm talking about."

But wait a minute.

Why do aircraft designations matter? Isn't it a tempest in a teacup? To most people, ignoring rules, history, and logic simply doesn't amount to much compared to the hardware itself. It's the same thing with the nonsensical names given to warships. The "system" for christening submarines is so convoluted that the boats are named for cities, states, politicians, and fish. Carriers are named for politicians nobody's ever heard of (Stennis and Vinson) and those who nearly destroyed naval aviation (Truman and Bush). But as one prospective skipper said, "I don't care if they name it the 'Good Ship Lollypop' as long as I get my command."

However, names and numbers can matter in the larger context. Beyond the serious enthusiasts and historical purists, there's the concept of rationality—rule of law rather than impulse or expediency. If the United States Department of Defense is incapable of adhering to a simple linear progression of aircraft numbers, what does that say about us? It tells the world that we are so arcane, so self-absorbed with our compartmentalized viewpoints that we continually make exceptions to the published rules.

The system is broken and it's not likely to change. But sometimes the suits who decide such things need to be held up to public scrutiny—and ridicule.

We Need "Prain Engrish"

During a Western Pacific naval exercise in the 1970s, the American admiral commanding the endeavor sought to standardize communications with his allies. After much dismayed discussion of the U.S. Navy's reliance upon Pentagon buzzwords and acronyms, a Japanese officer took the floor. In a plea for clarity, he asked, "Why cannot we just speak prain Engrish?"

It's an atrocity. The language beloved of Shakespeare, Churchill, and Hemingway has been seized by soulless merchants and careerists who babble among themselves in Pentagonese, the arcane argot of the military-industrial-political complex.

Exactly how the mutation began may lie beyond reckoning, but clearly it could not have occurred without the conscious collaboration of hundreds (perhaps thousands) of willing conspirators.

Retired Army General and Secretary of State Alexander Haig was often excoriated for his linguistic wanderings in "Haigspeak." They included such examples as "terminological inexactitude" (i.e., lying) but in retrospect they appear harmless enough, even colorful. "Rewickering" and "contexted" may not appear in Webster's or the OED, but at least the intent can be guessed at.

Not so for the following abominations:

"Throughput."

"Single-process owner."

"Human cross-functional strategy capital team."

"Value chain."

At a recent military-industrial conference, a board of admirals indulged itself in that sort of gobbledygook (you can look it up) for forty minutes or more. Two authors sitting in the back of the room—as far from the offenders as possible—slumped in their seats and not only tolerated the insipid language, but waited in vain for a hint of explanation. It never came. At length they occupied themselves by trying to fashion a grammatical sentence from the spew of Beltway buzzwords. The scribes labored mightily, and here's what they produced:

"The system's throughput relies upon a single-process owner to manage the human cross-functional strategy capital team in producing a viable value chain."

We had absolutely no idea what that means. Obviously neither did any of the admirals.

Nor is the Air Force much better. A recent publicity release touting "cost avoidance" policies for the F-22 stealth fighter. Later, reading between the lines, we can infer, "What the general meant was: savings."

Another blue-suit document referred to "noncurrence." By Googling, it's possible to discern among the 133 total hits (as of August 2006) that the nonword indicates plain old-fashioned *disagreement*.

Contrast that corruption with the clear, concise prose that the Combined Chiefs of Staff sent to Eisenhower before D-Day:

"You will enter the continent of Europe and, in conjunction with the other United Nations, undertake operations aimed at the heart of Germany and the destruction of her armed forces. The date for entering the Continent is the month of May 1944. After adequate Channel ports have been secured, exploitation will be directed toward securing an area that will facilitate both ground and air operations against the enemy."

Or consider the following list of military priorities:

"If it helps kill Japs, it's important. If it doesn't help kill Japs, it's not important."

Admiral Bull Halsey would turn apoplectic at today's political correctness, but his language was unmistakably simple. There was no room for misunderstanding either his priorities or his intent.

Today, the U.S. military is more managed than led, and perhaps we have no right to be surprised at the linguistic mutilation that has occurred over the past five decades or so. But how did that occur? *Somebody* made it happen.

Apparently Robert Strange McNamara presided over much of the mangling of military English, with Harvard Business School management schemes and a passion for quantification. "Systems analysis" became a mantra for all manner of numerical legerdemain, with data selected to "prove" the desired outcome. A Marine Corps general finally broke the code when he realized, "We were constantly told to resubmit our findings until they agreed with what Mr. McNamara really wanted."

So much for objectivity.

Ultimately, there are only three elements to writing, be it good, bad, or indifferent: clarity, brevity, and style. Certainly such phrases as "human cross-functional strategy capital team" are neither clear nor brief, and the style is noteworthy only for its silliness.

But why does phraseology matter?

Well, aside from the presumed purpose of language to communicate clearly, there's this from George Orwell: "If thought corrupts language, then language can also corrupt thought."

Assuming that our military-political-industrial leaders continue folding, spindling, and mutilating the dominant language of Western Civilization, they (and we) probably are due for some unpleasant consequences. Muddled phraseology is evidence of muddled thinking, and the inability to communicate ideas, concepts, and plans in easily grasped terms is bound to cause confusion leading to failure.

There's a historical parallel. The late Professor Paul Dull, a World War II Japanese linguist, was familiar with the workings of the emperor's warlords. He believed that the innumerable subtleties and nuances of their language sometimes led to confusion in drafting orders for the Imperial Navy. While he did not contend that the

Great Pacific War would have ended otherwise with more clarity from Tokyo, it's possible that avoidable errors occurred. The problem appeared to be systemic, from petty officers up the ladder to admirals.

Fortunately, the potential for trouble is recognized below the star-wearing level. A colleague of mine is a significant officer: a combat commander and accomplished writer with a PhD. Recently he bemoaned the growth of "transformational semantics," a phrase he placed in quotes to indicate his disgust at the calculated destruction of unadorned English. He recognizes the absurdity of trendy buzzwords among senior officers who warp the language as a verbal secret handshake among insiders, and vows to avoid such influences upon his subordinates.

Maybe it's not much, but at least it's a start toward a possible return to "prain Engrish."

Chapter Seven

The China Syndrome

"One needs the enemy."

—T. S. Eliot, 1940

I'm not talking about the 1979 movie with Jane Whatshername. I'm talking about DoD's love-hate relationship with the People's Republic of China as the conventional warrior's tar baby: it's just too hard to turn loose.

After the collapse of the Soviet Union, the Pentagon had no "go to" enemy. The Soviets were wonderful in that respect: big, ambitious, antidemocratic, threatening. Their huge military and their demonstrated willingness to cause trouble all over the world spurred the massive spending spree of the Cold War.

Then the five-decade-long windfall was gone, almost literally overnight.

What to do?

Answer: gin up the next world-class enemy. But auditions were severely limited, and China got the role just for showing up.

On paper, the PRC represents a significant military power. The 2005 figures alone are daunting: the world's largest military manpower pool, second biggest air force, and a growing, fourth-ranked Navy. However, it helps to look beneath the rankings to see what they really mean.

In terms of active military personnel, Iran leads the world with 11.7 million, followed by China with 7 million, and North Korea with 5.9 million. The U.S. ranks seventh both in total available and active duty personnel.

China's air forces (all services) poll number two on the global hit parade with 9,200 of all types. But that's barely half the U.S. figure, and ours are far more capable across the board. The People's Liberation Army Air Force is pushing hard to upgrade with Russian designs, but parking Su-30s on the ramp is a long-long way from making them competitive with Eagles and Hornets. Truth be told, most of Beijing's front-line aircraft are technically eligible for membership in the Antique Airplane Association.

The People's Liberation Army Navy (PLAN) (!), while looking impressive at number four, lags about six laps behind Uncle Sam's. With fewer than three hundred vessels of all types, China has fewer warships than Russia, and cannot begin to compete with America's. Even with other commitments around the world, the U.S. Navy still can bring enormous firepower to bear by sea and air. ("World Military Strength Ranking," *GlobalFirepower.com* [most recently accessed April 17, 2007].)

It's why we have more aircraft carriers than the rest of the world combined.

In terms of naval and air power, it's not even certain that a Sino-Russian alliance could meet us head to head because some Russian gear such as the Sukhoi 37, while technically impressive, remains in low-rate production with limited ability to maintain and deploy. Meanwhile, much of the Russian navy continues rusting at anchor.

A land war would, of course, be another matter entirely, even if we weren't fully extended in Afghanistan and Iraq. We're in no position to commit ground troops against China or Russia anywhere, least of all on the Asian mainland, nor do we have the remotest reason to do so.

Yet, as the Global Policy Forum noted July 20, 2005, "Air Force officials, fighting vigorously to preserve the budget for the Stealth F-22 fighter, have put emphasis this year on China's improved air defenses and the F-22's abilities to elude radar. 'You look at the Air Force's briefings, and they are all China, China, China,' said a senior defense official working on the Quadrennial Defense Review. Chinese officials have stressed that their government has no intention of threatening neighboring nations or disturbing regional stability. Its mission, they say, is to develop a credible deterrent so Taiwan doesn't declare independence."

Whether Mainland China is truly worried about Taiwan—and that's a real stretch—it begs the question of American concerns about a war with the PRC.

Nevertheless, we build platinum-plated aircraft and next-generation submarines on the basis of a supposed war with one-fifth of humanity. Despite decades of evidence to the contrary, the military and Congress continue funding wondrous machines (never mind if the performance matches the brochure) for a conflict that is extremely unlikely to occur.

Here's why.

The United States is not going to attack China. Neither is anyone else, for that matter. Aside from military folly, the reasons are far too obvious to enumerate, but Big Money ranks very high on the list.

Therefore, in order to believe that Washington will ever cross swords with Beijing, we must conclude that *They* will attack *Us*. Think about that for a moment. We're dealing with people who take the long-long view of history and plan accordingly. We, on the other hand, having invented instant gratification, try to look five years downstream and pat ourselves on the back.

Follow the Money

The PRC has no reason to wage open war against America because the Chinese have far too big a stake in the U.S. economy.

Beijing owns an increasing share of America's debt and is not about to cut China's own fiscal throat. If China will start a war, one must decide that the hard-eyed pragmatists in Beijing are willing to ruin relations with its second-biggest trading partner. Furthermore, our trade deficit with China runs five to one in Beijing's favor, topping a $200 million deficit in both 2005 and 2006.

Nor is that all. At the end of 2005, 60 percent of China's foreign reserves were U.S. capital. As of 2006 China held $240 billion among the $2.1 trillion in treasury securities owned overseas. (Zhou Shijian and Wang Lijun, "China, U.S. Complementary in Trade," *China Daily,* April 18, 2006.)

China's economic influence in and reliance upon the United States has been growing for decades. For instance, PRC exports to the United States increased 212 percent between 2000 and 2006—nearly $163 billion (American exports to China grew 157 percent in the same time). Moreover, consider the trade materials: we buy shoes and sweaters while exporting computers and jet aircraft. Simplistic? Yes. China's electronics industry is growing, but the high-ticket products largely flow from here to there, not vice-versa.

The U.S. government reported in 2005 that America imported $243.5 billion, or 32 percent, of PRC total exports. But look farther: after Japan and America, China's biggest individual trade partners are Hong Kong, South Korea, Taiwan, Russia, Australia, and Canada. Thus, if Beijing makes war on America, the effects would be felt in the PRC's first, second, fourth, fifth, seventh, and eighth biggest markets as well. ("Facts and Figures: China's Top Ten Trade Partners," *People's Daily,* August 6, 2001.)

Why would China do that?

The question should answer itself.

Yet even some well-placed observers ignore the fiscal aspects. In their 2006 volume, *Showdown: Why China Wants War with the United States,* a former undersecretary of defense and a congressional-Pentagon insider present several scenarios for a Sino-American war. Some are intriguing, including a

Chinese-Venezuelan alliance. But nowhere in more than two hundred pages do the authors even allude to America's huge, growing trade deficit with the PRC.

Apart from interesting war game prospects, most of which involve high-high tech gear, war with China needs to be discussed in context. What are the conditions that would lead Beijing to wage war against an essential trade partner and almost certainly alienate many others as well?

There's no room for doubt: China is upgrading its military as fast as possible. Frequently, when members of the American military-industrial-political complex are asked to justify DoD spending, the go-to answer is China: "Beijing is spending billions on high-tech weapons."

Well, so are we!

There are reports of a Chinese F-22 clone, and among the nations selling hardware to Beijing are our old friends the Israelis, Russians, and French. But that's all part of the global game. Everybody sells weapons, and though America perennially leads the world in that category, it's often overlooked that our sales go to our allies rather than merely the highest bidder.

So: what is China buying?

While the PRC has tried to hide the true amount of its military spending, intelligence analysts conclude that in 2006 the actual figure would approach $100 billion, or 7.5 percent of the nation's GDP. That's nearly twice the American ratio.

Since nobody but nobody threatens China, the foregoing seems to indicate that the PRC is headed for war.

Or does it?

Beijing is investing heavily in high tech, to the point that, Rumsfeldlike, it has reduced its manpower in recent years to make financial room for more gear. What the PLA is buying would find approval in many Pentagon offices and business boardrooms: satellites for navigation, communication, and killing other satellites; computers and network-centric warfare options; command and control aircraft; electronic warfare systems; and more.

What does that mean?

It is possible—even likely—that China seeks regional military superiority in order to assure itself of unfettered trade, especially by sea. Most Americans have no idea that China is heir to a centuries-old tradition of far-flung maritime commerce, extending as far west as Arabia. Thus, Beijing's steady growth of forces and capabilities could well be prompted by a desire to offset not just American actions, but those of America's Asian allies as well: Japan, Taiwan, South Korea, and others.

By pouring billions into high-tech systems such as satellites and network warfare, China may well be placing itself in a position of intimidation. Knowing that we realize our national life and economy could be ruined by a competent computer-communications attack, Beijing seems to have it both ways: continuing a lucrative economic relationship while preparing for low-intensity, high-scale warfare that sheds little or no blood.

War Gaming China

Let's ask the primary question: what would we fight about? Possibly excepting Taiwan, where would our interests clash militarily? It's not clear that Americans would support fighting China to defend Taiwan, but Beijing's risk-benefit analysis surely factors that question into the equation.

What are the other reasons that we might fight?

Conflicting markets? A replay of the opium wars with colonial powers vying for financial control of Asia? Today a unified China and the increasingly interdependent global market renders that nineteenth century scenario irrelevant. It just won't happen.

A resources war? Access to oil or natural gas? Since America lacks the will and ability to seize and hold new territory, that scenario defaults to a naval/maritime conflict that we probably would win hands down. Whether we could sustain the operation may be less certain.

Consequently, if we do fight China, it will likely be in a specific area under very peculiar circumstances. How else to preserve the trade relationship so important to both sides?

Consider this:

We stood toe to toe with the Soviets for half a century, all the while keeping the Kremlin afloat with food shipments despite the USSR's enormous (and grossly inefficient) agriculture industry. When we were eyeball to eyeball with the Russians in Berlin, Cuba, and elsewhere, we never came to blows beyond various "incidents." So why would China be any different?

I cannot answer that question, and apparently neither can anyone else. But for one moment let's assume that Beijing decides to go to war against its second biggest trading partner. Where and how will the PRC fight us?

Not on its own soil, that's for certain. For one thing, we would have trouble getting there, and for another, we will never have enough soldiers, sailors, airmen, and/or marines to get to first base. So where might we fight?

Look at the map.

The Strait of Malacca, between Malaysia and Indonesia, is one of the world's strategic maritime choke points, like Gibraltar, Suez, or Hormuz. About 80 percent of China's oil passes through Malacca, and a goodly share of the world supply.

In 2005 DoD identified China's "string of pearls" strategy in building military-political alliances in Southern Asia while constructing a series of bases to support naval operations in the region. They include a canal across the narrow isthmus of Thailand that would emerge into the Indian Ocean north of the strait. Other outlets involve an airfield on Woody Island between the Philippines and Vietnam; a maritime/naval base in the Indian Ocean; a large port at Chittagong in Myanmar (aka Burma); and other ports in Bangladesh and Pakistan.

It's no coincidence that Indonesia is the most populous Muslim nation, while Pakistan and Bangladesh rank second and third.

Even with half our naval forces deployed in European and Middle Eastern waters, China cannot hope to fight America at sea on anything resembling even terms. Whether our antisubmarine forces are as bulletproof as they appear, getting many points on the nautical scoreboard would be exceedingly difficult for the PLAN. In order to sink an American carrier, the Chinese might have to shoot tactical nukes, and the price for capturing a queen could produce a chilling escalation. If we're unwilling to retaliate in kind, then we deserve to lose.

One area in which the Chinese might score some points is mine warfare. The U.S. Navy has seldom placed much emphasis on mine countermeasures since the Korean War (perhaps to be renamed the First Korean War). Enemy mining of choke points such as Malacca and any number of ports could tie up a great deal of our combatant tonnage for days at a time, delaying transit or forcing long detours. That's why we need more mine hunters and sweepers (see Chapter Eight).

Another advantage accruing to Beijing is the ability to concentrate most of its naval forces at the crucial point. Being a true deep water, power projection creature, America has to keep much of its fleet deployed elsewhere or at home undergoing refit. Therefore, if China carefully chooses the time and place of an attack, Beijing could conceivably gain enough of a temporary advantage to achieve specific, limited goals.

Despite the seemingly impressive growth of the PLAN (presumably replacing most 1960s construction circa 2025), analysts note that China's new ships employ technology first seen on America's *Ticonderoga* (CG-47) class cruisers in the 1980s. Says one observer, "The PLAN regionally is very capable, and the ships contain a large amount of antishipping missiles, but very few have area SAMs or close-in weapon systems." Considering numbers and capabilities, for the foreseeable future the Chinese navy is not structured to fight a major war. We might say that its surface force remains a good welterweight with decent reach and a glass jaw.

But assuming the PLAN decided to fight, after the smoke cleared and the water settled, what would change? Trade pressure would dictate a return to something approaching the status quo ante, and if for some reason it did not, there still remain more circuitous routes around the area of contention. Therefore, the residual effects of open conflict with the PRC will almost certainly appear elsewhere.

Conclusion: if China decides to strap us on, we've probably already lost, but not at the point of contact.

Beijing will have years, perhaps decades, to plot its strategy and set things in motion. At risk of hyperbole, envision the following email to whitehouse.gov:

"Please to look under desk in Oval Office. Device you see there is like eleven others stashed across the Fruited Plain. Now leave us the hell alone while we annex Taiwan."

We would do well to remember that it's possible to win every battle as well as the war—and still lose the aftermath.

What Price Stealth?

Stealth technology represents the golden boy and the crown prince of the MIPC: it's the major growth industry and will remain so well into the foreseeable future. Because it is so often cast in context of a war with China, some observations may be pertinent here, but the principles apply elsewhere.

A bit of background: contrary to common perception, "stealth" does not render an aircraft or anything else invisible to radar, horizon to horizon. Rather, its shape and covering deflects or absorbs electronic beams until the platform is well within range of the target, permitting little response time. With standoff weapons such as air-launched cruise missiles, stealth aircraft presumably can attack important targets from beyond the defense's normal engagement zone.

That's the theory. The reality may fall somewhat short of that goal, but the facts are closely held secrets for good and valid reasons. But like any technology, stealth will grow old. Perhaps it already has:

Writes a retired air force colonel, a former bomber pilot working inside the Beltway: "Stealth birds are, in my opinion, one technological advance from being obsolescent. We seem to be spending a lot of money on this 'one trick pony' and have not really come to terms with the fact that one was bagged by something other than a lucky shot in Bosnia. It's a combination of 'The emperor isn't wearing any clothes' and 'Ignore the man behind the curtain.'"

Whether stealth lives up to the brochure remains to be seen. But in the meantime, the technology's immense cost continues absorbing vast quantities of the DoD budget, to the detriment of other, mundane (and often more useful) items: ammunition, body armor, batteries, even socks.

Stealth (aka "low observable" or LO) aircraft were designed for a Cold War doomsday scenario: penetrating the formidable air defenses of the Evil Empire in a world gone nuclear with mushroom clouds erupting across the Eurasian landmass and North America. The first such design was the now-famous Lockheed "stealth fighter" that first flew as the "Have Blue" prototype in 1978 and went operational as the F-117 five years later. However, the Nighthawk was more a tactical than a strategic attack aircraft.

The next design was a no-kidding strategic bomber, Northrop's Batplane lookalike, the B-2 Spirit that first flew in 1989 and was declared combat ready in 1994. Only twenty-one were built at an average price of $2.1 billion, with a B. It has been computed that an empty Spirit (roughly 150,000 pounds) costs about $870 per ounce—twice the going rate of gold.

Two genuine fighters are more recent entrants to the stealth stable: both from Lockheed-Martin. The F-22 Raptor is a dedicated air superiority machine though the Air Force claims a modest strike potential for it. The futuristic design was flown in 1997 and became operational at the end of 2005. Due to escalating costs, the "buy" steadily declined from 750 aircraft to 183, at which figure the program cost per airframe is $340 million and $187 million "flyaway" cost. By way of comparison, the stated cost of an F/A-18E Super Hornet runs around $60 million per copy. It carries most of the same air-air weapons as the Raptor, and vastly more air-to-surface ordnance, but lacks the stealthiness.

Insiders concede that the F-22, like the even spendier B-2, could have been handled much better. Instead of a progressive approach, as in the Cold War's F-102 and F-106 evolution, the Air Force decided on a "gross correction," dumping a bucket load of new technology into one platform at the same time. The decision was all the more peculiar considering that there was—and is—no comparable threat on the horizon. Meanwhile, other aircraft with real-world missions to perform often went wanting for spare parts and fuel, and the service began RIF'ing personnel (RIF: reduction in force; in other words, firing people) to pay for the new equipment, including the F-35 joint strike fighter. As of 2006 there were reports that as many as one-third of F-15s were grounded on a given day owing to lack of spare parts.

There are other factors in play. Not the least of them is political pork, with the F-22 as Exhibit Alpha. Contractors and subcontractors are found in forty-six states plus Puerto Rico, and by one reckoning in 88 percent of all congressional districts. Done deal.

That's the political aspect. The presumed military rationale has to do with the evolving threat: other high-high tech designs from Russia and France, among others. As noted previously, the ability of likely "opponents" to obtain, maintain, and employ their own fifth-generation fighters remains speculative. You can get an argument either way in any air force officers club—if it still has an officers club.

The one aspect of building stealth airplanes that actually makes some sense is neither military nor political. It's industrial. America needs to maintain its cutting-edge technology by keeping its industrial base up to speed with design, engineering, and production capabilities. And there's the dichotomy—the ultimate engineer's dilemma. Do we build something because we can or because we actually need it? There's serious question whether we need stealth equipment when our conventional aircraft totally dominate the opposition, and have done so approximately forever, certainly since the 1970s. But as a hedge against something currently unexpected, our research facilities should continue their work so that it can be translated into ships and aircraft ready to go when needed.

That in turn requires long-term, intelligent planning (and yes, dear reader, I share your cynicism).

Stealth in Combat

How would stealth aircraft likely be used against China?

In fact, would they be used anywhere at all?

When politicians pontificate that nothing is too good for "our fighting men and women" they're dead wrong. If we truly felt that way, we'd raise taxes to spend 49 percent of the GNP on military personnel, gear, and training. But the fact is, a gadget *is* too good for the troops if it's too expensive to risk in combat. And thus far, the high-end stealth platforms have seldom been exposed to serious risk.

Been There, Done That, Part IX

North Vietnam, December 1972.

It was called "The Christmas War," an eleven-day bombing campaign calculated to nudge Hanoi back to the Paris "peace" talks. Following the North's massive spring offensive into the South, the Nixon administration forsook its "secret plan to win the war" and sent the bombers back to conduct some no-kidding negotiations. The kind that the Politburo understood.

It worked. More than seven hundred B-52 sorties dropped fifteen thousand tons of bombs on selected targets, razing much of Hanoi's military power. At the end, North Vietnam had nearly depleted its stock of SAMs, and its inventory of MiGs had been seriously dented, though not without losses among U.S. fighters, especially the Air Force's. Even heavy antiaircraft guns were low on ammunition.

Out of options, Hanoi conducted further talks leading to a cease-fire in January 1973, and withdrawal of the last American forces. Before long the U.S. Congress stabbed Saigon in the back, withholding further assistance, and the forceful "reunification" of Vietnam occurred barely two years later.

Operation Linebacker II remains one of the few all-air-power victories in history. It achieved a significant foreign policy goal without recourse to land or naval measures, though in fairness it should be noted that the mining of Haiphong and other ports was accomplished entirely by navy and marine aircraft.

But at what cost?

The B-52s sustained heavy losses: fifteen Stratoforts destroyed by SA-2s in less than two weeks. By all accounts, including those of B-52 crews, the campaign was poorly conceived, flying "airline" profiles: predictable routes and schedules. After the first night the Vietnamese SAM shooters noted the pattern and took advantage of it. Furthermore, SAC pulled its punches in the electronic countermeasures department.

A few years later, sitting in air force officers clubs, survivors of Linebacker II still were bitter over the losses. Most were considered unnecessary because the '52s had the ability to deceive enemy radars. With sophisticated electronic countermeasure (ECM) gear, they insisted they could have rendered Hanoi's air defense net practically useless, but were forbidden to do so.

Why?

The Big Picture.

SAC knew that Hanoi's Soviet mentors would watch the B-52s with both eyes wide open. Consequently, the methods of a no-holds-barred strategic bombing campaign in Southeast Asia would presage what could be expected if the B-52s ever launched for Moscow. SAC headquarters in Omaha made a calculated decision to withhold the most effective jamming and deception measures to preserve its deepest-darkest secrets for Doomsday.

That was at the end of a major war lasting nine years, costing fifty-eight thousand American lives. Sixty-six of those were B-52 crew members killed or captured.

What are the odds that today's stealth secrets will be exposed in anything less?

What would have to be at stake in order to send B-2s or F-22s into hostile airspace today?

If anybody knows, none are willing to say.

Which puts us back to Square One in the stealth business.

* * *

Contrary to what's sometimes claimed, stealth machines do not go naked into battle, and part of the flail regarding stealth is interservice rivalry. In broad terms, the Air Force has it and the Navy/Marines do not. For a tailhooker perspective, here's "Rambo," a combat-experienced electronics warfare operator with dozens of Prowler missions in Desert Storm:

"*Repeat after me*: CentCom and EuCom will not let LO (stealth) platforms enter a moderate, let alone severe, threat envelope without standoff jammers. It is a fact." (CentCom—United States Central Command; EuCom—United States European Command.)

What electronic warfare operators concede is that stealth is a great door kicker, especially when the opposition is not expecting you. Rambo adds, "After Day One, I suspect that all bets are off. Unless we take out nearly all of the hostile air defense net, what's left on Day Two will know what to expect. The only way around that is to alter your tactics, but if you're fighting Mike Tyson, are you going to pull your punches in the first round? I sure wouldn't. So it comes down to who's smarter and who executes better."

We should never-ever assume that we're smarter than anybody, let alone the Chinese, who invented the compass, paper, gunpowder, and rockets.

So that leaves us to execute our plan better than they perform theirs—whatever it may be. But we won't know until the fight starts, and even then we can count on being surprised on

Day Two and beyond (remember, they're smart).

Other tactical considerations also arise, including the "LO" requirement to fly at night (F-117s and B-2s aren't painted black just for a nifty Darth Vader color scheme). Being subsonic—by quite a margin—they're unable to outrun interceptors and cannot defend themselves against enemy aircraft. Stealth birds also are vulnerable to visually directed defenses such as antiaircraft guns and optically guided SAMs. Consequently, old-fashioned gunfire can destroy the stealthiest aircraft if it's caught in the barrage pattern, and current thermal or acoustic sensors also remain a threat.

The F-22, with supersonic cruise, presumably can operate in daylight. Time will tell.

Meanwhile, you didn't read it here, but . . .

Stealth birds do not like flying in clouds because moisture *enhances* radar reflectivity. Therefore, stealth aircraft are kept in semiantiseptic hangars to avoid degrading their stealthiness. Yes, portable hangars are available to deploying units (they cost about $3 million apiece), but that does little good when radar-absorbent material can be blasted away in a two hundred–knot sandstorm.

There are also security concerns. No sooner had "Vega 21" hit the Yugoslavian dirt in 1999 than the F-117 wreckage was swept up by hostile scientists and engineers eager to retrieve the stealth coating. Are we really going to send our most sensitive military equipment over territory where its materials can be examined and its secrets deciphered?

That would require some extremely acute risk-benefit analysis. So ask yourself: What's worth destroying that justifies losing a $360 million platform—let alone an irreplaceable one that costs $2 billion?

Cost—it always comes down to cost. But the Air Force leadership has long been beloved of fighters, and the pattern is well established: the front office will nearly always buy the slickest, quickest "F machines" almost without regard to anything else. One example will suffice.

There's a popular poster showing a Boeing Superfortress in flight. The caption is: "Sacrifice: Being willing to retire half your B-52 fleet for two more F-22s."

The Air Force guy who sent it to me added, "And hey, for another thirty U-2s, fifty-two F-117s, forty C-21s, and seventeen North Dakota Air National Guard F-16s, you can get *two more* F-22s!"

The poster was inspired by a 2006 plan to save $16 billion for the F-22 program by retiring older Air Force planes and a bunch of people. The changes, approved for FY 2007–2011, represented what a Pentagon consultant called "a full frontal assault" on the bomber, attack, and transport communities. (It has been suggested that the seriousness of the measure is gauged by the Air Force's willingness to ground forty Lear jets kept for undersecretaries and generals.)

Perhaps the most telling cut involved B-52s, which had been considered as long-range (standoff) jamming platforms. The Air Force went out of the electronic warfare business with retirement of its EF-111 Ravens in 1988, and modified Stratofortresses were seen as an option. Now, the light-blue suits have to rely on the dark-blue suits for EW protection. But in a way that's all right, because the Navy painted itself into a corner by doing away with both the A-6 Intruder and F-14 Tomcat/Bombcat and, now lacking long-range strikers, must rely on USAF tankers.

The plain fact is, the Air Force has not been terribly astute in its acquisition policy. Midway through the B-2 program, the blue suits decided that they wanted a low-level capability for the stealth bomber. Lockheed was aghast: "That'll double the cost!" the engineers exclaimed. "It's what we want," the generals replied. Congress went along, and the taxpayers took a ride.

In private, smoke-filled rooms, some former star wearers occasionally concede, "We screwed up." But you won't hear it on Fox or CNN.

At present rate, we may yet see a realization of Calvin Coolidge's alleged aviation philosophy, circa 1925: "Buy one aeroplane and let the pilots take turns flying it."

Excessive reliance on stealth severely limits other, more urgent, funding.

Perhaps the best example attends plans for buying another thirty-five or so C-17s, raising the total to around 180, but here's a well kept secret: we need airlift far more than we need "aerospace dominance" (read: F-22s). Yet the ghastly prices we pay for stealth aircraft adversely affect everything else. That means fewer spares and less fuel for every other platform, including airplanes that start with "C" (cargo) and "K" (tankers).

Bottom line: should we do away with stealth and save a great deal of money and/or spend it elsewhere?

Answer: we couldn't if we wanted to. The research and development money is long since spent. Whether we fight China or anyone else, we can still save a great deal by refusing to spend further, unnecessary funds on high-high tech projects when the actual warfighters lack for low-low tech gear such as upgraded body armor, modern bandages, and training ammunition. Until we realign our priorities, every dollar spent on futuristic gear for international show-and-tell is a dollar withheld from troops headed for combat.

Chapter Eight

Some Suggestions

"People are smart when they agree with you."
—Captain Jerry O'Rourke, USN (Ret)

In *A Country Made by War* (Random House, 1989), British historian Geoffrey Perret identified three legs of American military success:

Professional education (not limited to the service academies).

Faith in firepower.

A dual technology serving both the military and commercial-industrial sectors.

Perret states that the triumvirate is enduring if not invincible: "It could survive even something as tragic and farcical as Johnson and McNamara's mismanagement of the Vietnam War."

Despite the centuries-long tradition of education, firepower, and technology, America typically is unprepared for "the next war." Certainly it was true of the current conflict: we were top heavy with aerospace technology while wanting infantry.

In the twentieth century, America was a creature of the sea and the sky. In the twenty-first it is undisputed master of both, and it matters little to the Terror War. We have unfettered logistics, limited only by the amount of tonnage we can deliver to a combat zone, but we're still fighting at the squad and platoon level. Major operations are conducted by battalions.

However, things can change mighty fast in the military-industrial-political world, but almost always it's due to external forces. For instance, in preparing the 2006 budget request, DoD had cut $1 billion from missile defense. But that summer the North Koreans began shooting long-range rockets in violation of previous agreements, and claimed that one design could reach North America.

It was just another reminder of the folly of relying upon diplomacy to affect the behavior of despots. After all, appeasement failed utterly with Adolf Hitler, but Moammar Gaddafi's attitude adjustment hour was effectively hosted by Air Force and Navy aircrews serving five hundred– and two thousand–pound *hors d'oeuvres.*

So: as long as we're going to maintain a large military establishment, let's have the most capable, most relevant one possible. While acknowledging that many of the following suggestions may be overtaken by events, here's a smorgasbord of options to consider. They're grouped under four headings: Land, Sea, Air, and Generic.

One: "If By Land . . . "

Because ground combat represents the low end of the military spectrum (there have been knife kills in Iraq), the Army and Marine requirements are far simpler than the Navy's and Air Force's. But "simpler" does not mean "easier." To cite von Clausewitz again, most things in war are simple but the simplest things are hard. Perhaps nothing is harder to get across to the DoD budgeters than the enormous need for improvement in quantity and quality of ground combat training.

We Need More Training

We need to acknowledge that far, far too many military personnel are poorly trained, especially with their basic weapons: rifles and pistols. Some are downright unsafe. That is shameful, but the kahunas walking the Pentagon's hallowed halls refuse to be shamed.

Most of our soldiers are pitifully trained as combat riflemen, nowhere near the basic infantry standard. Just some of the most egregious examples were cited in Chapter Two.

In the current "360-degree war" or, variously, the "three-block war," anybody can become a player at a second's notice. Therefore, we can no longer afford to assume that "rear echelon" troops need only qualify with their weapons rather than become truly proficient with them.

It's clear that the armed forces are not going to fix the problem: otherwise, it would have happened by now. The reasons are similar to those from the 1870s and 1930s: indifference and money. Many star wearers would rather put their budgets into big-ticket items that lead to postretirement contracts with industry. Meanwhile, we send kids off to war who literally cannot shoot to save their lives.

Consequently, military personnel are increasingly seeking training in the private sector. While most soldiers know when they have reached a comfort level in combat skills, the real outrage is that some of them do not know the difference. If nobody tells them, they continue mistaking familiarization for training. That situation is intolerable and needs to be changed before noon last Friday.

Solution: Change the Army's priorities regarding marksmanship and combat training, which have been far, far too low for much too long. Devote a lot more money to ranges, instructors, and training ammunition. If there is anywhere near as much fat in the complex, networked future combat system (FCS) as many observers believe, the shortfall in training could be made good from reallocating funds from that program (and if you read

Robert Heinlein's classic *Starship Troopers*, you have a good idea of what's behind FCS).

Expand the Civilian Marksmanship Program and allocate more DoD funds to civilian ranges, Boy Scout troops , 4H clubs, and even in schools. Most kids would welcome the chance to learn firearms safety, gun handling, and marksmanship. Think of it as "No shooter left behind."

Speaking of schools, our educators need to ask themselves a question: will they set aside their personal prejudices in favor of developing lifesaving skills among our future soldiers? (We teach driver education and sex education but recoil—pun intended—from firearms education.)

If teachers and administrators want to help more Americans survive the current open-ended conflict, there will be no delay. Schools will start supporting shooting programs, even if it's only with air guns. The fundamentals of breathing, sights, and trigger control can be imparted before students reach military age, with huge advantages once they put on the uniform.

If teachers and administrators are not interested in preserving the lives of future soldiers, that's worth knowing, too.

We Need More and Better Guns

We're going to war with a rifle well over forty years old, though its age is not *prima facie* a detriment (consider the matchless M1911 pistol). The trouble with the M16 and M4 carbine is that they fire a marginal projectile. Their erratic reliability does not require elaboration here, although most of the problems arise from inattention or improper maintenance. In any case, we're stuck with the M16 family until approximately forever. However, there are other options, especially for units whose primary purpose is shooting people rather than guarding places or moving stuff.

The U.S. armed forces now rely almost wholly upon foreign-designed light and medium machine guns. Again, that is not necessarily a Bad Thing in itself, but since we're engaged almost wholly in infantry combat, especially in urban areas, the trigger pullers sometimes want something else.

The advantage of Gatlings over single-barrel machine guns is a no-brainer. It should not even be a topic for discussion. Miniguns provide greater volume of fire, gain far more hits per rounds fired, and end the fight quickly.

The opposition has nothing remotely comparable. Therefore, the M134D represents a significant "force multiplier" both in its intrinsic value and the fact that we have cornered the market.

As noted above, urban combat means close quarters, which often translates to pistols. The issue 9mm weapon and, especially, the ammunition are marginal at best. Those who shoot for a living—and those who shoot to live—want a side arm that's easier to use and hits with more authority.

Solution: Consider purchasing more of the Special Combat Assault Rifle, taking advantage of its modularity. Where specialized needs exist, issue 7.62mm SCARs to units with a demonstrated requirement and competence, and provide 5.56s to others. Parts commonality between the two variants will offset some of the anticipated difficulty in switching some units from M4s and M16s.

A biggie: buy more miniguns, train more people to maintain them, and buy shiploads of ammo to keep the shooters well trained and the barrels warm.

There's official interest in a new military pistol, reportedly in caliber .45 ACP (Automatic Colt Pistol). That's definitely a Good Thing, and needs to be pursued. Meanwhile, acquire new-production 1911s and teach our professional military how to use them.

Next subject.

We Need Maintenance

The enormous shortfalls in deferred vehicle and equipment maintenance and repair are cited in Chapter Five. It's a safe bet that most motor pools have hummers or "tracks" that never move. As with the Air Force, they're called "hangar queens." They don't go anywhere but they take up space because they still show on the unit's TO&E.

Hangar queens do serve a purpose, however: they're cannibalized as a source of spare parts. Rather than going through the motions of filing a requisition form for a new distributor or cylinder or wheel, it's far easier to remove one from the immobile vehicle and put it to use in "curing" another "patient."

Such practices are by no means limited to the Army and Marine Corps. Air Force insiders confide that as much as 30 percent of F-15s are cannibalized at a given time because most of the budget goes to buying new stealth aircraft rather than keeping existing planes flying.

Solution: Before we buy many new vehicles, allocate more funding specifically for repairing hummers, trucks, tanks, and AFVs. That probably means providing more mechanics and technicians, but so be it. If there's a problem finding enough military personnel for the job—and undoubtedly there will be—then default to the civil option and hire contract maintenance.

It's worked before.

We Need Linguists

We need not only linguists in Arabic and Pashto but people who understand those cultures—and others. Britain fought three Afghan wars in eighty years (1839–1919) and the Soviets were mired there almost a decade (1979–1989) before pulling out. We've been engaged since 2001 and the end is nowhere in sight. Obviously, we're going to be there a long, long time, so we need a thorough understanding of the nation, its people, and its language.

There are far more Americans of Arabic descent than Afghan, so it's easier to recruit soldiers for Iraqi service. Almost every soldier or marine interviewed for this book said the same thing about Iraq: the ability to interact with the people is not only invaluable for any hope of a settlement there—it's absolutely essential. While there have been isolated instances of American Muslims turning on their comrades, we cannot allow those episodes to deflect us from the greater need to make friends.

Solution: It's obvious: increase the amount of foreign language training, but do so in both directions. While Americans are learning Arabic, Pashto, and other Islamic dialects, let's spend some money on teaching some of those folks our brand of English. DOD already has a well-conceived language program for selected public schools; expand that worthy effort.

We Don't Need Future Combat Systems

The Army is certainly not immune to boondoggles. Exhibit Alfa is the M16 fiasco during the Vietnam War. Not only did the ordnance bureaucracy change the ammunition's powder (without bothering to consult the weapon's designer), but the first rifles were issued without cleaning kits under the absurd notion that a combat weapon required no maintenance! How many GIs and marines died with jammed M16s will never be known.

In the 1980s the M247 Sergeant York was the last in a failed series of front-line air defense systems that chucked about $7 billion down the drain. The M247 Division Air Defense vehicle was plagued with insurmountable problems (among other things, its radar could not distinguish between a hovering helicopter and a cluster of trees). Not to mention the XM-2001 Crusader 155mm howitzer that had serious mobility problems and duplicated existing as well as future weapons. SecDef Rumsfeld properly canceled the $11 billion program in 2002.

The foregoing proves an arcane subject called engineering theory. Essentially, it's a philosophical question: "Should we build a widget just because we can?"

It may be the greatest widget ever. Hell, it might be the *only* widget ever. But does that mean that it's worth the time, effort, and expense?

The usual answer is: "If we can sell it? Hell yes!"

Meet the Army's Future Combat System.

Northrop Grumman's immensely complex FCS is described as "a network of networks." It includes Future Force Warrior for infantrymen; mounted combat systems with an infantry carrier vehicle; non–line-of-sight cannon and mortar; a recon and surveillance vehicle; command and control vehicle; medical transport; plus a recovery and maintenance vehicle.

Unmanned ground vehicles will include an armed robotic vehicle; a small unmanned ground vehicle; and Multifunctional Utility/Logistics and Equipment vehicle (MULE, ain't that cute?).

Wait. There's more: four unmanned air vehicles; a smart ("intelligent") munitions system, and "unattended" ground sensors.

Even with competing projects, FCS program cuts have been minimal: the 2007–2011 appropriation was reduced just $236 million from a $25 billion budget. As of 2006 the total program cost was pegged at $300 billion. It's bound to go higher.

A quick survey of operators who have left boot prints in Afghanistan and Iraq yields predictable impressions of FCS. *Nobody* interviewed was in favor of it, but not because of concern about complexity or cost. To reduce the shooters' comments to one response, "This thing is wide open to abuse. I guaran-damn-tee you that eventually there'll be a panel of brass and suits in the Pentagon monitoring a squad- or platoon-level action eight thousand miles away, telling some E-3 or O-2 if he can or can't do something. Can you spell m-i-c-r-o m-a-n-a-g-i-n-g? It's just an incredibly bad idea."

An industry consultant who has no dog in the FCS fight says, "As far as I can tell, FCS is not threat driven, it's driven by determining what they call 'the art of the possible,' where the engineers and other boffins sit down and try to think about how the Army should be linked together on the battlefield.

"The obvious question is, 'Did anyone ask the warriors?' I'm sure they'd say they have, but so much of it seems blue-sky that risks an eventual collision with reality. The theory seems to be that we'll be so good that the bad guys won't be able to respond. 'All of our soldiers will be linked, we'll know where they are and exactly what they're doing, their ammo state, their medical condition, all the time' is what I hear. But what if one gets captured or killed and the bad guys take his gear, won't they be on your link and identified as a good guy?"

"The response is, 'Won't happen. We'll be too good for that.'

"What if they jam your system? Response: 'Won't happen. It's a secure data link so they can't read it.' (I about fell out of my chair when I read that. 'Secure' and 'unjammable' are two completely separate things. It's easy to jam 'secure' links—the encoding is absolutely irrelevant—it's all about putting more energy over that frequency than the opposition has—which makes it unusable for anybody).

"My gut says this is becoming the biggest boondoggle in Army history, and I'm not the Lone Ranger. It seems designed by somebody who saw FCS in the movies—watch *Alien II* and the way the lieutenant sits in his APC (armored personnel carrier) to monitor his troops with no earthly idea of what's going on when the defecation hits the rotary oscillator . . . "

As noted so often before, the MIPC continues buying high- and *high*-high tech stuff while the troops lack adequate basic gear and training. Until every soldier has the latest body armor and knows how to load his-her weapon's magazines, we have no business spending billions on extravagant gadgets that drain funds badly needed elsewhere.

Two: "If By Sea . . . "

In the post–Cold War world, the Navy doesn't have much of a role in Iraq or Afghanistan. Or more specifically, navy *ships* have little role. We certainly don't need submarines to fight terrorists, and although aircraft carriers are mighty useful things, in recent years they've had little to do in the way of bombing and strafing.

Truth be told, the most valued naval aircraft are neither fast nor pointy. They're the Grumman E-2C Hawkeye, a sophisticated surveillance aircraft with a variety of sensors, and the same firm's bulbous-nosed EA-6B Prowler. Both types date from the

1970s, with the Prowler serving a variety of roles but most significantly "SEAD" (suppression of enemy air defenses). Its ability to jam electronic frequencies and destroy missile sites endeared the EA-6 to attack aircrews.

However, since al Qaeda has no radars and no SAM batteries, one might logically ask what Prowlers do in the GWOT. What makes them so valuable?

Some deductive reasoning narrows the field. The insurgents in Iraq and Afghanistan (and no doubt elsewhere) rely on radios and telephones for all the usual reasons: communication, command and coordination, planning and the like. Also, command-detonated bombs and booby traps often use cell phones and other electronic means. Prowlers, with their powerful jamming pods, probably can neutralize some of those methods.

When I posed that theory to a former EA-6B mission commander, he rolled his eyes, shook his head, and exclaimed "How 'bout those Red Sox?"

I withdrew the question.

Otherwise, there's not a lot for the "squids" to do, besides delivering marines and SEALs wherever they need to go. Maritime terrorism has been rare: al Qaeda and its cohorts have seldom achieved much success at sea. The reasons are varied, but they range from a scarcity of worthwhile, vulnerable targets to the vastness of the sea itself. Destroying or damaging a ship necessarily occurs beyond most media coverage, and if the terrorists understand anything, they comprehend box office as well as any bejeweled, finger-snapping PR flack. After all, 9/11 debuted in the Big Apple, baby.

Here's the recent record:

October 2000. U.S. destroyer *Cole* was attacked in Aden Harbor, Yemen, seventeen dead.

October 2002. French tanker *Limberg* was destroyed off Yemen, one dead.

February 2004. *Superferry 14* was bombed in Manila Bay, one hundred dead.

All the foregoing had one thing in common: they were conducted by very small groups operating in coastal waters. Even if al Qaeda were to develop a marine corps, specializing in capturing or sinking ships, the ratio of successes to the effort expended probably would not prove worthwhile. That's why there have been so few attempts.

However, the terrorist maritime threat is still out there, and has little to do with hijacking ships. Other than SEALs, who most often act as elite infantry somewhere above the high tide mark, our naval warfighters are most valuable in guarding the Middle East petroleum infrastructure. Most of the world's oil providers load their product at large ports that are vulnerable to sabotage. Holding tanks, pumps, and complex pipe networks are necessary to gather and dispense crude oil to the vessels that deliver the industrial lifeblood around the globe. Perhaps the prime example is "ABOT," the Al Basra Oil Terminal, which has been attacked on occasion, resulting in American deaths. It's a critical facility, often shipping more than half of Iraq's daily oil exports.

With no likely blue-water enemy on the horizon, our naval forces often appear excessive to probable needs. That is not to say that we should scuttle our battle groups and start building coastal gunboats. After all, eighty thousand tons of nuclear aircraft carrier buys a mountain of intimidation. But we're now well into a transition period in naval history, when open conflict between nations is increasingly rare—especially at sea.

Been There, Done That, Part X

Lieutenant Commander Bafford Lewellen commanded the submarine USS *Torsk* in the Sea of Japan. On a Tuesday morning he sank two Japanese frigates, each displacing about eight hundred tons, *Coast Defense Vessels 13* and *47*. The previous day he had put a small freighter on the bottom.

It was August 14, 1945. *Torsk* had fired not only the last torpedoes of World War II; they were the last ever shot in combat by a United States Navy ship.

Since 1945 only two submarines have sunk an enemy ship. Twenty-six years later—in December 1971, during the second Indo-Pakistani War—the French-built Paki submarine *Hangor* torpedoed India's British-built destroyer *Khukri*.

Eleven years passed.

Off the Falklands in 1982, Britain's nuclear-powered HMS *Conqueror* sank Argentina's American-built cruiser *General Belgrano*. Ironically, *Belgrano* had been USS *Phoenix* (CL-46) which survived Pearl Harbor and four years of Pacific combat only to succumb in one of the most peculiar conflicts of the twentieth century.

The only known combat losses of submarines in the sixty-plus years after VJ-Day occurred in those same conflicts. Pakistan lost *Hangor's* sister boat *Ghazi* in 1971, probably to Indian destroyers.

At South Georgia in April 1982, Argentina's *Santa Fe* was attacked by Royal Navy helicopters that forced her aground, where she was abandoned.

If the Cold War produced any submarine combat, it remains a closely held secret by both sides.

Therefore, from 1945 to the present, at least 1,500 men died aboard twenty-seven submarines lost at sea (excluding a few that foundered under tow), but only one was likely sunk by enemy action.

No American submariners have been lost to enemy action since then.

The foregoing demonstrates that submarines have been largely irrelevant to warfighting for six decades; their utility has been deterrence and surveillance. Consequently, disgruntled aviators note, "No U.S. submariner has intentionally killed anybody since 1945." (Whatever results ensued from sub-launched Tomahawk cruise missiles remain classified or unknown.)

During the Cold War, "boomers" comprised one-third of the deterrent triad, but we continue building and deploying nuclear submarines beyond their operational needs.

Why is that?

The reasons are diverse. Apart from the obvious military-industrial-political influences, submarines are the original stealth machines. They go almost anywhere largely unobserved and therefore can conduct covert surveillance and deliver "deniable assets" such as SEAL teams. Their nuclear missiles were a bulwark of our Cold War deterrence, and while that mission remains, its importance abated with collapse of the USSR in 1990.

For decades when the Navy's primary (indeed, almost only) combatants are aviators and SEALs, the service has been dominated by submariners and surface officers. Meanwhile, there's an often-overlooked naval community that could outstrip the others almost overnight:

We Need Minesweepers

The state of mine countermeasures in the U.S. Navy should be a disgrace, but it is not, because our admiralty refuses to be embarrassed.

Mines are the least glamorous of naval weapons—and the most cost-effective. Our enemies know that even if we do not. Today, minelayers are more likely found in small navies rather than large, especially since America's offensive use of mines tends toward air delivery. Planting the fields around Haiphong in 1972 provided an excellent example of mines' economy of force, since nine carrier aircraft bottled up Communist (and other) ships supplying North Vietnam and deterred fellow travelers from entering the harbor.

We did not learn our own lesson.

Mine warfare craft come in three flavors: layers, hunters, and sweepers. As of 2003, America had fourteen minesweepers and a dozen mine hunters, few of which were considered deployable. In sweepers alone, the U.S. was outnumbered by Poland, Turkey, and Japan. The U.K. and Taiwan had nearly as many. (Andrew Toppan, database creator, "World Navies Today," *Haze Gray and Underway* [hazegray.org], March 10, 2003.)

Today, the *Avenger* class sweepers are highly capable, ocean-going vessels but reportedly they are complex, troublesome craft. The last of the dozen *Osprey* hunters will be gone by the end of 2008. In partial compensation, mine countermeasures (MCM) devices operated by Aegis destroyers are expected to take their place.

If we have to go to war against a capable coastal enemy, we will be caught short and we will lose expensive ships to cheap mines, "weapons that wait."

It's happened before.

Been There, Done That, Part XI

During World War II the Navy maintained a force of more than five hundred minesweepers. Five years later, when the bell rang for Round One in Korea, there were ten. The shortage of minesweepers came home to roost in the cold, gray waters off Wonsan when Communist minefields forced nearly a week's delay in landing there in October 1950.

Throughout the Korean War, five U.S. Navy ships were sunk with forty-three sailors killed or missing, all by mines. Most were involved in sweeping North Korean minefields around Wonsan Harbor. Three more ships were damaged with 133 additional casualties, including seventeen killed.

Korea was no exception. From 1946 onward, the Navy has lost four times as many ships sunk or damaged by mines as by any other method. During Operation Desert Storm (1990–1991) two American ships were seriously damaged by mines, including the flagship of the mine countermeasures commander. On February 18, 1991 a helicopter assault ship, USS *Tripoli*, was badly damaged before dawn and a few hours later the missile cruiser *Princeton* also fell victim. The latter ship, costing some $1.2 billion, had been sidelined by a $14,000 Italian-made "Mantra" mine.

Subsequently about 1,300 Iraqi mines were counted in an area that had been declared a "mine-free zone." The option for an amphibious landing was deterred, though clever manipulation of the media caused the Iraqis to keep significant forces watching their coastal flank for most of the short conflict.

However belatedly, the Navy took note. The next year Mine Warfare Command assessed the situation and drafted the Mine Warfare Plan. It was more organizational than technical, putting all antimine units under one admiral, including surface, air, and disposal forces. Furthermore, standing countermeasures staffs were established for rapid deployment to oversee sweeping activities almost anywhere on earth. The dedicated "miners" also could plan deliveries against hostile areas on short notice.

It worked. The Navy learned the right lessons, and since 1992, it has avoided loss or damage from mines.

The trouble is, mine craft are like antifreeze: you can never have too many, only too few.

By 2005 the Navy had just fourteen mine countermeasures craft (MCM) for hunting and destroying mines. It's almost certainly not enough.

Time and again, mines emerge as the weapon of choice in naval guerrilla warfare. Small wonder: they are cheap, relatively easy to produce, and therefore are plentiful. By one recent reckoning, fifty navies dispose of a quarter-million mines in enormous variety. There are all kinds of detonators: contact, magnetic, acoustic, timed and numeric (X number of days or ships pass before the mines go active) to name a few.

Today, people forget that "the first Gulf war" (aka the tanker war) was fought in the 1980s mainly by Iran, though Iraq also was involved. The naval guerrillas dispensed mines in the Persian Gulf and ran around in Soviet-built speedboats, shooting up oil tankers. In all, nearly 550 commercial vessels were damaged plus two U.S. Navy warships. No single nation had enough mine craft to counter the threat.

Consequently, mine hunting and sweeping is a collaborative effort. British, Australian, and Polish vessels all have been involved in recent years—an acknowledgement that America's MCM capability has diminished.

In 2006, the Navy announced plans to consolidate underwater concerns into a joint antisubmarine-mine command. Bad idea. While it might make some sense from the outside looking in, there are far more differences than similarities. Yes, submarines operate under the surface. So do mines. That's about it. Otherwise, subs move; they operate best in deep water; they're big, very expensive, and seminoisy. Mines are stationary, work best in shallow water; and they're dirt cheap, extremely small, and totally silent.

Consider the record: According to defense analyst Scott C. Truver, since the Korean War, most U.S. ship losses have been from mines. None have been due to submarines or enemy aircraft.

What more do we need to know?

Solution: Our naval doctrine is titled *From the Sea*, focused on "littoral warfare" in the world's coastal areas. That concept just screams "mine warfare." Consequently, we should build more mine hunters and sweepers and forward-deploy them to likely trouble spots.

As of 2005 we had about 280 ships, down from 568 in 1987. There are plans to build up to 313 or so.

But raw numbers may matter less than types. We do not need submarines to fight the war on terror but we do need to keep building some in order to maintain the industrial base as a hedge against another conventional war. (That's a separate issue from political pork concerns revolving around jobs and local economies, but it's like political hypocrisy: it's here to stay.)

So . . . what kind of ships do we need?

Ask six naval analysts what our fleet should look like and you'll probably get nine answers. But based on various sources, here's as good a take as any:

Aircraft Carriers. Cancel the next-generation CVN-78, scheduled to begin building in 2009, and revert to the CV-77 type (now named for George H. W. Bush), the transitional design between the standard Nimitz class flattop and the follow-on concept. It will mean a delay of a couple of years to restart the CVN-77 reactor program, but that's all right. Establish a force level goal of perhaps ten CVNs in fifteen years, yielding five or six deployable at a time.

Surface Combatants. Reconsider whether the new stealth destroyer (DDX) is worth the cost, but proceed with the related LCS littoral combat ship (*nee* support landing craft) at about the same rate, probably three per year. Whatever it's called, LCS is a corvette or perhaps a light frigate in size and function, with stealth features. No doubt it makes economic sense to put modular packages aboard the hulls for various roles including logistics, coastal ASW, mine countermeasures, and surveillance. But it's extremely doubtful that one LCS crew can master so many tasks, leading to questions as to just how modular each hull will be. More likely individual ships will receive specific roles which, while denting the one-size-fits-all concept, would enhance mission performance.

Meanwhile, certainly continue with DDG-51s (the improved *Arleigh Burkes*) to yield two or three surface combatants per year. That gives us sixty to ninety destroyers and similar numbers of LCS in about fifteen years.

Attack Submarines. Continue Virginia-class nuclear-powered submarines (SSNs) at the rate of one per year but push the technology-design community for a combination nuclear power and "air-independent propulsion" (AIP). Alternatively, produce a small nuke submarine, building at the rate of one per year for an ultimate force of a few dozen nuclear-powered hunter-killer submarines (SSN/SSKs). The "combo" would have a very small reactor (called "teakettle" in the trade) to keep a continuous charge on the battery.

Boomers. The submarine's strategic deterrence mission still remains, but in nothing like the scale of the Cold War. Since there is almost no credible threat to our boomers (which have considered replacing some of their nuclear missiles with conventional warheads) we can streamline our force and save some money.

Therefore, reduce the current fourteen *Trident* ballistic missile (SSBN) subs to ten. In a few years, start an SSBN variant of the *Virginia* class SSN, the same as in the late 1950s we modified the *Skipjack* SSN design (not actual submarines) to the *Polaris* SSBN.

Amphibious Assault. Stop the landing platform dock (LPD)-17 program at four or five landing platform ships, which should be adequate to meet requirements. The *San Antonio*s are big, capable vessels roughly comparable to World War II fleet carriers, intended to replace three older types of vessels. Possibly build two or three more configured as fleet flagships. Considering the historic trend of actual 'phib usage, we can afford to produce amphibious assault ships (LHAs) and amphibious assault ships (LHDs) ("dry" or no docking well) at the rate of one every other year. They can operate vertical short takeoff and landing (VSTOL) aircraft (likely including the new F-35 Joint Strike Fighter) and drones as appropriate. In fifteen years the 'phib force would have a dozen LSD/LPDs plus fifteen to twenty big-deck ships (LHAs and LHDs).

Mine Craft. This should be the Navy's growth industry. While the emphasis understandably is upon finding and sweeping enemy mines, we should not neglect our own offensive capability. After all, we may want to bottle up some ports that harbor hostile forces, and we should be able to do so by sea or by air.

If funding becomes a problem, we should reexamine our submarine requirements in light of how often the "boats" are used in combat (approximately never), and consider reallocating some of those funds.

Bottom Line: Most importantly, America should devise a "steady state" shipbuilding plan *and stick to it.* Without one, we cannot develop the related science and technology, nor accurately profile our funding and manpower efforts.

Three: "If By Air . . . "

As previously noted, we're still buying extremely expensive airplanes for which there is precious little use—nor is there likely to be. The vastly wasteful high-high tech projects such as F-22, let alone F-35, address a "threat" that is largely nonexistent, and with each passing day our stealth technology grows older and moldier. Meanwhile, hostile radars and other sensors continue developing.

On the other hand, in combat the most useful aircraft are helicopters and unmanned "air vehicles" (UAVs) or drones. The latter are increasingly capable, evolving from purely reconnaissance machines into long-ranged strike platforms that can hurl precision lightning bolts from beyond the target's visual range.

The fighter pilot had his day, and it was a glorious run—from 1915 into the 1980s. But history and sentiment are poor measures of military priorities. For decades now, by far the most frequently employed airmen are found in helos, transports, and tankers—and those who control UAVs from thousands of miles away.

Let's recognize the facts and spend accordingly.

We Need Less Stealth, More ECM

Here's a flash: The Cold War is over, and we won.

But we're still buying enormously expensive aircraft designed for battling the Evil Empire in a galaxy right here at home.

Sometimes less is more, and that concept applies to stealth airplanes.

We've already noted the technical and doctrinal history of stealth technology in Chapter Seven, concluding that we do not need nearly as much high-high tech stuff as we're buying, whether we ever fight China or not. There's little or no mission for it, and it drains huge amounts of defense dollars that could be better spent elsewhere.

The thing is: depending on your sources, current stealth technology is twenty to thirty years old. And you don't add it on to existing platforms: it has to be built into the machine from Day One. The specifics are classified Beyond Top Secret, but as radar and other sensors continually evolve, stealth's effectiveness diminishes. It's already acknowledged that the F-22 is optimized for air-to-air stealthiness; it's more detectable from the ground.

Before we proceed with options to stealth, we need to define our semantics.

What used to be electronic countermeasures (ECM) now is electronic attack (EA) and electronic counter-countermeasures (ECCM) is electronic protection (EP). What used to be electronic surveillance measures (ESM) is now plain old electronic surveillance. Quips a navy commander, "I am sure someone got a Legion of Merit for that nomenclature change!"

In any case, jamming pods and other deceptive measures literally can be hung on a nonstealth airplane, assuming there's a spare hardpoint beneath the wings. And the marvelous thing is, EA and EP can be upgraded vastly easier and immensely cheaper than any stealth iteration. When time and technology (and maybe nature) take their inevitable effect upon stealth birds, we'll be stuck with $190 million race horses that have become very high-priced one-trick ponies.

Solution: We should be investing at least as heavily in EA as in stealth—and probably far more. If we cannot pry the blue suits' hands from the stealth tarbaby, at least trim the high-high tech briar patch to manageable levels.

The short answer: get the Air Force back in the electronic warfare business, in a big way. And fund it with savings from chopping a bunch of wasteful high-high tech brush.

We Need Close Air Support

Besides the Raptor, an even bigger project is the F-35 Joint Strike Fighter (JSF). A true multiservice machine (Robert S. McNamara would adore it), the Lightning II is hailed as the replacement for current close air support (CAS) planes: the A-10 Warthog, F-16 Fighting Falcon, and AV-8 Harrier. It's far from certain that the U.S. Air Force, Navy, Marines, and Royal Navy can ever afford enough JSFs, or that its cost and sophistication will in fact permit it to be used in the down and dirty role of CAS. Presumably standoff ordnance will provide pinpoint accuracy from beyond the hostile threat envelope—that's the theory. But when the duty

Lightning IIs are out of PGMs, are the pilots really going to flip their armament switches to "gun" and go strafing in a high-high ticket stealth machine?

At one point DoD priced an F-35 at $45 million, but that figure was based on a total buy of six thousand aircraft. If that was a big leap of faith then, it's downright delusional now. As of 2006 the combined USAF-USN-USMC-UK deal looks more like 2,500 Lightnings, with a commensurate increase in unit cost.

Meanwhile, the FA-22 "strike fighter" will only pack half the internal ordnance of the F-117 (one ton versus two) and loses its stealthiness if extra bombs are hung under the wings. But the Nighthawk is being retired, leaving the field to the Raptor and Lightning II.

Bottom line: we need affordable CAS birds, "affordable" meaning that we can afford to lose some of them without affecting the federal budget deficit.

At the squadron and wing level many aircrews—perhaps most—want a "bomb truck." Something along the lines of the A-6 Intruder or A-7 Corsair II that hauls a lot of ordnance several hundred miles unrefueled or remains on station for a comparable period closer to base. We don't have it. The F-16, designed as a lightweight fighter, almost immediately became an attack airplane (the Air Force would never-ever burden the Falcon with the F/A designation) and it's done good work but United States purchases ended in 2005.

Says a naval flight officer: "What we need is a twenty-first century A-6 Intruder that can carry a *big* payload of standoff weapons or iron bombs, and (with minimal mods) double as an ECM, tanker, or even ASW aircraft. We went from the A-6 capability to having an F-14 with immense strike potential to an all-Hornet fleet with limitations. We (the Navy) failed to buy an adequate tanker and now are stuck with the Hornet because there is nothing else. The E/F are good airframes—we've done a lot with them—but they also work because of advances in sensors and weapons. F-35 may work whenever it arrives, but I just don't see us being able to buy enough of them. Look at the continual reduction in the F-22 buy, let alone the B-2. Additionally, no airplane that expensive can withstand ordinary attrition for very long."

However, a navy squadron commander takes another view: "The lesson of the Cold War seems to be that money and high-tech wins, and we seem to be sticking with that strategy, regardless of the situation. Without money and high tech at your disposal, finding the counter for stealth isn't all that easy . . . so far."

Unfortunately, the factor taken for granted in the foregoing assessment is: money. We spent the Soviet Union into the gutter, but those days are gone. With no "peer opponent" (we don't admit to enemies anymore), the United States is undisputed master of sea and sky.

Trouble is, the Air Force has seldom been enthused about CAS. Consequently, the Army and Marines operate attack helicopters, which are certainly useful in some situations but lack the capacity and ruggedness required of the CAS calling, especially in the era of hand-held SAMs.

If we started at noon yesterday to design a built-for-the-purpose CAS bird, it could not become operational for a decade or more. One interim solution might involve "re-procuring" A-10s; build a couple hundred more to tide us over until the new machine is parked on the tarmac. In fact, there's sentiment in the Army for more Warthogs, likely because soldiers are the beneficiaries of the A-10's services. This 2005 email came from a National Guard source in Afghanistan:

"For the war on terror we do not need stealth fighters, stealth bombers, or stealth anything. We hardly need fighters or bombers of any description to fight al Qaeda or the Taliban, because even when airpower is appropriate, it is often denied owing to concerns about collateral damage.

"Therefore, we need counterinsurgency (CoIn) aircraft, both fixed and rotary wing, numerous and fast enough, or with sufficient duration, to keep up with Chinooks, the heavy lifters. USAF still isn't adequately interested in COIN/CAS, but then neither is army aviation!

"We do not need F-35s; we need more A-10s: tough, potent, 'loiterly', and blessed with an assortment of nice hardpoints from which to hang ordnance and targeting pods and stuff."

Get a move on. We're burnin' daylight.

Meanwhile, let's look at the problem from another perspective.

We Need to Change the Law

That's right: change the damn law. Since 1947, amid the post–World War II flail about service roles and missions, the Army was deprived of its air arm. The Defense Unification Act that established DoD prohibited the Army from operating fixed-wing combat aircraft. So . . . the newly independent Air Force was granted a mission that it did not covet. And that's putting it nicely. Strategic bombardment was the sine qua non of the AAF, and became the primary focus of the USAF. Just ask Curt LeMay.

Meanwhile, along came Korea, and guess what? Things were so fouled up that the Air Force couldn't talk to the Army much of the time. The Navy could talk to the Marines because flying leathernecks lived, ate, slept, and dreamed close air support. The integrated air-ground team was up and running when the starter pistol went *bang*. But the Air Force, not being institutionally committed to CAS, had to play catch-up early in the first quarter.

(On the other hand, a flying buddy of mine logged a pretty happy tour in F-80s in 1950–1951. Hap said, "I learned in Korea that if you're going to be in a war, you want to get there early, before things get too organized.")

Since then, things certainly have improved, but sometimes doggedly. Of the major USAF missions, CAS comes well down the list behind aerospace dominance (that's air superiority on steroids); global reach (B-2s and all that); and airmobility (transports, of which we clearly do not have enough). CAS is down there somewhere neck and neck with special operations, those rugged individualists who can call in an A-10 or F-16's ordnance loadout within two hundred meters of their own position and talk about it next day.

If you doubt the Air Force's lack of interest in CAS, just check the designations. Uncle Sam's Air Force has no attack units because Air Combat Command claims to possess only fighters and bombers. Its only remaining "Type A" aircraft (Warthogs) are found in "fighter" wings. It had some attack aircraft, but because of image and front-office semantic games, the true strikers were "F"-117s, which possess no air-to-air capability. Zero, zip, nada.

So then: consider changing the law, returning the fixed-wing CAS mission to the Army, including some of the combat controllers. It can only benefit everybody: greater coordination, less need for "jointness" and "interoperability." The only difference evident to those on the receiving end would be jets labeled "U.S. Army" instead of "U.S. Air Force."

However, since that's less likely to happen than the Arizona Cardinals winning the Super Bowl, there's another option. Change the focus of the Air Guard to CAS: units specifically assigned to supporting Army and other grunts. We really need a CAS guild: aircraft optimized for the mission, pilots thoroughly trained in it, with indigenous FACs to put them on target. (F-35 is not the aircraft: it's going to be far, far too spendy to risk in a "Warthog environment." Some CAS practitioners still insist that the best aircraft for the A-10's mission is the A-10.)

Intercepting enemy bombers has become a hugely improbable mission that the Air National Guard has practiced for decades. Therefore, transfer the assets elsewhere and tweak our SAMs, especially since the likely threat is a sub or ship-launched ballistic or cruise missile, extremely difficult or impossible for fighters to intercept.

We Need Airlift and Tankers

If we're going to have a "real" war, we're going to have to get there in a hurry. The reason should be obvious: since we're not going to start it, we'll begin at a deficit much as we did in Korea in 1950

194

and Kuwait in 1990. That means, in order to stabilize the situation, let alone reverse it, we require the long-range airlift to plug the hole in the dike while awaiting the heavy sealift and maritime prepositioning assets.

As noted in Chapter Three, we're running short of strategic airlift. The reasons (excessive funding of stealth airplanes) need not overly occupy us here: it's enough to recognize that the C-5 and C-17 both have problems that are not soon corrected. Consequently, we'll have to rely on the Civil Reserve Air Fleet, but how many commercial airlines want to fly the unfriendly SAM skies? Our enemies (let's be honest enough to use that term) can read a map as well as we can: in order to choke off our reinforcements, they need only pop off a couple of antiquated SA-7s, let alone the long-range double-digit variety, to shut down a given airport.

The cost of installing chaff and flare dispensers in commercial airliners ensures that it will not happen. So we're back to Air Mobility Command.

Since we cannot assume that our airlifters can get where they need to go on their own (landing or basing rights may not be taken for granted), they need in-flight refueling. But we don't have enough tankers, either.

It's a problem of our own making; we brought it upon ourselves.

Solution: Stop buying extravagant "F" machines and put more of that money where it does some demonstrable good. Buy more transport and tanker aircraft with the personnel and infrastructure to support them.

Next question.

We Need Hypersonics

Though some airmen and engineers salivate at the thought of a next-generation superfast manned bomber, there is simply no mission for it. As one Pentagon civilian notes, "A bomber or manned system of any sort is a nonstarter precisely because it is hugely expensive and hugely complex, and hugely huge as well—probably bigger than the XB-70." Truth be told, there's precious little work for the manned bombers we currently own."

However, in Ralph Peters' war of faith, flesh, and cities, there is still room for some high-high tech weapons. It has to do with TOT: time on target.

In the information age, we're able to survey enormous areas of the earth's surface in considerable detail. With some three thousand unmanned drones in startling variety (as many as eighteen by one account), we have the potential to watch many of our enemies in real time, day or night.

That's the good news.

The perennial bad news: it takes a while to act upon the intel.

A promising answer is hypersonic missiles coupled with extreme precision guidance—weapons traveling well beyond three times the speed of sound that will pinwheel a Volkswagen.

The trouble with funding such ordnance is the image it usually conjures. Many people in the acquisition process hear "hypersonics" and immediately conclude that we're trying to sell something like a new Space Shuttle, and their minds close to the weapons options, which are numerous.

Says a D.C. based analyst, "Against very high-end threats, the guy who has a missile and isn't afraid to use it (read "Iranian nut case"), you can make a real case for a six hundred– to nine hundred–mile range air-breathing hypersonic missile coming out of a tube on a ship, an upgraded army tactical missile system, or off something like an F-15E or a B-1.

"Right now it seems silly to be talking about closing the 'sensor to shooter loop' when, once we pull the trigger, we're waiting for an hour to an hour and a half before we get a cruise missile on target. And for a target that is deep in somebody's country, you need to reach them in ten to fifteen minutes max, which says hypersonics. And, incidentally, for all categories of naval vessels and even our air mobility bridge, we need to have counters to the hypersonic antishipping and antiaircraft threat—it'll come and a lot sooner than we think, given the number of programs and interest we see around the world."

Therefore, let's invest some of our discretionary high-high end R&D in closing the sensor-shooter loop. Perhaps a modular system like a sub, air, or ground-launched cruise missile; something with parts commonality to get costs down, sized to fit a tube (maybe a new tube, though, not the Standard PAC-3 size), and be deployed as well out of a weapons bay with commonality for the B-52, B-1, B-2, and rack-deployed off an F-15E Strike Eagle and P-3 Orion.

Such a weapon might be too heavy for a ship-launched F/A-18E/F, and it's definitely not in the future of F-35, as the size would be excessive. But if it has a highly energetic rocket booster and a scramjet for sustained Mach 6–8, the warhead (if any) could be relatively small, since the kinetic energy delivered to the target would be awesome. Visualize a five hundred–pound pill moving a Mach 8: now, *that* will ruin somebody's day, and if it fragments over the last two thousand feet and deploys spin-stabilized explosive flechettes . . . triple your pleasure.

There's a flip side to hypersonics—those that we might find inbound to one of our ships or bases. Reportedly such a capability is possible if a wealthy country or countries are willing to invest in it. Planners admit to concern about the vulnerability of our sea and air lines of communication from surface and "platform air" (think an Airbus or 767) launching beyond our battlespace management area, or at least beyond the capabilities of defensive air. Then we are confronting an incoming Mach 6 or 8 weapon.

Solution: Drop whatever black program involves a super-fast manned bomber and invest in hypersonic weapons, which puts us all the way back to Square One in the old Star Wars debate: the Reagan-era antiballistic missile (ABM) treaty. But the era of asymmetric warfare defies categorization, especially with rogue entities collaborating with nation-states hostile to our interests.

We Need Helicopters

More specifically, we need big, capable helicopters that can haul lots of cargo and troops at high altitude.

We need more Chinooks.

Depending on how you count it, the aged, venerable, and highly valued CH-47 has been around since the Eisenhower or Kennedy administration. Its replacement is not even on the drawing board. But it's the go-to machine in Afghanistan, where the floor often is pegged at eight thousand feet and it's uphill in both directions.

However, the existing airframes are old, tired, and in need of replacement. Boeing continues low-rate production in Philadelphia, using modern composite materials, and that's fine as far as it goes. But it doesn't go far enough. Here's why:

Retired Warrant Officer Morrie McCormmach is a Vietnam helo pilot and long-time army instructor. Speaking of Afghanistan operations he says, "I think the aviation troops go reasonably well trained, and since all our recent conflicts, they are pretty well experienced. The problem is that we keep using the warrant officer system in the Army, hence a bunch of new captains and lieutenants run the aviation units. They all want to be a general someday; they don't fly much; but make all the decisions and want to get medals, good fitness reports, etc. So they keep making the same dumb mistakes.

"Our lessons learned don't seem to sink in to the next captain that comes along. Why are we doing these things in daylight? Why are we exposing a Chinook—a corps level asset—to small unit actions where the cost-return ratio simply doesn't equate? Why are we flying in air movement corridors at low level when there is no reason for airspace C3 (no arty, no fast movers to speak of, and nothing else to deconflict) and the high altitude threat has a countermeasure and the low level RPG threat is an optical weapon that can be almost eliminated by NVGs? Why must we land the infantry on the objective when they have almost new boots and are capable of walking, then calling for extraction when they have the area secured? Or stay until it is secured. The more bad guys they kill in the process, the fewer trigger fingers are left."

So let's buy more Chinooks. There's little reason to build a new machine, which would only cost more for a questionable increase in capability.

While we're at it, we also need to replace the Air Force's HH-60G Pave Hawk, which entered service in the early 1980s. Special operations units require newer construction, and with expansion of SpecOps forces, they're going to need more lift. And they're used globally. In fact, two-thirds of the helo rescues in Hurricane Katrina's aftermath were accomplished by Pave Hawks. But due to continual demand and very high usage, most remaining HH-60Gs will reach their expected service life in 2007 to 2010.

For the optimum mission profile, combat rescue helos require thirty minutes on station 325 nautical miles from base, getting there at 135 knots. Says an air force operator: "We need these capabilities yesterday."

The tactical world has been stood on its head, but once again, we need highly capable helicopters far, far more than we need new fighters.

Four: "If By . . . Other Means"

Some problems, and presumably their solutions, apply across the board. Consequently, let's examine some generic situations, many of which seldom receive much attention. The subjects are found in most or all of the armed services, so we needn't worry overmuch about specifics.

We Need Institutional Knowledge

Institutional knowledge vanishes at approximately the speed of light. It's an amazing situation, probably dating at least from Varro and the III Legion in 216 B.C.

Throughout American history, there exists no better example than the start of the Korean War.

In 1945 the U.S. Army stood astride the world, from Western Europe to the Western Pacific. It was a large, competent, well-trained and well-equipped force that had garnered an immense amount of knowledge and ability, defeating world-class enemies.

Yet somehow, in five short years, the U.S. Army forgot how to fight. The communist steamroller that left the Pyongyang station southbound in June 1950 was very nearly unstoppable. Though operating in a situation of American air supremacy, the North Korean juggernaut nearly pushed U.S. and ROK troops off the peninsula. America was handed a humiliating reversal by a second-line opponent. We needed a masterful amphibious landing at Inchon to save the day.

True, the U.S. and ROK forces were surprised, outnumbered, and outgunned. But they were also outmaneuvered and, more importantly, out-trained. The first American units committed to Korea had been garrison forces in Japan for five years. Once committed to combat, they had to make up for years of neglect, literally overnight. That they performed as well as they did is a credit to individual soldiers and unit leaders.

But so much had to be learned, absorbed, and disseminated in a very short time. The learning process began at the squad level and worked its way upward through platoons, companies, and battalions.

The seminal works on Korea were produced by field combat historian S. L. A. Marshall, who had perfected his trade in World War II. (His oft-quoted figures on infantry firing ratios were almost certainly manufactured. As more than one officer has said, "If only 25 percent of my guys were active shooters, I'd be dead.") Nevertheless, "Slam" Marshall identified serious deficiencies in the U.S. Army: poor basic skills, such as fire and maneuver; poor communications; inadequate unit cohesion. The list was long and dolorous.

Nevertheless, changes were made. The situation improved: allied forces got sufficient numbers of troops, well supported by artillery and air. The front line stabilized along the prewar boundary straddling the 38th parallel, and an uneasy truce descended upon the Land of the Morning Calm.

Time passed.

A decade later Vietnam came along. The same thing happened again. Because of the "ticket punching" mindset in the Army (and to an extent in the Marines), officers frequently rotated in and out of platoons, companies, and battalions. With as little as six months in command of a unit, lieutenants, captains, and lieutenant colonels rolled out, receiving the obligatory Bronze Star as an I-was-there gong. Meanwhile, the grunts—the trigger pullers at the sharp end of battle—came to rely increasingly upon noncoms. The NCOs had the "bush knowledge" to fight and survive, but they had no influence upon the Army's policies and what passed for strategy.

Hard, bloody lessons were learned, forgotten, relearned, and reforgotten, on and on. Ad nauseam.

It's better today. The Army established the Center for Lessons Learned, with professional, lucid assessments of what works and doesn't work. The information is there, but frequently it's overlooked.

Before leaving the smorgasbord of suggestions detailed above, it's only fair to consider some of the many things we do not need in the military. And right at the top of the list is star wearers.

Who Needs Generals?

We do not need more generals. Or admirals, for that matter. As of 2006 the Navy had some 215 admirals; the Marine Corps 100 generals. Relatively few of those officers actually command anything. Taking the Marines as a sample, 42 percent fill command positions and 14 percent hold the title of "director" of an office or program. The others are deputy or assistant commanders, staff officers, or representatives to legislative and other offices.

For comparison, at the end of World War II the Marines had seventy-two generals to command 669,000 leathernecks. Today, with one-third of the personnel, the Corps has 52 percent *more* star wearers. In the Navy, there are about two-thirds as many "flags"—342 in 1945 to 215 today—with barely *one tenth* the force structure. (However, the Navy's World War II count is skewed by 109 commodores, a one-star position now called "rear admiral lower half." Honest.)

Generals are uniformed politicians—they don't pin on the stars if they don't play the game. Nevertheless, no system is perfect and a few good ones are bound to slip through the cracks. Very few.

When you consider how many thousands of flag officers we have had since the end of World War II, it stands to reason that some of them must have disagreed with something strongly enough to dissent from the administration they served.

I know of three.

In 1949 the chief of naval operations, Admiral Louis Denfeld (a nonaviator) resigned in protest over the Truman administration's anti-Navy bias and cancellation of the first supercarrier, the USS *United States*.

Nobody resigned during the Vietnam fiasco. Nobody. Curt LeMay might have done so had he not reached mandatory retirement in early 1965. To quote the late Marine Major General Marion Carl, some senior officers remained in place "to prevent us from doing something stupid," but no one bucked the system at the four-star level.

In 1977 Army Major General John K. Singlaub committed de facto suicide by dissenting from Jimmy Carter's troop reduction policy in Korea. (Subsequently, Carter expressed his regrets over the death of Kim Jong Il, who started the Korean War and killed at least 34,000 Americans.)

Twenty years later, Air Force Chief Ronald Fogelman put his four stars where his ethics were. When he considered a subordinate unfairly blamed for American deaths in the Khobar Towers terrorist attack, Fogelman retired a year early in protest.

It remains an exclusive club.

There's been a debate in professional circles as to whether

even retired officers should criticize the policy of a sitting president. It seems a tempest in a teacup: just because a general hangs up his suit doesn't deprive him of his citizenship. He (or she) still has the same rights as anyone else, in John Wayne's words, to "live free, talk free, go or come, buy or sell, be drunk or sober, however they choose."

That was from *The Alamo*, pilgrim.

The problem, from a credibility perspective, is that if the star-studded dissenters truly held strong feelings, they would have stated them while still wearing the uniform. They would have made a public statement like John Singlaub and accepted the consequences. Instead, they tend to protect their retirement and wait months or years before speaking up. Unquestionably some speak from the heart—equally unquestionably some await consultant fees and book offers.

Who Needs Promotions?

We need to stop promoting people so quickly.

You read it correctly. Do not promote everybody—at least not out of their position. "If they're doing a great job, leave them there." That's the advice of many veterans who have seen careerism triumph at the expense of competence. Vietnam was a classic example: young captains rotated in and out of rifle companies in a matter of months, punching their professional tickets. Says one noncom who spoke for many, "Just as soon as you broke in a new CO and he was starting to learn the ropes, zip! He was gone and you'd have to start over."

If there's a way to change the rank structure, let's look at it. But on the other hand, if a lieutenant colonel or Navy commander is doing a magnificent job running a critical logistics operation, why harm the unit's efficiency and rotate him-or-her out just to check the next box for eligibility as an O-6? Hell, keep him-or-her in that job as an O-6 with suitable pay and seniority. Then when he-or-she has trained his-or-her successor, let the water walker jump to the next level.

We also need to give more of our people some credit for brains.

The conventional wisdom holds that the all-volunteer force is composed of the best-educated and smartest (not necessarily the same) personnel of all time. That may be true, but whether it is or not, there's room for improvement.

Among most career officers, the "up or out" dilemma is unavoidable. The cycle in the Navy, for instance, has evolved (some say mutated) from warfighting to engineering to management. (Recently the Proctor and Gamble company was consulted by a board of admirals interested in learning about more efficiency in corporate management. By itself that's not a bad idea, but somehow it's unseemly for the U.S. Navy to be seen squeezing more toothpaste from the institutional tube.)

Slicing the Terrorism Pie

Everybody wants a slice of the terrorism pie, because that's seen as the big job these days. Even those programs with a key to the congressional coffers feel obliged to justify themselves in terms of the Terror War. Some of the more egregious examples:

Project Noble Eagle (and a nobler sounding name was never coined) touts the F-22 stealth fighter as a homeland security asset. Just what role the Raptor might play in an internal threat scenario seems vastly uncertain, considering that a $190 million fighter cannot do much more to intercept domestic airliners than a $50 million F-16. Since the target of such an intercept—a hijacked airliner—has no air-to-air radar, the F-22's stealthiness is irrelevant.

With no genuine war to fight, the Raptor continues scouring the skies in search of other missions.

So does the Silent Service. As far back as 1990s the Navy floated (!) a proposal to arm sub-launched Trident missiles with conventional warheads. The theory held that with time-critical targets, a submarine-launched ballistic missile (SLBM) could arrive before the intended victims could move.

If ever there was a Pile On concept, that's it. Nevertheless, it made the 2007 budget request, intended to replace two conventional Tridents (i.e., nukes) with high-explosive warheads on each boomer.

The cost of launching a single high-explosive SLBM would be enormous. According to former missileers, the unit cost of a nonnuke Trident is a shade over $29 million. That would have to be *some* high-value target! Quipped an Internet poster, "If this had been in place, El Zarqawi could have been nailed from the Sea of Okhotsk. He wouldn't have known what hit him and the cost of two 500-pound bombs could have been saved."

Another blogger conceded, "Yes, you could put a conventional warhead on a sub-launched missile and use it to hit a high value target (HVT) somewhere within six thousand miles of the sub. You could also use a nitro-fueled dragster to go to the supermarket for a gallon of milk, but why would you?"

(Ask yourself: who needs $29 million worth of killing? At that rate the Mafia or Mossad would be glad to do the job for ten cents on the dollar.)

Aside from the enormous cost, there are also strategic and geopolitical concerns. For instance, what high-value target is worth revealing the location of a $2 billion submarine and therefore its capability? Not to mention the understandable concern over an SLBM launch in places like Moscow, Beijing, Pyongyang, and Tehran, to name a few.

Just another example of the "me-too" syndrome: high-high ticket items with no immediate mission looking for a way to justify their expense. While the Silent Service was insisting, "Our contributions to the Global War on Terror are significant," no details were forthcoming. In 2006 Congress denied major funding for the concept, in the FY 07 budget. (Paul X. Rutz, "Conventional Trident Missiles Will Aid Terror War," *Military.com*, June 8, 2006.)

Then there's the Space Marines.

(Yes, there was a television series, *Space: Above and Beyond*, Fox

Network, 1995–1996. The episode with Chiggy von Richthofen was especially memorable.)

Meanwhile, back on Earth: Uncle Sam's Misguided Children have proposed a small space shuttle capable of delivering a marine rifle squad anywhere on earth in two or three hours. In 2004 a brigadier general told Congress, "The Marine Corps needs this capability." The best scenario: deployable by 2025–2030. (Article by "John" on *Op-For*, "Marines Want Space Plane," posted on July 10, 2006, http://op-for.com/2006/07/marines_want_space_plane_1.html [most recently accessed April 17, 2007].)

The vehicle is called Small Unit Space Transport and Insertion, yielding the cute acronym SUSTAIN.

Thing is: what can the Space Marines do when they arrive?

Having delivered Twelve Good Men (following one or two sonic booms) somewhere populated by unfriendly locals, the hugely expensive vehicle has to be guarded while the balance of the team proceeds on mission assigned.

How many does that leave? What would that mission involve, i.e., what can fewer than twelve marines expect to accomplish deep in Indian country?

SUSTAIN's advocates cite counterterrorist strikes and hostage rescue scenarios, though the operational details are notably nonspecific. (And if the rescue effort goes south, turning into a cosmic dustoff on a hot landing zone, how much room does the space ship have for hostages?)

But the problems accumulate.

How can the ship come and go without being detected and zapped by missiles?

Where can it land? If it needs a two-mile runway, that facility has to be secured. If it has a VTOL capability, that adds immensely to the cost.

Since one SUSTAIN clearly is insufficient for any task, how many others would be needed? Let's say four to deliver a reinforced platoon, more or less.

How many billion dollars per copy?

What can forty-eight marines accomplish? The Internet was full of redneck puffery descending to the level of One United States Marine Is Worth . . . fill in the blanks.

Before totally dismissing the Space Marines, let's give them credit for vision and innovative thinking. But that sort of brain-power needs to be directed elsewhere, especially in the most cash-strapped branch of the combatant forces.

First get us more ammo, maintenance, socks, batteries, and bandages. Then we can discuss space ships.

Who Needs Ribbons?

"Give me enough ribbon and I will conquer the world."

Napoleon's famously cynical statement has been quoted frequently since the nineteenth century, but it still holds true. Pass out enough gongs and ribbons, and everybody feels good (well, almost everybody). It's self-esteem over professional pride.

One example will suffice.

Williams Air Force Base, Arizona, 1990. A World War II veteran was looking at the new hardware, but he noticed something else. Something that made him edgy. He was a short, twitchy sort, and finally he could stand it no longer. He hailed a passing female airman.

"Excuse me, Miss, I'd like to ask you something."

"Yes, sir. How may I help?"

The old timer cocked his head and said, "I was a fighter pilot in World War II. I shot down six enemy aircraft and at the end of the war I had two rows of ribbons including the Silver Star and DFC. Now, I see that you have two rows and I wonder what they're for."

The young lady glanced down and shrugged. "Gosh, sir, I don't know. They just give them to us from time to time."

True story. I was there.

At the same event we talked to an air force recruiter. The NCO had six and a half rows of ribbons and had never served outside the continental United States (Curt LeMay had nine rows when he retired). Obviously embarrassed, the sergeant explained, "I have to wear these. Uniform regulations."

My fighter ace friend just shook his head. "I guess the Air Force gives medals for perfect attendance these days."

Wait, there's more. Since the 1980s soldiers and airmen have received a ribbon upon completing basic training—an outright absurdity considering that the *uniform* says they finished basic!

When noncoms' "fruit salad" resembles that of Soviet field marshals, something's wrong. But there are about forty current ribbons for medals and decorations, and—get this—four of the top ten are noncombat awards. A fifth, the Bronze Star, may be awarded for combat but often is not.

Like our friendly air force recruiter, there are still active duty personnel who know the awards system is far out of control. Says a navy officer, "I'm only required to wear two rows of ribbons, and that's as much as I'll do. Nothing's going to change, but I refuse to wear any more ribbons than I'm required to, especially since I've never been shot at."

Who's Elite?

In 2001 the chief of staff waved the Magic Waiver and declared the whole danged army to be "elite" (never mind that, by logic and definition, if everybody is "elite," then nobody is elite). Just to "prove" the concept, the general mandated that henceforth all soldiers would wear berets, previously the mark of true elites such as the special forces, rangers, and airborne. The rangers, who had worn black berets for many years, had to give up their patent on that color because the rest of the Army usurped them. (In one of history's minor ironies, the change occurred just in time for the Second Iraq War, in which both sides wore black berets, prompting speculation as to the influence of a pudgy presidential intern as a military fashion maven.)

The rangers switched to tan berets. (Gary Sheftick, "No Chinese Berets for Army, Fielding Phased Through Fall," special to *American Forces Press Service*, May 3, 2001.)

My sampling is not scientific, but nearly 100 percent of soldiers hate their black berets. They really do. It's difficult, bordering on semi-impossible, to overstate the matter. I know a first sergeant who hates his "pet beret" so much that he carries it whenever he can get away with it. Soldiers call them pet berets because, like dogs and cats, berets need grooming from time to time.

Besides looking silly (they resemble shriveled croissants), berets also lend themselves to institutional embarrassment.

After some American suppliers defaulted on their contracts, the Army of One went to a British firm that subcontracted to the Peoples Republic of China, and that caused serious discontent among U.S. labor unions. Some 618,000 of the damn things were ordered, half of which were issued, recalled, and sold surplus— at a loss. The balance was trashed, the deficit made up by contracts to foreign suppliers. One soldier, tongue firmly in cheek, noted "We're getting our new berets from Third World places like Sri Lanka and Arkansas."

In any case, it appears that We the People paid twice the money (or more) for the same product.

In the MIPC, that seems to make perfect sense.

Suggestion: get rid of the damn things except for the green, maroon, and original black versions.

Not everybody is elite. Deal with it.

We Need Innovators

Three years after the invasion, perhaps the most-cited complaint from friendly or neutral Iraqis was, "You Americans have gone to the moon and back. Why haven't you repaired our sewer and electrical system?"

It's a fair question.

In fact, it's a crucial question.

There is already too much work for the Army engineers, and evidently too few civilian contractors, so other options were considered.

Consequently, a few innovative unit commanders have used

some of their stateside training time to go to school. Making use of local plumbers and electricians, officers have found ways and means to teach some of their soldiers how to conduct basic repairs in Mesopotamia. At this writing the jury was still out, but the fact that somebody in authority thought of the option is a Good Thing.

We need more original thinking like that.

If you talk to the troops, you learn that we have plenty of people willing and able to think outside the box. In the words of the late, great Vice Admiral Jim Stockdale: "Think big, think basics, and cheat like hell."

The trouble as seen from the "Seven-Eleven" perspective (where GIs and airmen and sailors hang out and kibbitz) is that innovation is a hard sell.

A case in point:

One of the marines interviewed for this book was an unusual young man, a thirty-two-year-old lance corporal. He said, "I enlisted at twenty-eight because I wanted to serve my country. But I've been to Iraq a couple of times and now I'm getting out. Mainly it's because of the attitude in the Marine Corps. It's like nobody expects you to know anything—just follow orders even if you have a better way to do things. I mean, I understand the need for discipline, especially in combat, but I'm a lot older than most of the guys. I guess it's my age catching up with me because I just don't want to be around that attitude anymore."

"Biff" is intelligent, focused, and motivated; the kind of man we need to keep in the military. But he's gone by now, and he won't be back.

We Need Old Stuff

At an airshow in the 1980s, a lady looked at my restored 1940 navy trainer and asked, "My goodness, is an old airplane safe to fly?"

"Yes, ma'am," I replied. "How else would it get so old?"

Sometimes the old gear works best.

Just to demonstrate that this book can be objective, it's time to acknowledge the weapon systems that have more than paid for themselves over the decades. These are the prime examples, though there may be others.

In aviation the byword is, "Never trust an aircraft under forty." Boeing products have proven especially durable, including the B-52 Stratofortress (first flown in 1954) and KC-135 Stratotanker (1956), as have two helicopters, the Boeing-Vertol CH-47 Chinook (1961) and Sikorsky CH-53 Sea Stallion (1964). The outstanding transport of the post-World War II era is Lockheed's C-130 Hercules (1954), still in production seven presidents and fifty-three years later. All are enormously long-lived designs that appear ageless. In the Chinook's case, there's not even a replacement on the drawing board.

The Chinook is produced by Boeing Philadelphia, which has delivered some 1,200 aircraft since 1961. It remains a multigenerational design, in service over forty-five years and likely to remain thirty more. It's in low-rate production, about two a month. It carries twenty-eight thousand pounds: two humvees or thirty-three soldiers, and that's why operators love it. So do the Brits: they kept their 1982 Falklands campaign going, partly due to one Chinook that survived the sinking of *Atlantic Conveyor*.

If old airplanes are good, old guns are better.

The only conventional American-designed machine gun remaining in service is the timeless Browning M2 .50 caliber, which dates from the 1920s. The 1960s 7.62mm "minigun," a six-barrel Gatling design, was resurrected by the civilian sector in the 1990s, and has proven invaluable.

The M1911 pistol, firing a century-old cartridge, is still the finest side arm ever made: potent, reliable, and "shootable." Owing to NATO politics, it was largely replaced by the inferior M9 in the 1980s, but the Colt is staging a comeback.

Incidentally, the M2 and the 1911 both came from the fertile mind of John M. Browning, who died in 1926.

Among army vehicles, there's the M113 armored personnel carrier, which has been laying tracks since 1960. It's still used in Iraq (it featured in the first Medal of Honor action there) and is employed by more than thirty other nations. Though vulnerable to increasing threats, with some 80,000 produced it's the all-time champion best seller of armored vehicles.

At sea, you simply cannot do better than Nimitz class aircraft carriers. The first entered service in 1975 and the tenth is expected to be launching jets in 2058, when I'll be 110 years old. However, due to serious mismanagement on Bush 41's watch, the Navy was deprived of the deep strike mission, leaving tail-hookers dependent upon air force tankers to get to the fight. The very capable F-14 Tomcat, which first flew in 1970, possessed range and performance, but was retired in 2006. By B-52 standards, the Tom was just getting warmed up, though hundreds of eleven feet per second crunches onto a carrier deck tends to frazzle the best airframes.

If the previous examples prove anything, it's the wisdom of sticking with proven winners rather than discarding them just because they've been around for decades. In one case, we could do worse than buying more F-15s rather than all the stealth aircraft we're committed to purchase (the original Raptor program posited 750 aircraft, now we can afford about 180). First flown in 1972, the Eagle already owns the best air combat record in history. With current upgrades plus new airframes, improved sensors and weapons, supported by jammers, it should be *augmented* by the F-22, not *replaced* by it. The same applies to the F-15E Strike Eagle versus the massively expensive F-35 strike fighter. Considering who we're likely to fight (and therefore the probable type of conflicts), the less-than-best option makes a great deal of sense.

Which leads us to . . .

Down With The Best

According to Tom Clancy, who should know, during the Cold War the commander of the Soviet navy displayed a sign in his office: "The best is the enemy of the good enough."

Admiral Gorshkov was on to something.

He reckoned that the Evil Empire would go broke trying to

compete with the capitalist West on a qualitative basis, and he was right. Therefore, he structured his fleet as a consortium of many players, most of which were less capable than their opponents but were good enough to inflict serious damage. In the overall scheme of things, the Red Fleet only had to break even. If it expended itself in gaining a zero-sum result against the NATO navies, Moscow won. Facing massive superiority in European land forces, the United States and its allies needed uninterrupted sealift to reinforce against any Soviet attack.

No sealift equals no reinforcement equals T-72s parked in Calais.

But Americans are technocrats down deep in our bones. We are also sentimental to the point of self-delusion, assuring ourselves that Nothing Is Too Good for our fightingmenandwomen (it's become one word in recent years).

It's not true.

For one thing, if we truly believed in nothing but the best, we would never send *anybody* to war without knowing how to load magazines or zero a rifle. But we do it all the time. So let's get over that emotional-factual hurdle and look at equipment.

We fought and won World War II with just a whole lot of stuff, and it wasn't all first-class. In just three examples:

The Curtiss P-40 was obsolescent at Pearl Harbor;

Our best tank was second-rate;

And our submarine torpedoes were semiuseless until late 1943. (That was a genuine scandal, but service politics and careerism prevailed. Whereas the German ordnance engineers responsible for similar failings went to prison, ours were promoted to admiral. Honest.)

Nevertheless, we won the war. True, after Pearl Harbor it took the Greatest Generation of Americans and the rest of the world almost four years to beat Germany and Japan, but there's a lesson in how we did it.

We had a lot more stuff. But that was then; this is now. We have long since shunned that philosophy because we're economically, institutionally, and culturally gadget-happy. If it's newer and costlier, it must be better. Right?

We've already examined the cult of stealth and what it has cost us. Not merely the R&D and acquisition costs, but the mountain of other things (gear, programs, logistics, and training) that go wanting because the money was spent elsewhere, feeding the voraciousness of the MIPC.

Consequently, Gorschkov's shade beckons from beyond the ghostly bastion of the Red Banner Fleet. *The best is the enemy of the good enough.*

If something is too expensive to risk in combat, it *is* too good for our fightingmenandwomen. In that situation the irony cackles aloud, sending peals of laughter down the halls of the Pentagon: to do justice to the troops, we need to give them something less than the best.

That's right—give our forces what's good enough; and more of it.

We Need More Medical Care

The historical irony holds that while battlefield lethality has increased tremendously, combat deaths have declined. Throughout World War II, one-third of battlefield casualties were killed or died of wounds. That figure dropped to one-quarter in Korea and Vietnam and now hovers around 12 percent.

With an eight-to-one WIA-KIA ratio, today the system is often overloaded. The situation places further burdens on requirements for transportation, facilities, near and long-term care, and rehabilitation. But the bottom line remains: more critically wounded troops are surviving. A big factor is jet transport aircraft. The worst injured service members from Iraq can be rolled into an operating room in the United States in as little as thirty-six hours.

A DoD study of nonmortal casualties from Iraq through early 2007 showed 23,400 wounded, of whom 7,000, (30 percent) required medical air transport. But the 16,400 who were not medevaced were more than offset by 25,500 noncombat cases, including 18,700 victims of various diseases. The balance had been injured in vehicle or machinery accidents, negligent weapon handling, and a myriad of other causes.

To summarize: of 32,500 military personnel requiring evacuation from 2001 to early 2007, barely one-fifth were combat casualties. Therefore, if peace is established in Iraq at noon tomorrow, accidents and disease will continue inflicting thousands of hospital cases upon the medical system as long as Americans are deployed there. Furthermore, thousands of routine injuries will continue stateside, as they always have, especially when teenagers operate complex equipment. (More military personnel are killed in automobile wrecks than all other noncombat causes combined.)

In 2004 SecDef Rumsfeld mandated a 50 percent reduction in accidents over the next two years. To many service members it was a grandly optimistic expectation, partly because the personnel and even equipment losses already were fairly low. For example, the Navy and Marine Corps had averaged one noncombat death per month over the previous eighteen years.

When the 2006 results were posted, the figures had improved only marginally. Far from a 50 percent accident reduction, the Army's overall safety record showed an 11 percent improvement between 2004 and 2006, while fatalities were down about 9 percent. In the Navy, total mishaps (aviation, ashore, and afloat) increased 6 percent in those two years. Clearly, DoD's mandated improvements were unrealistic, as predicted by operating forces at the time.

Whatever the result of attempts to impose safety by dictate, the injured still require treatment. With the DoD medical system facing a greater influx of patients than anytime in more than thirty years, innovation was called for. And many organizations and individuals rose to the challenge.

In a prime example of medical "jointness," marine casualties from Bethesda Naval Hospital often are seen at Walter Reed Army

Medical Center and vice versa. The two centers frequently swap casualties according to the needs of individuals, and one observer writes, "In that regard, bureaucratic turf doesn't seem to exist, a great example of interservice cooperation. Hoo-rah!"

However, throughout the system patients still report many bureaucratic hoops, including endless forms to be filed, onerous waiting periods, lost records, and repeated procedures or mixed-up schedules. Concludes a combat infantry vet, "In the long run the soldier usually gets screwed by The System, so read Kipling's *Tommy*."

Says a National Guard NCO with partial paralysis, "At Fort Bliss they didn't seem to care when I got my evaluation and release as long as they knew where I was most of the time. So I became an ace at crossword puzzles and read every science fiction novel I could find. Finally, I guess my name worked its way to the head of the line and they let me leave."

Among other concerns, there's a new category of patients. Due to rapid response and advancing medical technology, people are surviving wounds that would have been fatal a few years ago. That poses new challenges for the "downstream" aspects of treatment and care. In just one instance among dozens, a visitor to Walter Reed described meeting a young woman whose skull was partially destroyed, and with it part of her brain. "She's walking around, talking, sometimes even joking," says my contact. "But the docs don't know if she'll be able to learn new skills or hold a job."

If we can influence others who are genuinely interested in helping the current crop of casualties, we'll do more good than any of us can individually. The problem appears to be a shortage more than a lack of postrehab focus, and given the case load perhaps that's understandable. Continues one of the Walter Reed visitors, "These casualties are going to need a job or something productive to do with the rest of their lives. The need is when they are near the end of recovery and will emerge from military hospitals. That especially applies to the younger ones, sometimes under twenty, with little premilitary work experience. Okay, we put him/her back together. Now what?

"How about a job arranged by those who didn't have to man the ramparts for the rest of us? How about a nationwide chamber of commerce interested in promoting and implementing some 'return home' place of employment to fit the individual's abilities? No legs? We have a desk job for you. No arms? We have a speaking or proof-reading job for you. Blind? We have a Braille section in the library."

If more Americans were committed to helping injured service members return to satisfying, productive postmilitary positions, the entire nation would benefit. It's a challenge for everybody, military and civilian alike.

The VA Option

Once the service member is released from military control, he or she usually encounters the Veterans Administration system. The organization's ups and downs are too well known to revisit here, but suffice it to say that the VA is simultaneously part of the problem—and the solution.

Those VA patients with service-connected disabilities receive priority treatment, followed by individuals with postmilitary problems. (However, there is no VA bump for Medal of Honor recipients, though one army man quips, "Fortunately, most of us already have Purple Hearts.")

A quick survey of the veteran community reveals a need for more knowledge of the system. Many eligible individuals simply do not know the benefits to which they are entitled, which indi-cates a need for more veterans benefit counselors. However, counselors require three to five years experience to maximize their ability to help vets get what they're entitled to receive.

To take just one outstanding example, to this day many Vietnam veterans don't know that twenty or more illnesses are almost automatically granted service-related status due to Agent Orange exposure. The list includes lung and prostate cancer, Hodgkin's disease, and diabetes.

The ignorance factor is not limited to "grunts" or "snuffies." In one instance an air force general, a Vietnam War POW, accepted 30 percent disability upon retirement. Years later, when informed of his eligibility, he was reevaluated and received a 70 percent disability.

Veterans' advocates insist that the services need to do better in "capturing" military personnel before separating from the military. Says Fred Ferguson, a Vietnam Medal of Honor recipient and former Arizona veterans administrator, "Especially in the Guard and Reserve, outgoing soldiers are told they can wait around for two weeks to take an exit physical, or they can go home now by signing a release. Most of them fall over themselves to sign, not realizing they're depriving themselves of benefits downstream.

"Sometimes DoD doesn't care much about its broken toys. The Pentagon spends all kinds of money getting kids to sign up, but when they come back in pieces, it's often a different story. However, part of the problem is with the soldiers, too. Sixty percent of those who plunked down $1,200 for the Montgomery GI Bill's education benefits don't use it. And the government isn't in any hurry to remind people that they have money or benefits due them."

Other than treatment and eligibility, lesser problems seem to resist cures. One of the most-cited concerns in VA hospitals is communications. The phone system is often so fouled up that one can spend hours trying to get something done. Sometimes it's impossible to get through. One veteran who functions as a patient advocate lives in suburban Maryland. He found that he could drive to Walter Reed, personally address a soldier's problem, and return home faster than he could accomplish anything by phone. As he reports, "Twenty minutes driving there, twenty minutes yelling at somebody, and twenty minutes back usually does the job."

Whether the problems be large or small, each affects soldiers and veterans, and by extension their families and friends. If the Terror War does in fact result in more boots on the ground in Iraq, Afghanistan, and elsewhere, the people who fill those boots will require increasing funding, facilities, and care providers for decades to come.

Time to get going.

Chapter Nine

Guessing the Future

"A nation that does not prepare for all the forms of war should then renounce the use of war in national policy . . . A people that does not prepare to fight should then be morally prepared to surrender. To fail to prepare soldiers and citizens for limited, bloody ground action, and then to engage in it, is folly verging on the criminal."

—T. R. Fehrenbach, *This Kind of War*

Fehrenbach was writing of Korea. But he might have been addressing the situation more than fifty years later, because we are now engaged in a limited, bloody ground action for which we were poorly prepared. How might it progress?

It's a bold prognosticator who presumes to predict what will happen in one year, let alone generations downstream in the war against militant Islam and its allies. Even the best guesses of life-long professionals gang aft agley (to quote Robert Burns) and there is no better example than the immediate post-World War II period. In 1949 atomic bombs and rockets were clearly the wave of the future. No less an authority than General Omar Bradley, the army chief of staff, declared that amphibious operations would be impossible in the nuclear age.

Then came the frozen hell of Korea, the Inchon landing, a three-year rifle fight for the ridge tops, and then a decade wasted in the rice paddies of Vietnam. The Cold War came and went. Then came Desert Storm. Then came 9/11, Afghanistan (another perennial rifle fight for the ridge tops), and the urban quagmire of Iraq.

No nukes. Not even close. Deterrence worked, but in the long run the experts had been wrong, wrong, wrong.

In fairness, as responsible officials they planned for what Vice President Dick Cheney called "the 1 percent solution" based on the least likely of worst case scenarios. But even after the collapse of the Soviet Union, they kept on doing what they knew best—buying high-high priced gear long after the high-high threat had disappeared.

Today we're still preparing not merely for the last war, but for one we've not fought in two generations—against a conventional enemy who can fight us as equals.

Today we face a global enemy, but he's incapable of meeting us on even terms so he fights the battle of David versus Goliath. Hence the discussions of asymmetric warfare.

Today we have the greatest airpower on earth, but we use helicopters vastly more than fighters or bombers.

Today we have the world's most powerful Navy, but it hasn't fought a genuine sea battle since World War II.

Today we have the finest armored force in history, but it lacks an opponent.

Could any of the foregoing change?

Yes, it could. Some day.

But that's conjecture. It's somewhere downstream, if ever. Meanwhile, we have our hands full—and then some—managing the present conflict.

Military history turned a corner in 2003. In Iraq the American-led coalition defeated a nation with a large, experienced army, and when that enemy was destroyed, the real war began. We're still engaging in it, every day, but not against any nation.

Our current enemies represent no country and no army. They possess no navy and no air force. They do not even wear uniforms. Imbued with religious fervor, they are willing to die in large numbers not for any specific goal but for the purpose of killing some of us.

Against such enemies, what should be the purpose of the U.S. armed forces?

Defining the Mission

According to DoD's quadrennial report of 2006, the U.S. military has four primary missions:

1. Defend the homeland.
2. Fight terrorism.
3. Conduct asymmetric warfare.
4. Shape the choices of nations at strategic crossroads.

Pay attention, because what follows is important.

The most significant factor is the mission that is absent: fighting "peer opponents." That's because there are none. The Pentagon tacitly acknowledges that fact but continues its ravenous purchasing of high-high tech gear that would only be useful against such an enemy.

So where does that leave us?

The first three missions appear self evident, but the fourth requires some interpretation. The short version is: manage the evolving situation in China. As frequently noted in this book, the true nature of the Chinese threat is likely far less than the MIPC likes to describe it, for a variety of reasons. But it's worth repeating: Beijing has no reason to inflict vast economic harm upon itself by picking a fight with a major trade partner.

Logically, if China represents little military threat to American security, then no lesser nation can pose a comparable conventional threat. (Threats to our economy may be far more serious, not only from Beijing but from al Qaeda and other terrorist groups. Osama bin Laden has long since identified the West as vulnerable to financial boycott, trade sanctions, and computer attack.)

Since homeland defense and counterterror operations necessarily involve intelligence agencies as well as the military, we'll only touch upon Mission One and Two.

National security goes hand in glove with counterterrorism, so the first two missions are interrelated. It says much about the convoluted nature of American politics that it took five years after 9/11 before the president finally signed legislation authorizing an incomplete fence along the Mexican border. Mexican nationalists and American liberals predictably found common cause in deriding the common sense measure, however effective it may prove. Absurd comparisons with the Berlin Wall inevitably were made on the left, which remains stunningly unable to distinguish between measures to keep people out from those that keep people in.

Consequently, in the realm of approximately conventional conflict, we need to focus on Mission Three: asymmetric warfare against an often shadowy enemy.

Whom Shall We Fight?

Wars between nation states are becoming passé. Nobody is saying that it will not happen, but that's the trend.

It's for certain: in this century we will face two opponents— radical Islam and somebody else.

Since we're already heavily engaged against the former, and will be for decades if not longer, perhaps that's where we should place our focus.

Some background:

In 1900 Christians accounted for 27 percent of the human race; Muslims 12 percent. A century later the figures were 30 and 19; relative growths of 11 and 58 percent, respectively.

Once upon a time, Western troops could rely upon vastly greater firepower to offset a numerical deficit in battle. Nowhere was it better illustrated than the 1898 Battle of Omdurman, when British and Egyptian forces chopped down thousands of Muslims near Khartoum.

The litany went:
"Whatever happens
We have got
The Maxim gun
And they have not."

The Mahdi's warriors fell in heaps to machine guns and artillery, with an entirely satisfactory kill-loss ratio of about two hundred to one in favor of the Brits.

Things are different now. Islam's warriors have learned to fight us in other ways, but at rock bottom their greatest weapon remains their fertility. Not that the West is going to find itself cast against every Muslim or even every Muslim nation, but the faith's increasing numbers ensure a growing pool of dedicated enemies.

Let's consider some specifics.

In the global campaign against Islamist states and entities, the West begins the contest with an inherent deficit: population growth. Islam is on the rise, especially in Africa. For instance, Sudan leads most nations with a 2.5 percent population growth per annum, a 34/1000 birth rate, and a 4.7 fertility rate (births per woman). Sudan is 70 percent Muslim.

Meanwhile, the U.S. and western European nations yield an annual population growth of well under 1 percent (in Germany, it's essentially flat-line at 0.2 percent). In contrast, most Muslim countries add 2 percent annually, though Iran has a lower growth figure (1.1 percent) and birth rate (17/1000) than almost any Islamic society. Nevertheless, the Persian figures exceed the western democracies.

According to CIA figures, Muslim nations are producing more children than America and Europe by considerable margins. Consequently, many Islamic populations average half the age of the West. The net gain of those youngsters translates into more warriors. It takes less than eighteen years to grow a jihadist; sometimes a lot less.

In the twentieth century, world population grew from 1.65 to 6.06 billion, an increase of about three and a half times. During the same period, demographers reckon that Islam increased nearly five times.

So what do the demographics mean?

In *The Looming Tower* (2006), Lawrence Wright noted that, despite some spectacular terrorist successes and remarkable staying power, in the past sixty years Islamic extremists have not established a radical theocracy in the Arab world. However, such entities have emerged elsewhere, notably Afghanistan and Iran (contrary to many Americans' impressions, neither are Arab).

In some ways, Afghanistan remains the central front in the Terror War, for that is where al Qaeda grew up. Its Taliban allies succeeded there, dominating the country and demonstrating a gritty determination not only to survive but to arise from its defeat in 2001. Islamist fighters continue resisting in Afghanistan today.

Therefore, the absence of a new, radical Arab theocracy should not lead us into complacency. Ralph Peters' war of faith and blood is conducted by individuals and groups rather than nations, however much covert support some countries may provide. Meanwhile, young, uneducated, impoverished Muslims will see a demand for fewer resources with more shortages; more poverty; more anger and therefore more fodder for the global jihad.

Guessing the future: We will continue fighting Islam in ever greater numbers. However, it would be a mistake to assume that followers of the Prophet represent our only enemies. There are other "opponents" on the horizon, and they are well known to one another.

We should recognize the potential of an alliance between Muslim entities such as al Qaeda and well-established nation-states such as Iran and North Korea. While it could make for a messy display on DoD charts and graphs, with a lot of dotted lines demonstrating unofficial lines of command and control, it might also reflect reality.

Nobody said that the world has to be orderly to be understood.

The Ghosts of Tsushima

Where will we see the greatest revelation in twenty-first century warfare?

Probably at sea.

There has not been a naval battle worthy of the name since

1944. (Context: after a live-fire exercise against Iranian gunboats and small craft in 1988, the American admiral declared Operation Praying Mantis "the greatest naval battle since World War II." Enough said about puffery and careerism.)

We are now in much the same position as one century ago: the Russo-Japanese War of 1904–1905. A new generation of ships, weapons, tactics, and doctrine remain untried in combat. In fact, entire generations of naval hardware have come and gone without ever spilling blood. We do not know how well we have prepared until we have to sink and get sunk.

My prediction: if it happens, we will be surprised and frustrated.

At Jutland in 1916, the Royal Navy scored about 3 percent hits against the Kaiser's High Seas Fleet and steamed home disappointed because prewar gunnery exercises generated much higher expectations. In fact, 5 percent hits would have been exceptional but the Brits didn't know that.

The U.S. Navy learned much the same lessons in World War II, belatedly realizing that the gamesmanship that won peacetime gunnery pennants did not produce ship-killing results in combat.

Let's take a brief look at 1905 and a century later.

When the Emperor's and the Czar's fleets clashed in Tsushima Strait, neither side had experience of modern naval combat on that scale. Actually, nobody did. True, the Yankees had easily whipped the Spanish in Cuban and Philippine waters only seven years before, but the naval art had advanced considerably in that brief time. In 1898 the Spanish navy's best ships displaced seven thousand tons, mounting eleven-inch guns. America's finest at Santiago Bay were eleven thousand tons with eight-inchers, but off Manila the U.S. flagship was less than six thousand tons with eight-inchers. Her opposite number was merely 3,500 tons, firing six-inch guns.

At Tsushima both fleets possessed new combatants of twelve thousand to thirteen thousand tons with twelve-inch naval rifles. That was a major evolution in a very short time. The difference was that Japan had spent that period far better than Russia. The results showed in combat: Admiral Togo's practiced gunners sank more than twenty Russian ships and captured others while his force lost three torpedo boats.

The results were eye-openers for the global naval community. Seen in context, prior to 1898 there had been no real naval battles since the American Civil War, and those were small. The subsequent main events had been Turko-Greek feuding and occasional South American posturing, often with no ship losses. Nobody really knew what to expect of early twentieth-century combat until it actually occurred.

Today, we find ourselves in a similar situation. We are forty years into the missile age of naval warfare (an Egyptian boat sank an Israeli destroyer in 1967) but there have only been a handful of small engagements since then. As of this writing, most likely the first missile-era naval *battle* will involve nations other than America. The China Syndrome (see Chapter Seven) still looms large in the Pentagon's menu of scenarios, but where blue-water combat might occur between the United States and Beijing remains dubious. However, China versus Taiwan remains a possibility (officially there have been four Taiwan Crises, 1954–2000), as does China versus other players, not to omit the perennial prospects of India-Pakistan. But if history is any indicator, a genuine war at sea may come out of "port field" with unlikely antagonists (witness Britain-Argentina).

Guessing the future: It stands to reason that after more than sixty years, there's going to be another surface engagement, possibly involving the U.S. Navy. It may be a small, isolated event, or part of a larger campaign in a strategic location. But whenever or wherever it occurs, stand by to be surprised.

"The Air War"

Reporters are fond of commenting on "the air war" or even "the carrier war." Balderdash—there's no such thing anymore.

What journalists perceive as "air wars" or "carrier wars" in fact are air or carrier *operations*. In order to have a war, you need two sides. In that regard, there is almost no chance of another aircraft carrier battle—ever. There have only been five (perhaps six, depending on semantics) and they all occurred between 1942 and 1944.

Since neither al Qaeda nor the Taliban has airplanes, no aerial combat is going to occur within the Terror War. Therefore, only national air forces (or conceivably some well-funded and well-organized freelancers) can pose an air threat to American or Western militaries. Consequently, barring a hostile alliance of historic proportions, the next air war is bound to remain terrifically lopsided in our favor. Not that it's a bad thing—it's just the way it is.

Some perspective:

May 4, 1999, may become a landmark event in aviation history. As of this writing, that Tuesday night was the last time an American fighter pilot shot down a hostile aircraft.

During Operation Allied Force, Lieutenant Colonel Michael H. Greczy of the 78th Fighter Squadron was flying an F-16CJ from Aviano Airbase, Italy. He was partnered with Grumman EA-6B Prowlers, protecting a mission against Batajnica Airfield in Serbia. Following the attack, allied controllers noticed a lone bogey closing on the "strike package" and alerted the escorts. Greczy acquired the intruder, confirmed it as hostile, and fired a radar-guided missile that destroyed the "Yugo" MiG-29B. It was the sixth confirmed kill for an American-flown F-16 since the type entered service in 1979.

For a larger perspective, since the last MiG kill over Vietnam in 1973, American pilots have claimed just fifty-five shootdowns, including trainers and helicopters. That's a record spanning thirty-three years—a trend if ever there was one.

Yet the theory holds that our limited number of F-22s will offset the numerical advantage of China—or whomever we're supposed to fight in a conventional war. But what are the likely numbers of hostile aircraft that we can expect to encounter?

In other words, how big is a really big dogfight?

Let's pick a number: say, twenty smoking holes in the ground.

To find a one-day air battle involving twenty fighter kills, we have to look back a quarter-century. The bloodiest aerial combats of the post-World War II era occurred over the Bekaa Valley in 1982. In a six-day shootout the Israelis notched eighty kills, including twenty-nine on June 9 and twenty more on June 10.

The biggest day for American pilots in the jet age was logged over Korea on June 30,1953. To find more than sixteen U.S. victories you have to default all the way to August 15, 1945—VJ Day.

Now, could we be surprised someday and find ourselves facing a skyfull of MiGs, Sukhois, Mirages, and other assorted bandits? So many that our fighters might run out of missiles and have to resort to guns?

Well, yes, it's theoretically possible. It's equally possible that Madonna might take vows of chastity and enter a convent. Meanwhile, can anyone say who would be flying all those sophisticated airplanes, and with what goal in mind?

Me neither.

"The air war" involves ground-based guns and missiles vastly more than hostile fighters. From 1975 through 2006 the U.S. armed forces lost thirty-two airplanes to ground defenses (averaging one a year) versus one to enemy aircraft. About twenty choppers were shot down from 1975 to 2001, but since then the figures have been hard to acquire since the Army appears reluctant to identify combat losses. In Desert Storm we lost fifty-seven aircraft, but barely half were combat related.

To place things in perspective, no American soldiers have come under air attack since Korea, and those were small, ineffective efforts by nocturnal biplanes. Meanwhile, army air defense has shot down just two airplanes since 1945. In the 2003 invasion of Iraq, both Coalition fixed-wing losses were "blue on blue," victims of a U.S. Army Patriot missile battery. We own the air— whether the enemy flies or not—but we've now become our own worst enemy for our own jets.

Guessing the future: based on the world trend spanning decades, another major air-to-air campaign is extremely unlikely. While we should not take air supremacy for granted, neither should we obsess over theoretical future scenarios while more pressing needs remain under funded or ignored.

High time to get our priorities straight.

The Pols and the Press

In the summer of 2006 a senior marine NCO responded to a query about what was needed in Iraq. The question was gear oriented, but here's what the gunnery sergeant wrote:

"What I think we need is the politicians (to) stay out of the way and let us do our job. Because of them listening to all those bleeding hearts, they have put so many restrictions on us that we can not effectively do our jobs. In return it takes us longer to do the job which in turn is one of the reasons we are still over here. Second, I think we should kick out all the press, because all they are doing is reporting on the bad things and not talking about any of the positive things that have happened. Also every time we find a way to defeat the enemy the press/news is all over it. And all they are doing is telling the enemy how we are operating or defeating them, which in turn is getting us killed or injured."

The gunny's antimedia attitude was by no means unique. Several respondents voiced similar opinions based on the belief that most of the news media and many liberal politicians were opposed not only to the war but to the military (that was about two months before Senator Kerry's botched joke regarding the intellectual capacity of armed forces personnel).

It was possible to discuss the matter with some troops, but not all. Some are downright vehement in their opposition to any media coverage. I noted that a press blackout would deprive the taxpayers of information about the war they fund, because the government certainly is not going to provide unbiased coverage, regardless of the administration. Furthermore, it's not only unrealistic to expect the pols to keep their mitts off the military, it's unconstitutional as well. Our system is based upon the primacy of civilian control of the armed forces. ("The president shall be Commander in Chief . . . " Article II, Section 2.) While some wars unquestionably would have ended more satisfactorily had the president gone fishing for several months, that's just not in the cards, and any volunteer soldier should know that.

Perception of media and political bias was not limited to soldiers on the ground. In 2006 a civilian contractor said, "We need more accurate reporting. The majority of reporters are still sitting in the Green Zone and filing second-hand reports from the field."

The fact that many troops do not understand either the media or political aspects bodes more problems for the Republic than may exist in any combat zone. One of the least examined concerns for the Long War is not what happens Over There, but the mindset among embittered soldiers who may return home to become policemen, carrying a simmering anger alongside a badge. In the words of a former SWAT instructor, "I saw it after Vietnam, and I'm starting to see it today. Some of these guys are ready to go out and make war on the citizens they swore an oath to serve and protect."

Guessing the future: In time, growing resentment among veterans of the Terror War may aggravate the political and cultural divisions that are already apparent. But the potential is likely to remain diminished or ignored by the military and civilian authorities.

Iran

Nobody needs a crystal ball to predict trouble with Iran. Ever since we turned on the Shah in the 1970s (having deposed the previous ruler in his favor) we've had continuing problems with Tehran. Now that the theocratic regime has aligned itself with Pyongyang and called for Israel's destruction, there is little reason to expect anything but more trouble.

Whatever the merits of invading Iraq in 2003, Washington

clearly misunderstood the consequences: internal resistance (much of it supported from Iran) and more trouble with Tehran. In other words, when we strapped on Iraq we strapped on Iran.

Q: Since Iran sits on a lake of oil, why does Tehran need nuclear power?

A: It doesn't.

Yet Iran operates more than a dozen nuclear facilities, civilian and military. That's a major program by any standard, though it includes innocuous sites such as uranium mines and waste storage. While America's foes (and some supporters) ask how Washington can keep its own nuclear weapons for sixty years and deny them elsewhere, the policy makers are not obliged to justify what has gone before. Rather, the American leadership needs to formulate options for addressing a problem that may—literally—reach critical mass.

In 2002 the West learned of an Iranian uranium enrichment facility at Natanz and a heavy water facility at Arak. Just how far the rest of the world will tolerate enrichment in Persia remains to be seen, but it is questionable whether Israel will permit the project to reach completion. At that point, it's anybody's guess: all-out war in the Middle East might be the lesser of various devils.

Clearly, Tehran's actions prompt suspicion. In 2004 the Iranians leveled their Lavizan military research facility, allegedly after the International Atomic Energy Agency wanted to inspect the site. When European investigators reported traces of enriched fuel, the Iranians explained it as residue of a nearby facility unrelated to military use. Subsequent analysis apparently was inconclusive.

Some Iranian facilities are underground, which almost certainly equals military use. Reportedly such plants feature eight-foot-thick, reinforced concrete walls, plus air and ground defense sites. "Bunker buster" penetrating bombs would be necessary to reach them and inflict significant damage, if not actually destroy them.

But we live in a world where nuclear "all-up rounds" are available for merely millions of dollars. Even if it were possible to disable or destroy Iran's large nuclear power and weapons programs, the mullahs still could obtain ready-made nukes on the global market.

That fact points increasingly toward regime change. But it will not come from within.

Which means . . .

Invading Iran

The only way to ensure that Iran does not complete its nuclear weapons program is to occupy the country. International inspectors can be deceived or deterred, as they were for so long in Iraq.

That's a *very* large order, invoking consequences both varied and unknowable.

Considering that America is mired in Iraq, the problems of tackling Iran appear huge. For starters, Iran has three times Iraq's population living in four times the area—a region larger than Alaska.

Depending upon sources, the Iranian armed forces number between 540,000 and 770,000 personnel, active and reserves. Reportedly the Mobilization Resistance Force (the *Basij*) maintains some ninety thousand full-time plus three hundred thousand reservists with a total call-up of one million men. Any invasion would likely be met with near-total mobilization, and if history is any guide, the mullahs would not care about casualties.

Some American estimates run as high as three hundred thousand troops to invade Iran, which means a multinational force. Whatever the numbers, a Western or Coalition attack against Iran would rely upon technological advantages and massive firepower to offset the manpower deficit. But if the 1990–1991 coalition that freed Kuwait could not agree upon how to proceed in Saddam's Iraq, what are the prospects for a unified policy against Iran?

Just for drill, let's assume that America goes it alone.

In fairly specific terms, it's possible to determine the maximal amount of force we would need to conquer Iran. It can only be done on the ground, if at all, so here we go:

We would own the sky, no question, even without stealth assets.

We would own the sea but might pay a price in some ships lost to Iranian mines and submarines. Frankly, our antisubmarine warfare community needs some attention after years of neglect—especially ASW helicopters, which have been burdened with other tasks including transport and humanitarian aid. (In 2005–2006 naval MH-53 and H-60 units, *including training aircraft*, were deploying to Afghanistan and Iraq for combat support duty because the Army needs some rest.)

We should not take the Iranian navy for granted—nor any other. The embarrassing episode in November 2006 when a Chinese submarine surfaced undetected five miles from USS *Kitty Hawk* was explained as greater need for communication between the two navies rather than need to mend our ASW fences.

The fence contains huge gaps. Since most American surface ships lost their acoustic "tails" (towed arrays) that troll for submarines, airborne platforms inherited the task. But now that no carrier airplanes retain the ASW mission, and land-based P-3 Orions have been halved, we rely largely on our own submarines. Open sources state that only SSNs retain a significant ASW capability, and that is limited because of active sonar emphasis, especially in coastal waters.

We have already discussed mines, but shallow coastal waters also are where we'll tangle with Iran's half-dozen or so capable, quiet submarines. Yes, undoubtedly we could destroy them, but what's a "fair exchange" in the bargain? How many ships could an amphibious force afford to lose, sunk or crippled, and still accomplish its mission?

For the moment, let's assume the best and move inland.

We could invade with four corps although more would be better. But that's not possible at present since we should leave a corps in reserve for South Korea. (The skeleton I Corps' two understrength active divisions include one in Korea, from which we've rotating brigades, and another in Hawaii, parts of which have been used in Afghanistan.)

The U.S. Army currently maintains ten active divisions:

Five heavy: 1st Armored, 1st Cavalry (armored), 1st, 3rd, and 4th Mechanized.

One medium: 2nd Infantry in Korea.

Four light: 10th Mountain, 25th Light Infantry, 82nd Airborne, and 101st Air Assault.

Those divisions make up four corps (I, III, V, and XVIII Airborne), and the Marines form another. Each corps requires three to five divisions, so fully arming four U.S. Army corps would require more than our present ten active divisions. The guard and reserve are supposed to field ten division equivalents, but of course do not. However, we also have active airborne and special forces brigades, plus independent ranger and armored cavalry regiments.

Minimum requirements for an Iranian invasion would put XVIII Airborne Corps into Northwest Iranian Kurdistan; V Armored Corps into Southwest Arab Khuzistan; marines into the same area (with PhibRons off the Arabian Sea coast as a diversion), and III Armored Corps out of Afghanistan.

Occupying all of Iran lies beyond our ability, but holding the ethnic minority fringe provinces may be feasible. We could probably capture the oil-rich Shi'a Arab southwest fairly quickly, and Kurdish northwest, although the mountainous terrain favors the defense. Iranian Azerbaijan is less restive and would require the nation of Azerbaijan letting us attack from there, but that may be a diplomatic possibility. We might drive the heavy division (3rd Mech) of XVIII Corps down the Caspian coastal road through Iranian Azerbaijan to hook up with the corps' three light divisions (10th, 82nd, and 101st) pushing through the mountains east out of Iraq.

It's possible that occupation duties could be handed over to Kurdish and Shi'a Iraqis, plus perhaps Turkish, Azeri, and Turkomen troops in regions of Iran with Azeri, and Turkomen majorities. In any case—to repeat—solid allies would be absolutely essential, except that no Israelis need apply.

Guessing the future: If we invade Iran, then (as in Iraq) we would have an even bigger problem. "Okay, coach, we won the main event. Now what happens in post season?" We had no obvious Plan B in Iraq; we'll need C, D, and E for the more complex problems in Persia.

The Twenty-First Century Swan Threat

When I was in college in the 1970s, one of my political science profs liked to posit some off the wall concepts. Her favorite was the Soviet Dolphin Threat of the 1980s. Just as in the Great Patriotic War, when Russians trained patriotic dogs to run under German tanks and detonate backpack explosives on contact, the Soviets were said to be training dolphins to attack NATO vessels. Apparently nothing came of the Dolphin Threat, but the concept of animal-delivered weapons still remains—in far more frightening form.

In the twenty-first century, Tehran doesn't need nukes to inflict grievous harm on the West. For instance, Iran is a biotech-capable country able to develop bird flu virus. Swans from Iran migrate north to Scandinavia and even Alaska. If the elegant birds are injected with avian flu virus, deaths in the hundreds of millions could result in infidel land.

Basically, it's the same dilemma with Iran's nuclear program: talk, plead, and threaten. The only significant difference is that Iran cannot claim "peaceful civilian uses" for the bird flu virus.

What to do?

Invite Iran to join efforts to create and use the avian antidote. Point out the advantages: eradicate the virus or risk destruction of the nation's oil industry via cruise missiles. (Naval Strike Warfare doctrine: "Never send an aviator where you can send a bullet.") State with crystal clarity, and as much of our depleted credibility as we can muster, that in event of a bird flu epidemic in the West, retaliation will be forthcoming.

But threats only go so far. Mutually assured destruction (MAD) worked with the Soviets for a half century, because they were merely evil, not crazy. Negotiating with religious zealots poses vastly greater problems, since many Muslims eagerly await Paradise. Yet perhaps therein might lie our advantage: the men running Islamic petrostates might value their oil profits even more than their souls.

Guessing the future: Absent a credible deterrent, a bird flu offensive against the West likely would succeed, assuming that "success" is measured by a massive death toll and chaos. We might consider that the goal of such a campaign may be limited to just such malevolence, unrelated to broader concerns.

The Tehran-Pyongyang Connection

The Zealot's Dilemma: whether to remain true to the Faith or to invoke convenience in dealing with one Devil to destroy another. The Great Satan, of course, is America and the West generally, but the Islamic ideologues in Tehran and elsewhere are not above consorting with the most godless Communists remaining on the planet: those who reside in Pyongyang, North Korea.

Forget political-religious philosophy and Islamic ideologues: Tehran and Pyongyang talk to each other. They have exchanged nuclear and missile technology for years, and we would be insane to assume they have not discussed mutually supportive actions against the West.

If North Korea tests missiles for Tehran, then anything that Pyongyang owns can wind up in Iran. If Kim (or the Pakistanis or anyone else) has provided Ahmadinejad with a bomb or a weapon design, it is likely a Chinese design already well proven.

For the moment, however, let's step back from WMDs and consider a lower order of conflict.

As events have shown in Iraq, there is no rear area in the Terror War. Nor should we presume that the situation will improve or that it would not exist elsewhere. If we ever strap on North Korea, we will have to deal with Communist infiltrators and very capable *Spetsnaz* units. Reportedly Pyongyang has more special forces than anyone: perhaps one hundred thousand. They are the ones who murdered seventeen members of the South Korean government in Rangoon in 1983.

We can only assume one thing—they will not remain idle.

Let's take a huge leap of faith and assume for a moment that things settle down in Iraq, and the Afghan rebels—ignoring centuries of contrary evidence—trade in their AKs for goats. What will we need then?

Exactly what we need now. Many of the same problems will occur whether confronting North Korean commandos or more urban mujahadeen.

The geostrategists inform us that there are about 1.4 billion Muslims on Planet Earth. Their presence extends far beyond the Middle East, including Indonesia, the Philippines, Africa, and the Balkans. (Remember Kosovo? It was in all the papers. We're still there.) All represent potential hot spots.

Then there's Latin America. Ignore the open sieve along the Mexican border for a moment (but no longer than that). There are people in our southern hemisphere who devoutly wish us ill, and Venezuela only tops the list. It is by no means the only potential troublemaker. (At this moment, U.S. SpecOps troops are operating way south of the border, keeping an eye on things.)

Few of the world's other regions lie outside of America's area of interest. Yes, there are conceivably very specific scenarios in which it would be mighty comforting to have some B-2s; maybe some F-22s; and even a submarine or two. But none of the problems we're likely facing in any of those areas will be solved by high-tech, high-budget gadgets. As in Iraq, Afghanistan, and elsewhere, once we've gained entry to the theater of operation, the flashy, pointy hardware goes away, and the arbiter of decision becomes the ancient and honorable infantryman.

Guessing the future: This one's easy. Gadgets come and go; riflemen are here to stay.

Sealing the Border

"Militarizing the border" is good for a cyber feud on most blogs and Internet forums. But suffice it to say that defending the nation from foreign intrusion is certainly within DoD's realm, however much or little the armed forces may support the mission.

Determining the force needed to seal our borders is of course conjectural. To guard against conventional military invasion might require three million troops on the Mexican border alone, but that's not the threat level. We are more concerned with catching or deterring hostile individuals or groups who illegally come here with something besides employment in mind.

In some areas it makes sense to employ National Guard or regular units as lookouts for *La Migra*. Presumably the basic asset would involve a small company per kilometer with perhaps some headquarters and support units.

Assume that two soldiers can adequately scan or patrol one hundred meters or more per shift; three shifts equals a small, six-man squad, call it seven with leader, or eight to ten to compensate for certain undermanning. A thirty-man platoon (three nine-man squads plus platoon leader, NCO and radioman) would then cover a kilometer per shift, or about one hundred troops total, possibly a few more with a company HQ element or squad.

If the border is three thousand kilometers, then three hundred thousand troops are needed, or maybe 10 percent more with minimal battalion, brigade, and division or higher echelons and support units. Since there's no need for fire support and little for service support, formations would be much smaller than the normal combat allotments. However, with sufficient technology, probably we could use fewer troops, given technological aids (surveillance and sensors) plus physical barriers in some areas.

Where would we get three hundred thousand more troops, or even one hundred thousand?

As the saying goes, "Hey, I'm Plans. You're Operations."

Meanwhile, we need to remember that putting military personnel on the border is not a substitute for adequate law enforcement. But the fly in the bureaucratic ointment becomes evident if you talk to Border Patrol agents, who for years have reported poor morale and retention. Aside from perennial under funding (U.S. Border Patrol has one-tenth the people of New York Police Department) the agency frequently punishes or ousts agents for doing their job. Its internal feuding and dissent is, of course, beyond the scope of this study, if not beyond the realm of our concern.

Guessing the future: If the porous border cannot be sealed under a neoconservative Republican administration, it certainly will not be done under Democratic leadership. Therefore, the situation will remain unchanged until there's an immigration related terrorist incident.

The Short Version

In order to condense the lessons and conclusions drawn in these pages, here's "the short version."

1. We're spread thinly across the globe. As of 2005, a quarter-million American service personnel were deployed overseas with another 100,000 routinely serving in Britain, Germany, Italy, and Japan. They're not all combat forces by any means, as humanitarian aid continues in "distressed" places such as Haiti (since 1994) and Kosovo (1999).

Therefore, let's recognize that we're short of troops and start planning accordingly. We talk about the Long War but continue assuming there will be some sort of "victory" in the foreseeable future. Maybe there will, but that's happy-puppy optimism, not detached realism. At some point we will have three options: continue exhausting our all-volunteer force; cut back severely on overseas commitments and bring most people home; or augment the regulars with a combination of more guard and reserves and/or a limited draft.

Unpopular? Definitely.

Politically impossible? Probably. But we need a lot fewer Republicans and Democrats and a lot more Americans in government.

In a conventional war we'll still inherit most of the problems we face in Afghanistan and Iraq. Shortages in maintenance, airlift, basic equipment, and especially proper training for all troops will be an even greater challenge in any "real" war scenario. The time to start fixing that perennial problem was approximately twenty years ago.

Let's saddle up and put the spurs to that pony.

2. Buy what we demonstrably need *now* more than what we may never use later. This book has repeatedly examined the inverse relationship between Pentagon purchases and troop requirements. Yes, we should plan for other contingencies, but while we're focused on World War IV (against a major conventional power or powers) let's not forget about World War III—the one we're engaged in today, however our "conflicts" are numbered.

As long as Americans continue going to war zones with inadequate training, support, and equipment, parents and voters should demand change of the military-industrial-political complex. While it's barely conceivable that someday we'll actually use stealth fighters and next-generation submarines, the fact remains that our sons and daughters are engaged in gunfights today and will be tomorrow and next year.

As already noted, "Business as usual" represents a losing philosophy.

3. Acknowledge the likely development of ICBMs funded by Islamic governments and other petro dollars, and continue investing in ballistic missile defenses. The "Star Wars" debate of the 1970s and 1980s has been settled—antiballistic missiles (ABMs) are needed but remain controversial in some quarters. The current Patriot system can work against aircraft and tactical missiles such as Scud, but is not intended to destroy far more capable ICBMs arriving from outside the atmosphere. Therefore, we need to continue developing advanced ABMs for the Missile Defense Agency, plus airborne lasers, or both. ABMs do not, of course, prevent "suitcase" or "backpack" nukes from being deployed, and those low-end weapons may represent the greater threat.

One of the surface navy's most urgent missions could be missile defense with Aegis destroyers or cruisers deployed off Korea and elsewhere (ships always possess the advantage of "territorial independence," freeing us from dealing with wavering allies). ABMs include sea-based SS-2s and land-based kinetic energy projectiles, both of which merit continued development.

Similarly, invest in hypersonic weapons able to take advantage of real-time intelligence and distant targets. For example, if satellites or other sources show North Korea or Iran ready to launch a warhead, we need to destroy that bird on the ground in minutes, not hours. If we have to "defund" (that's probably a DoD word) some mysterious projects to obtain hypersonics, by all means do so. At the same time, we should be looking at ways to defeat hypersonics coming our way, because some day—they will. At Mach 5 or more, speed equals range: a launch beyond our early detection sensors degrades our ability to intercept. That's indicative of the high-low threat: AK-47s and IEDs coupled with high-Mach missiles and stealthy submarines.

4. Drop the political correctness and admit the obvious: we are engaged in a long-term conflict with Islam. No other threat is currently as great, and if that means "profiling," so be it.

The focus of the Terror War is geographically contradictory. As a global movement, al Qaeda can choose any place on earth to launch its next strike. That situation forces America and the West to disperse their forces, trying to remain strong everywhere. It's a losing proposition. On 9/11 we were strong nowhere, least of all in New York and D.C.

In order to fight Muslim fundamentalists, it is necessary—it is essential—to understand their culture, faith, and languages. Fortunately, the U.S. and other Western combatants are allied with friendly forces in many Islamic countries. But how far any of them will go in opposing fellow Muslims remains to be seen—especially where economics hold sway.

Meanwhile, our greatest need is intelligence. However, over the years, some politicians have either naively or darkly sought to prevent U.S. intelligence services from obtaining information from various shady characters. (Now-deceased Senator Frank Church of Idaho is most frequently cited, as his 1978 legislation turned intelligence gathering from electronic and others sources at the expense of "humint.") In the twenty-first century, anyone who clings to the concept of "good guys only" probably has no business in the intelligence community. Frequently we gain information by appealing to the opposition's self-interest, not its higher values—as they do to us (street cops will tell you that the feds most often crack cases by throwing money at the target mob and seeing who picks up the cash).

In short, we need the best information we can obtain by any means.

5. Stop supporting North Korea. Pyongyang is one of the very few nation-states posing a serious risk to America, and the inane notion that providing food, fuel, and *nukes* would calm a rabid Stalinist regime was clearly doomed to anybody with two gray cells to rub together. If the rest of the world wants to support the Kim dynasty, at least we do not have to contribute to our own problems. The logical conclusion to be drawn from three presidential administrations supporting North Korea can only be extortion: "Keep feeding us or we'll attack." Instead of ceding the obvious, we propped up Pyongyang under the guise of "engagement" and "humanitarian assistance." As if *any* of the food intended for North Korea's starving population would ever reach the needy.

Granted, our options are limited. As long as Seoul wants to play patty-cake with Pyongyang, we're not going to invade, and we're not likely to take unilateral action. But at some point we'll have to decide whether to get along with our allies or defend ourselves against a determined, growing threat. If our eventual action forces hordes of refugees into China and South Korea, that's far preferable to a nuke on Honolulu or Seattle.

In any case, appeasers get what they deserve. And that includes the United States of America.

The Greatest Loss

Everyone who has lost a family member or friend in war knows the piercing pain and the nagging question, "Was it worth it?" Some people never recover; it haunts them to the grave. One example:

A friend of mine was a P-47 Thunderbolt pilot in Europe during World War II. His brother disappeared in a B-24 Liberator, and their father spent the rest of his life believing that the missing son would show up one day with a marvelous tale to tell. Of course, he never did.

At least we won that one, returning freedom to a continent that otherwise would still exist under the tyrant's heel. It was possible to assess the personal loss against the greater good.

Not so in Vietnam. In the depths of that "conflict" it was even harder for many of us, as the war seemed endless, and Washington had no intention of trying to win. As the grunts used to say, our losses were "wasted, man."

Today it's not much easier. The current war surely will outlast Vietnam—-at this writing we're six years and counting. But regardless of what happens in Iraq or Afghanistan, the effects of the Terror War will remain here, within our borders.

The greatest loss remains unknown, though its nature is evident. We hear a great deal about "winning the war on terrorism." But without sounding too Clintonian, what does win mean? And what constitutes losing?

Presumably just holding the status quo ante would represent a victory of sorts, but that's been a dead issue since that Tuesday morning in 2001. Whether the 9/11 terrorists intended it or not, they were handed a victory by We the People, who not only tolerated greater infringements of constitutional rights in the name of security, but many of us demanded them, embraced them, and called for more.

We got it. The result was called "Uniting and Strengthening America by Providing Appropriate Tools Required to Intercept and Obstruct Terrorism." The shorthand version is the Patriot Act, proving once again that some of the cleverest people in Washington are anonymous congressional staffers.

Through 2003 between 60 and 70 percent of Americans were satisfied with provisions of the Patriot Act. But in 2004 public support began waning, dropping below 50 percent in 2005. However, through most of that period, roughly half the people polled admitted they knew little or nothing about the act's provisions.

In truth, much of the act focuses on routine criminal activity that may be connected to terrorist groups, especially money laundering and drug trafficking. Few Americans have practical or philosophical problems with such measures, especially when directed against foreigners. But other concerns arose regarding proposed "sneak and peek" searches and unannounced access to personal records such as library withdrawals and bookstore purchases, plus medical or financial records. Wiretaps and email surveillance also were areas of concern among civil libertarians on both sides of the aisle.

However, there were earlier calls for limits on individual rights. In 1995, the future Israeli Prime Minister Benjamin Netanyahu published *Fighting Terrorism*, calling for complete firearms registration, disbanding of organized militias, and suspension of some traditional civil rights.

He was talking about America; the book was endorsed by Teddy Kennedy and Bob Dole.

But Israel is a democratic socialist state (some would say a theocracy) under perennial attack by nations and forces hostile to its existence. That would seem a poor comparison with America, presumably a constitutional republic that has largely been free of direct attack since the Civil War. In that era, Abraham Lincoln suspended habeas corpus and otherwise trod upon individual rights, even though the North was never in peril of conquest. During the Great War, Woodrow Wilson's administration clamped down on German-American organizations (though America was never in peril), and Franklin Roosevelt's draconian measures against Japanese-Americans are all too well known from World War II.

However odious (or necessary) the foregoing actions, they occurred within a finite period. The median was less than four years, with most rights reinstated after victory.

In the present circumstance, we cannot even define victory, let alone contemplate a date for it. Consequently, whatever further restrictions we accept are likely to remain indefinitely. That is, permanently.

In the 1990s the late Lieutenant Colonel Jeff Cooper wrote, "In our lifetime the American people will decide whether to continue living free."

A prediction: a great many Americans will prefer feeling secure to retaining their freedoms.

The Price

Walter Reed Army Medical Center faces Georgia Avenue in Northwest Washington, D.C. It's not for the faint-hearted.

A friend of mine—a veteran in his seventies—often goes there. Following is a brief account of one visit by one old soldier offering support to one young man suddenly grown old.

"He's a really good kid, just nineteen. An IED got him. It destroyed his face and one eye, and left him blind in the other. It's a good thing. If he could see in a mirror he'd probably off himself.

"He wears a mask most of the time just as a courtesy to the staff. I don't think that most of the soldiers there from Iraq or Afghanistan would ever say anything.

"I made friends with the kid—he was actually eager to talk. As combat vets we share a bond, though his war was a lot shorter than mine. I finished my tour in Korea but he was only in Iraq a few weeks.

"I asked if he'd like to go outside, and he said he would. He likes the breeze when it's blowing because the mask gets warm indoors. But just as soon as I led him down the steps he took off his mask without warning me. Two women were coming up the sidewalk, and they gasped out loud. The kid heard them and I think he was a little embarrassed, but it's impossible to tell from his expression. I mean, my God, he doesn't *have* an expression.

"He asked me to take him back inside. I did, and said I'd come see him again soon.

"And I will."

The final prediction in this chapter can be made with dreadful certainty: there will be thousands more visits in the years and decades ahead. Therefore, moral support for our casualties and their families will continue ranking high on the lengthening list of what we need.

Glossary

AMC: air mobility command
ASW: antisubmarine warfare
AWACS: airborne warning and control system
BTDT: been there, done that
CBN: chemical-biological-nuclear (defense)
CNO: chief of naval operations
CV: aircraft carrier
CVN: nuclear aircraft carrier
DDG: guided-missile destroyer
DoD: Department of Defense
ECM: electronic countermeasures
FCS: future combat system
GWOT: Global War on Terror
HARM: highspeed antiradiation missile
HVT: high value target
IAEA: International Atomic Energy Agency
ICBM: intercontinental ballistic missile
IED: improvised explosive device

JCS: Joint Chiefs of Staff
JSF: Joint Strike Fighter (F-35)
KIA: killed in action
LHA: amphibious assault ship
LHD: amphibious assault ship (well deck)
LMG: light machine gun
LO: low observable (stealth)
LPD: landing platform dock
LPH: amphibious assault ship (helicopter)
LSD: landing ship dock
MAD: mutually assured destruction (deterrence)
MIPC: military industrial political complex
MOS: military occupation specialty
NAS: naval air station
NCO: noncommissioned officer (sergeant, etc.)
NFO: naval flight officer
OEF: Operation Enduring Freedom (Afghanistan)
OIF: Operation Iraqi Freedom
OSD: Office of the Secretary of Defense
PGM: precision guided munition(s)
POW: prisoner of war
SAW: squad automatic weapon
SLBM: submarine-launched ballistic missile
SSBN: ballistic missile submarine
SSK: hunter-killer submarine
SSN: nuclear-powered submarine
TO&E: table of organization and equipment
UAV: unmanned aerial vehicle (drone)
VSTOL: vertical short takeoff and landing
VTOL: vertical takeoff and landing
WIA: wounded in action

Index

GENERAL INDEX